WOMEN WHO STAY BEHIND

# Women Who
# Stay Behind

## *Pedagogies of Survival in Rural Transmigrant Mexico*

RUTH TRINIDAD GALVÁN

THE UNIVERSITY OF
ARIZONA PRESS

TUCSON

The University of Arizona Press
www.uapress.arizona.edu

Printed in the United States of America
20  19  18  17  16  15    6  5  4  3  2  1

ISBN-13: 978-0-8165-3145-5

Jacket designed by Leigh McDonald
Jacket art: *Four shades* by Xiomara Ortega-Trinidad

Library of Congress Cataloging-in-Publication Data
Trinidad Galván, Ruth, author.
Women who stay behind : pedagogies of survival in rural transmigrant Mexico / Ruth Trinidad Galván.
     pages cm
  Includes bibliographical references and index.
  ISBN 978-0-8165-3145-5 (cloth : alk. paper)
  1. Rural women—Mexico—Social conditions.   2. Wives—Effect of husband's employment on—Mexico  3. Foreign workers—Family relationships—Mexico.
4. Immigrants—United States.   5. Mexicans—United States.   I. Title.
  HQ1462.T75 2015
  305.40972—dc23
                              2014024125

♾ This paper meets the requirements of ANSI/NISO Z39.48-1992 (Permanence of Paper).

*In honor of the life, work, and activism of the late Guillermina López Bravo.*

# Contents

# Illustrations

# *Preface*

This research study initially set out to examine Mexican rural women's empowerment and the role of a grassroots popular literacy organization in facilitating women's personal growth and learning. My first visit in 1998 to one of Guanajuato's rural communities served as an initial glimpse into the impressive work of women who had ample community organizing experience. The manner in which the women presented their stories and accomplishments to a complete stranger was impressive and, at the time, intrigued me to learn about their journey. Their work and participation with Proyectos Laubach de Alfabetización Popular en México, Asociación Civil—Laubach Popular Literacy Projects in Mexico, Civil Association (PLAMAC)—was clearly long-standing and consistent.

Guillermina López Bravo, codirector of PLAMAC, was my point of contact during that first visit a year before moving to the region and formally beginning the research study. At the time Guillermina oversaw the organization's rural community projects in the outskirts of the city of Irapuato and in neighboring cities, while her sisters, Silvia (codirector) and Alicia, oversaw the city projects. Guillermina, and that initial visit, would form my first impressions of PLAMAC's critical literacy and community projects from campesinas (rural women)* in a nearby rural community.

---

* *Campesina* is the term the women used to refer to their social positioning as rural women regardless of whether they resided in the *rancherías* (rural communities) or in town.

The women of La Casita,[*] who at the time worked with PLAMAC for over seven years, voiced impressive learning experiences and accomplishments. Because of their extensive experience organizing their community, their time with PLAMAC, and the numerous in-services and training they received from the organization, they served as excellent spokeswomen. I was immediately impressed with their stories, which they proceeded to voice without apprehension, through their engaging mannerisms and take-charge attitude.

During that July visit Guillermina drove my family and me to La Casita to meet and listen to these women's stories. Just ten miles outside highrises, paved roads, and green communities was La Casita with its dirt roads, flat treeless land, and roaming farm animals. We briskly passed a woman attending to her family business, who from the vehicle Guillermina instructed to convene the group. As we rolled up to a home around the corner, women began to arrive and settle into the front room of the house. It was there that a group of women had established a communal sewing space and fabric store. Among fabric, thread, and a sewing machine we sat around the small room and listened to the women of La Casita share their experiences as leaders and organizers.

Aurora Pérez, in her early forties and the owner of the family store, was the first to speak. As one of the most vocal women in the group she proceeded to speak with passion about her experiences with PLAMAC and the ideas and tools she gained to free herself from her abusive husband. Although she and her husband continued to live together, their relationship changed since she learned to assertively defend herself. From her role as the *animadora* (educator/motivator) of the only male *pequeño grupo de ahorro* (small savings group[†]) in her rural community and from the knowledge she gained from PLAMAC, she opened a small family business that she and her husband administered. She hoped one of her two sons would eventually take it over. Her eldest son, however, had migrated to the United States some time ago, and that year her younger son would also leave. Her attempts at creating employment opportunities for her sons would not deter them from migrating as she hoped. On this day though, she described with pride how she and others organized the implementation of a community

---

[*] With the exception of PLAMAC—a public state institution—pseudonyms are used throughout to protect participants' anonymity.

[†] Community groups, whose main purpose was bringing community members together to save money, engage in critical literacy activities and dialogue, reflect on community problems, and *convivir* (live life among others).

water system, raised money to add classrooms to their middle school, and organized their first 15 de septiembre ("Cry of Dolores," marking the beginning of Mexico's independence). Her greatest satisfaction was that she yelled out those famous words—*Viva México, viva la independencia*—in the main courtyard of her community during the country's independence celebration. She sat comfortably with one leg over the other and moved her hands around as she expressed how she went from being *tímida y tapada* (timid and dim-witted) to *alguien que no se deja* (assertive). During the two-hour conversation she and her younger sister Araceli overpowered the meeting.

Araceli Pérez was just as passionate and forceful. Her animated expressions and humorous laugh were sheer joy. Araceli was also the leader of her own group, and as with her sister, her participation in PLAMAC's workshops and in-services transformed her life. She was the first woman to run for local office in the history of the community, and even though she did not win, her defiance served as an example for other men and women. As a result, another candidate won and removed a community delegate who served in office for over thirty years. Between Aurora and Araceli it was difficult to get a word in. Rebecca's quiet and warm words served to close the meeting.

Rebecca González was also an animadora in La Casita. Unlike her colleagues, she did not need to yell or speak over someone to express her ideas. As with other meetings she participated in during the year, she allowed her colleagues to fight over their turn to speak and then took the opportunity to voice her experiences. On that day, she shared that leading her small savings group was a "work in progress" that required commitment and creativity. Rebecca participated in many of the same workshops and consciousness-raising activities as her colleagues but also remained cemented in ideals she found valuable. Albeit less abrupt, she was also not timid about voicing her opinions. She often clarified points that Aurora and Araceli argued about or corrected them when what they stated was not reminiscent of all of their experiences. For instance, on many occasions Aurora would speak of her personal liberation from her husband and disapprove of women who did not break from equally oppressive relationships. Almost immediately Rebecca would answer, "*Pues, yo también me siento liberada y puedo ir y venir a mi gusto, per a mi todavía me gusta atender a mi esposo. Me gusta tenerle su ropa bien ordenada para cuando él la necesite*" (Well, I also feel liberated and have the freedom to come and go as I please, but I still like to care for my husband. I like to have his clothes tidy for when he needs them.) Although I did not come to know any of these three women as those of the communities of Sierra Linda, we interacted almost every other month at various meetings during the year. During those encounters Rebecca's insight was always a breath of fresh air, and so I approached her with all the respect she was due.

Indeed, upon meeting La Casita's women and hearing narratives of leadership, strength, and resiliency, it became clear that I would focus on PLAMAC's work and its contribution to these narratives of communal empowerment. I set out to discover PLAMAC's educational philosophy, method, and practice that in turn critically transformed campesinas and their communities. Rebecca, Araceli, and Aurora's narratives of empowerment led me to assume that I would find similar women in Sierra Linda and that their knowledge and ideas would be reminiscent of PLAMAC's deeds. My initial encounter with the women of Sierra Linda a year later was actually quite different. They were timid and hesitant campesinas who had only worked with PLAMAC for less than a year. It required time and *convivencia* (living among them) in our everyday activities to know and see them for the formidable women they are. Consequently, the study uncovered no less powerful women but more complex narratives that could certainly not be revealed during a one-week visit, as in La Casita's case. During the eighteen-month ethnographic study and a relationship of over ten years with Sierra Linda's women, the purpose of the research changed. Upon living with Andrea, Julieta, Jovita, Carolina, and other equally formidable women, it became apparent PLAMAC was simply one fraction of the story.

# Acknowledgments

No research endeavor or written work is accomplished in isolation. That is certainly the case with a fourteen-year venture like this one. The book is the result of the support, encouragement, and extensive dialogue, feedback, and recommendations of family, friends, mentors, colleagues, and students. First and foremost I want to recognize and thank the women of Sierra Linda for their immense support and generosity. They shared more than stories and life histories; they imparted spiritual knowledge, shared their homes, and provided *cariño* (affection). I am grateful to my academic community and close friends and colleagues who read numerous iterations, especially Sylvia Celedón-Pattichis, Douglas Foley, Rick Meyer, Glenabah Martinez, Marios Pattichis, Tryphenia Peele-Eady, Ann Nihlen, and Leslie Poynor. I benefitted from conversations with Rebecca Sánchez, Troy Richardson, Amy Sweet, Charise Pimentel, Melissa Moreno, Nancy López, Teresa Guevara Beltrán, Leila Flores-Dueñas, Carlos LópezLeiva, Enrique Murillo Jr., Juan de Dios Pineda, Luis Urrieta Jr., Leroy Ortiz, Patricia Rosas Lopátegui, and Tracy Stevens. Mentors Donna Deyhle, Frank Margonis, Audrey Thompson, Edward Buendía, and most especially the constant mentorship, support, and encouragement of my dear friend Sofía Villenas were invaluable. As an instructor of courses in qualitative research, feminist epistemology, Latina/o education, and globalization and education, I benefitted from my students' questions, and their feedback encouraged me to revisit and reconsider my assumptions, interpretations, and (re)presentation of women's lives.

Ultimately, my family is the inspiration for everything I do. My daughters Xiomara, Anayansi, and Nemiliztli are the cornerstones of my continual commitment to historically underrepresented communities, efforts to unmask inequities and advocate action. The lived experiences of a long line of women in my life—aunts, cousins, and maternal grandmother—are a constant reminder of our past and the resiliency of our people. In particular, my mother, Socorro, and my loving sister Esmeralda inspire me daily. I especially want to recognize my partner, Brad, who with patience and unwavering love made this process bearable. I also have brothers, brothers-in-law, uncles, and my father whose challenges and experiences in a society that scorns brown men compel me to question gender roles and expectations. For this I look to my brothers Teodoro Jr., Juan Carlos, and Abraham and my brother-in-law Carlos Chavez. I also counted on the constant support of my second family—Sophi, Stacey, Earl, Brian, Christopher, and Britteny.

This work was also possible thanks to the support of the University of New Mexico's College of Education Summer Research Initiative and the Overhead Funds Allocation Committee (OFAC), the AERA/Spencer Fellowship, and the University of Utah's Presidential and Steffenson-Canon Fellowships.

# WOMEN WHO STAY BEHIND

# Introduction

*Once the causes for certain obstacles in her life are identified and worked through, she does not flounder about as merely a "survivor," such as one who has survived a plane wreck and awaits a rescue team (which may never be forthcoming) but uses the new affirmation, that she is and has always been a part of the intricate network of life on this planet, to strengthen herself and to share her knowledge with others.*

—CASTILLO 1994, 160

How do women and families who stay behind survive the migration of loved ones to the United States? Migration is one of the biggest social phenomena impacting Mexico's populace and most heavily felt in rural communities in central states like Guanajuato. While migration in general is closely studied in the United States as a host country to immigrants of all races and nationalities, studies on the impact that migration has on sending communities are uncommon (Durand and Massey 2006; Hondagneu-Sotelo 1994; Kearney 2000; Salazar Parreñas 2005). What's more, narratives relating the survival of communities left behind in their home country are relatively unheard (Battistella and Conaco 1998; Stephen 2007).

This book fills the gap in the literature by foregrounding women and families who stay behind. It presents women's use of cultural knowledge, community activism, and teaching and learning spaces to creatively survive the conditions created by the migration of loved ones. I offer a decolonial Chicana feminist analysis of campesinas' (rural women) pedagogies of survival as they were enacted in their collective groups, reflected in their transborder social relations and daily interactions, and founded on their cultural knowledge. The book addresses the following research questions: How does the migration of loved ones alter community, familial, and gender dynamics? And what social relations (*convivencia*), cultural knowledge, and women-centered pedagogies sustain women's survival (*supervivencia*)? Based on an eighteen-month ethnographic study and over a ten-year relationship with rural communities in the small city of Sierra Linda, the book focuses on the myriad ways campesinas who stay behind creatively draw on convivencia, spirituality, activism, and the support of collective groups and transborder community to survive.

This ethnographic study initially began as a study of popular education and the critical literacy work of a nonprofit organization with ample experience and work in rural communities in Guanajuato. The work and commitment of Proyectos Laubach de Alfabetización Popular en México, Asociación Civil—Laubach Popular Literacy Projects in Mexico, Civil Association (PLAMAC)—codirected by sisters Silvia and Guillermina López Bravo since 1986, had a long history in the area. Thanks to my affiliation and initial focus on PLAMAC, I had the fortune of meeting and interacting with almost one hundred women during my year-long stay in Guanajuato. Living in the town of Sierra Linda meant I interacted with over forty of them regularly and cultivated a strong friendship with half a dozen of these formidable women. It was from four women in particular that I learned about la supervivencia, not survival but that beyondness—the ability to live happy, creative, and full lives while defying the hardships of poverty, loneliness, and overwork. Just like Ana Castillo's (1994, 146) words reveal, "Survival should not be our main objective. Our presence shows our will to survive, to overcome every form of repression known to humankind. Our goal should be to achieve joy." Castillo's words resonate with what I saw, heard, and experienced firsthand, namely, la supervivencia as beyond being a survivor of domination and repression but a continuation, a beyondness, of what lies ahead and beneath plain victimry (Vizenor 1999). One does not merely survive domination, but chooses to *saciar* (satiate) one's hopes and dreams in creative and joyful ways. And so the focus turned to the pedagogies of survival these campesinas enacted in their community groups and lives.

## The Small Savings Groups

*Los pequeños grupos de ahorro* (small savings groups) were the foremost organizing mechanism PLAMAC implemented and used to engage communities in critical literacy and grassroots organizing. It was in the small savings groups (SSGs) where I first began my research and fostered relationships with dozens of women. PLAMAC's aim, in its various projects, was the development and education of poor communities and its populace. Their wide view of education encompassed literacy in the written and oral form, personal growth, basic and technical skills, and a critical vision. PLAMAC's work attempted to incorporate all these forms of education in order to advance participants' critical consciousness and prepare them to assume leadership roles in their communities. In order to do this, PLAMAC launched its work in Sierra Linda by introducing the small savings groups. The SSGs were community groups that served many purposes—of which saving money, reading and writing, conversing, reflecting on community problems, and *conviviendo* (living life with others) were only some. The small savings groups attracted community members to save money and engage in consciousness-raising discussions and critical literacy activities.

Three leading coordinators—the *animadora* (educator/motivator), the *vigilanta* (guard) in charge of the key, and the *tesorera* (treasurer) in charge of the box—led the group in the saving of money and engagement of literacy activities and consciousness-raising themes. The group gathered at a site of their choice (e.g., a community store, community chapel, or member's home) for about a two-hour period. As the leader of the group, the animadora was charged with the task of not simply having the group save money during their time together but also engaging in literacy activities, critical reflections, and dialogue. The animadora introduced a literacy activity or theme of discussion prompted by PLAMAC in the animadora meetings (special in-service meetings conducted by PLAMAC) or other workshops. The group might work on a particular group of syllables, certain words, or a theme from their literacy booklet, such as migration. At times the animadora began a group discussion from conversations she discussed in an animadora meeting or engaged the group in ideas she was working with, such as the use of alternative medicine. Once the time to save approached, the animadora instructed the vigilanta and tesorera to open the box (either a wooden box or a toolbox). The actual savings box was an investment the group made collectively during the initiation of their small savings group. In order to keep the process honest and everyone's money safe, the vigilanta, who was responsible for the key, could not also serve as or live in the same home as the tesorera. When prompted, the vigilanta handed the key over to the tesorera, who then proceeded to unlock and open the box and distribute members' small bags of money. Members took their bags and placed in them whatever amount of money they were capable of saving that week. Upon saving their money, the tesorera placed the bags back in the box until the next meeting. The SSG bylaws also determined that if on any occasion any of the three leaders were not present at the meeting, members did not save on that particular day.

While saving money was an excellent organizing mechanism, PLAMAC also understood community members were interested in acquiring skills that enabled them to grow personally and increase their opportunities for self-sufficiency. Consequently, PLAMAC incorporated the acquisition of professional skills, such as sewing and cooking lessons, into its general and animadora meetings. For example, the sewing classes, if learned well, could generate income. Women were encouraged to save money by tailoring their own clothing and in the future generate an income as seamstresses. This was certainly the case in the rural community of La Casita where women managed to establish a communal fabric and seamstress store and become professional seamstresses. After several months of working with PLAMAC, many women in Sierra Linda also considered the seamstress profession and took a loan with PLAMAC to purchase their own sewing machines.

The SSG and animadora meetings always included consciousness-raising discussions that Silvia or Guillermina initiated. Silvia and Guillermina's experience in rural communities was evident in the appropriateness of their lessons. Silvia, for example, was always prepared with a story or anecdote to spark a discussion, while Guillermina seemed to approach people in a more personal manner. The stories Silvia shared were almost always closely connected to the women's lives and intended as reflections of their lived experiences, problems, and cultural values. These reflections were also meant to generate questions and explore solutions. Although the SSGs aimed to teach people to save money, PLAMAC's goals favored educational endeavors and social activism. In order to engage community members in educational endeavors and activism, PLAMAC trained the animadoras who were responsible for motivating and imparting the educational aspect of the group's activities. Animadoras worked the closest with PLAMAC, because PLAMAC trained them in those roles personally. The animadora meetings provided training on critical literacy methods, guidelines on how to engage group members, and the opportunity to attend other PLAMAC events and trainings held across the state with other grassroots organizations. On one occasion, for instance, animadoras participated in a workshop on the meaning of personal and structural power led by a local feminist organization.

Since PLAMAC was my initial focus and point of contact, all participants consisted of members of the small savings groups and their families. Generally, I was closely involved with three of the six savings groups. Jovita, Andrea, and Carolina were the animadoras of those SSGs. Two other groups were in neighboring rural communities, but their meetings fell on the same weekday as Jovita and Carolina's. The overlap made it difficult to consistently visit every group, so after four months of attempting to participate in five of them, I opted to visit only three. Membership ran from twelve to twenty-five members per savings group. All the groups included women ages fifteen to eighty, with the exception of Andrea's group, which included her father as the only male. Andrea's father, Alberto Acosta, saved in Andrea's small savings group and also led a SSG in town on Sunday afternoons. His group, which consisted of *ejidatarios* (communal land-owners), like Carolina's in-town group, was not counseled by PLAMAC. Rather, these in-town groups originated out of the interest and desire of their initiator. I attended Alberto's group on one occasion almost at the end of my stay. Not until Alberto was completely comfortable with me did he invite me to his group in the hope that I would attend regularly and lead the group.

With the exception of Andrea Acosta Valdéz, most animadoras initiated their group from a genuine interest in the SSG's objectives. As one of two animadoras in her rural community, Andrea accidentally fell into her role. When PLAMAC initially visited La Vereda, Andrea was chosen by PLAMAC and her community to make a list of those interested in joining an SSG. That initial responsibility involuntarily placed her as animadora of her community SSG. Jovita Gomez, Andrea's aunt and the other animadora in their community, initiated her SSG from the interest of women in the community who were not invited to participate in Andrea's group. Unlike Andrea, she gladly initiated her own group and participated in all of PLAMAC's trainings. Carolina Acosta Valdéz, Andrea's older sister and the only animadora in one of Sierra Linda's neighborhoods, initiated her SSG as an established community organizer who consistently sought out opportunities for herself and other women in her congregation.

The animadoras, however, were not very different from other women in the groups. Like other campesinas in Sierra Linda, they participated in primarily church-related activities and were almost exclusively at the forefront of all the work in their homes, family subsistence, care and education of their children, and—with the migration of so many men—the leadership of their communities. The real everyday chores, responsibilities, and activities these campesinas carried out were a constant concern in and outside their meetings.

## The Setting

Although residing in La Vereda or one of the other rural communities would have been idyllic, my family and I lived in the town of Sierra Linda just three miles from La Vereda. Sierra Linda (see figure 1) is a small town-like

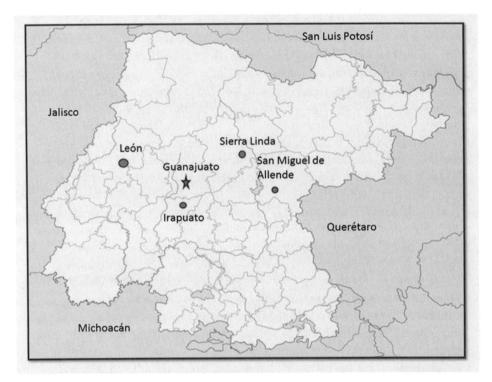

*Figure 1.* The state of Guanajuato.

city nestled in Guanajuato's mountain range northeast of the state's capital city of Guanajuato. Its surroundings are made up of clusters of rural communities, like La Vereda, that mirror many peasant communities across Mexico whose residents make their livelihood as farmers. With the exception of one woman, most of the women I interacted with lived in Sierra Linda's rural communities. Due to drought, the country's changing economy, globalization, and a host of other factors, families could not financially subsist from their small lot of land.

Sierra Linda has an important place in Mexico's independence history. As the site that initiated the country's independence from Spain in 1810, the small city relies on its place in history and local production of *talavera* (porcelain-type pottery) for its small-scale tourism. With a population under 150,000 in 2010 (with about 60,000 concentrated in the city), the municipality's main economic foundation continues to be agricultural and commercial, including the production of ceramic pottery (Municipio de Dolores Hidalgo Cuna de la Independencia Nacional 2012). Over the last few decades, however, these economic activities have not sustained rural communities, and more and more individuals and families resort to migrating to other cities in the republic or to the United States. Since Sierra Linda's region is the second poorest in the state, some point to poverty as one of the main reasons for the migration of so many of its citizens (Rionda 2000). Sierra Linda holds twelfth place in the state for emigration, and approximately 30.4 percent of the families in the municipality have a migrant father or mother (much higher than the state average of 24.5 percent) (Municipio de Dolores Hidalgo 2012). The state also does not fare much better when it comes to poverty and emigration.

During the period of study, the state of Guanajuato ranked sixth in the nation in population and thirteenth in poverty, particularly prevalent among rural communities (Rionda 2000). Considering the state's poverty, it is not surprising that Guanajuato leads the country in number of migrants to the United States with a total of 366,123 from 1997 to 2002 (see figure 2). Guanajuato also calculated that 1,800,000 of its citizens reside in the United States, mostly in Texas (Rionda 2000). Even now in the latest report period of 2005 to 2010, Guanajuato holds the highest level of international migration, at 10.8 percent, of any state in the Mexican republic, and among municipalities in the country, Sierra Linda comes in twelfth (Instituto Nacional de Estadística y Geografía 2011).

| Mexican State | Seasonal Migrants | Migrants who did not return from the United States | Total |
|---|---|---|---|
| Guanajuato | 152,492 | 213,631 | 366,123 |
| Jalisco | 127,401 | 164,256 | 291,657 |
| Michoacán | 97,208 | 150,832 | 248,040 |
| San Luis Potosí | 49,656 | 85,727 | 135,383 |
| Zacatecas | 44,988 | 71,363 | 116,351 |
| México | —— | —— | 111,837 |
| Oaxaca | 21,085 | 88,608 | 109,693 |

*Figure 2.* The top seven Mexican states with over 100,000 migrants to the United States from 1997 to 2002. (Consejo Nacional de Población n.d.)

## The Women

Andrea Acosta Valdéz was animadora of one of the two small savings groups in her rural community of La Vereda and one of three prominent Acosta Valdéz sisters. She had two daughters, ages fourteen and six—Lorena and Mayela—whom she raised with the help of her parents and sisters after her husband's migration to the United States. She was by far the most active woman in her community, and part of her introverted nature and insecurities stemmed from the community's criticism of her very public community organizing life. Actually, her role as animadora of her SSG emerged precisely because she was handed the charge of putting together a list of people interested in joining a small savings group. Although she was not initially interested in leading the group, the community's perception of her as involved and interested in *those* types of things meant community members gladly assigned her group leader and PLAMAC designee. She eventually took her role very seriously and tried arduously to motivate and educate her group on the social ills of the community and the benefits of organizing members to address some of their most basic needs. Andrea's insight, knowledge of community politics and local entrepreneurship, and close relationship to PLAMAC meant she was at the forefront of the projects that took place in her community.

Although Julieta Acosta Valdéz, Andrea's younger sister, was not an animadora, she was the center of several SSGs and my entry into the groups and community. Like Andrea, she was also the wife of a migrant man. Her husband Manuel Alvarez, however, migrated to the United States years before their marriage and consequently had the opportunity to legalize his residency status. This, of course, afforded him privileges other migrant men in La Vereda did not enjoy. For instance, his formal residency and time in the United States assured him a stable job, paid and unpaid vacations—which he took three times a year—financial security, and the opportunity of legalizing his family and eventually relocating them to the United States if he wished. Because he met his economic duties consistently, he and Julieta were able to purchase property in La Vereda and Sierra Linda. Julieta also learned to manage their money well and make do with what little they had. Manuel and Julieta had four children that included daughter Miztli, the oldest and fourteen years old, and three sons ages four, seven, and ten.

I met Jovita Gomez for the first time during a workshop Guillermina and Silvia conducted in La Vereda while I was still living in PLAMAC's office. Guillermina, Silvia, and I entered La Vereda to find Jovita in her yard attending her garden. She was also an animadora in La Vereda—a charge she shared with Andrea in her community. Jovita had nine children, five girls and four boys. The two oldest, a young woman and young man, were out of the house and working. Karina and Reina, who followed, attended the local middle school, which they graduated from during the year of the study. Her other three boys and two girls attended the local elementary school. Her husband, Anselmo, was Alberto's younger brother. Anselmo and Jovita counted only on the income from and personal use of their seasonal crop. Undoubtedly, for a family of eleven this meant living under economic straits.

Carolina Acosta Valdéz was the eldest of the Acosta Valdéz sisters and the *animadora* of the only SSG in a new neighborhood in Sierra Linda. Our first encounter took place after meeting her sister Andrea, who guided Guillermina, my family, and me to Carolina's home in the hopes of finding housing in Sierra Linda. At the time Carolina had seven children, two boys and five girls. Her eldest son, only eighteen, had worked in the United States for over a year. Her second child, Lupe, was a sixteen-year-old high school student. Her third child, a daughter, attended middle school, her other three attended elementary school, and the youngest stayed at home with her. Her family subsisted from both a family mill business that either her husband Agusto or daughter Lupe managed early in the mornings and the income from her husband's traveling sales business. While Agusto spent most of the day on his bicycle selling alternative medicine around town, Carolina contributed to both businesses by at times minding the mill, consulting patients, and selling alternative medicine from their home.

## Convivencia as Methodology

Like all good feminist ethnographic research, the focus and narratives emerged from the participants' experiences, social conditions, and teaching and learning spaces. Indeed, the study stopped being an exploration about women's empowerment to that of *supervivencia* (beyond survival) and the social relations (*convivencia*), cultural knowledge, and women-centered pedagogies that sustained their survival. To fully understand the role of *convivencia* and *supervivencia* in the lives of these formidable women required a methodological approach that privileged women's everyday experiences (Saavedra and Nymark 2008). *Convivencia*—living life together—became that methodological approach.

I entered the field in July 1999 initially living in PLAMAC's office until my family and I found housing. PLAMAC's office was located in the city of Irapuato about a two-hour drive from the rural communities of Sierra Linda. Since distance prevented PLAMAC from attending to these communities on a regular basis, they suggested I live in Sierra Linda. PLAMAC's recommendation could not have been more ideal since living among the women meant experiencing firsthand the meaning of convivencia the women talked about with such frequency. I entered the field first as a learner and began as an "observer as participant," being mindful of my outsider position and respectful of their teaching and learning spaces (Glesne 2006; Wilson 2008). Initially, the study and our interactions—strictly in the teaching and learning spaces that PLAMAC led—were awkward and structured. Those PLAMAC-led meetings kept my researcher role as an observer in tact and the possibility of an emic view minimal. Living in town, then again, meant I could attend meetings and other functions regularly without PLAMAC and *convivir* in the everyday activities. As a result of those convivencias (social gatherings), our relationship soon evolved outside the research focus of PLAMAC to genuine engagements as friends and women. I moved from observer to participant. Our convivencias were an opportunity to spend time in each other's company, discuss personal and collective problems, and share meals together. In those one-on-one engagements it was two women in particular who taught me about convivencia.

Andrea and her younger sister Julieta were those women. With Julieta— who lived in the city of Sierra Linda—our convivencias were jovial interactions of two women who "got" each other and felt comfortable in each other's company. Julieta's friendly nature made it easy to commingle and truly connect as women. Andrea, however, taught me the most about convivencia as methodology, because her quiet, unpretentious demeanor and hard exterior made it difficult to get close. For a researcher this can be a true predicament and the most difficult part of human interactions in the field. It took almost the extent of the study and true convivencia to know her. With her, research as convivencia required the arduous work of being completely in the moment and attentive to her reactions to others and me. Our relationship forced me to be a researcher conscious of my presence, what I said, how the women responded, and how I needed to *be* in their presence. This conscious state of being with others makes one present in the moment and enables true connections. As Andrea would eventually state to me, "*La convivencia nos lleva a reflexionar, a ser positivos. Te enseña a ser más sociable, a saludar a las personas y conocerlas. Te ayuda a ser mejores personas . . . te lleva a tranquilizar el espíritu*" (spending time with others [la convivencia] leads us to reflect, to be positive. It teaches you to be more social, to greet people and know them. It helps you be better people . . . it calms the spirit). Our convivencia certainly made me a better researcher, friend, and human being.

Meetings were often referred to as convivencias precisely because, as Andrea mentions, they were meant to create a positive and reflexive space where women experienced "living." While the meetings were about learning and creating community, the opportunity to experience life and learning among and with other women was the most crucial part of women's participation in PLAMAC and community groups. Just like getting to know Andrea on a personal level meant being present and conscious of our mutual *vivencias* (lived experiences), I needed to be equally attentive in PLAMAC's and women's meetings. This meant "using the self as much as possible" and going from observer to full participant with Julieta, Andrea, and the other women in family outings, *quinceañeras*, and *bautismos* (Buch and Staller 2011, 188).

It took our convivencia outside of the meetings to redefine my role beyond the confines of PLAMAC and establish myself as friend, researcher, woman, and mutual learner. As the year progressed and our convivencia became part of our daily interactions, my role changed to "participant as observer" and ultimately to companion and close friend (Glesne 2006). This closeness was especially felt with Julieta who was my point of contact and with whom I stayed during all of my visits since 2000. However, I eventually also felt that closeness with Andrea. In those last months in the field, Andrea and I took trips together and were comfortable in each other's company without others. I also felt we picked up where we left off upon my numerous returns over the last fourteen years.

Convivencia also required existing in that place of discomfort that makes you agonizingly aware of each other's vivencias and mutual humanity. Because Andrea was not open and jovial like her sister Julieta, those initial struggles with her were a reminder of not only her vulnerabilities but mine as well. In essence it was a reminder of our mutual humanity—my insecurities with the colonizing history of research and privileged position as a "paper-holding" bordercrosser and her deeply denigrated self-assurance and sense of womanhood (*lo que es ser mujer*). And so, we needed "to develop habits of coexistence: conversation in its older meaning of the word, of living together, association" in order to get at those deep insecurities and move beyond them (Appiah as cited in Abu El-Haj 2007, 312).

Our convivencia in the field also required the use of diverse methods of data collection, such as casual or conversational interviewing, oral life histories, and focus group interviews, in order to elicit women's views on education, their involvement in different community projects, and their role as women who stay behind (Angrosino 2005; Fontana and Frey 2005; Hesse-Biber 2011; Leavy 2011). In these conversational interviews—often done during everyday interactions—I stepped back and let the women take the lead and go "where they wanted to go" with the conversation (Hesse-Biber 2011, 115). Conversational interviews worked best during our convivencia because they worked alongside everyday conversations. After several months of convivencia, formal semistructured interviews were conducted with Julieta, Andrea, Carolina, and Jovita—the four main participants of the study—and with Guillermina and Silvia López-Bravo, codirectors of PLAMAC. Open-ended questions were used to elicit the women's roles in PLAMAC's activities and as leaders, mothers, and community members. Formal interviews were tape-recorded and took place in the privacy and comfort of participants' own homes among the sharing of food and while they attended to their numerous obligations. Each interview lasted from an hour and a half to two and a half hours. For instance, because of my closeness with Guillermina, Julieta, and Jovita, the interviews mirrored our usual convivencia and conversations together. Overall, I did all of the translating of the women's narratives and in many cases consulted expert colleagues in the Spanish language for accuracy in translation.

Focus group interviews were also conducted about the women's concerns, reactions, and experiences on mutual themes (Leavy 2011; Visweswaran 1994). In one case, women's activism was explored with Julieta, Andrea, and other community leaders. That conversation revealed the immense pain and community antagonism that was a common part of being a female leader in a traditionally male-dominated public sphere. After leaving the field in June 2000 and engaging in several months of data analysis, I returned to Sierra Linda in December of the same year to conduct one last focus group interview on women's perceptions of the migration of loved ones to the United States. During that focus group interview conducted in Julieta's rural home, Chuy—Julieta's mother—Jovita, Andrea, and her sisters Sara and Sandra reflected on their experiences as women who stay behind and the trials of transmigration in their families and the area. Life history interviews were conducted during a visit in 2006 with Julieta, Andrea, Carolina, and Jovita. These life histories captured valuable information concerning the women's formal schooling, upbringing, and familial relations and are reflected in their individual chapters (chapters 1, 3, 5, and 7, respectively). While the life histories were an important aspect of that visit, its foremost intention was maintaining our friendship and convivencia. Even now I try to preserve those relationships and periodically contact or visit Sierra Linda (Pillow and Mayo 2007).

In the summer of 2012, for instance, my colleague Patricia Rosas Lopátegui and I led a group of students to the city of Guanajuato for a two-week intensive course titled Transborder Feminist Literary Representations, where we engaged students in Chicana and Mexicana feminist works. Part of the course also included tapping into community activism reflective of a transborder reality, such as that of the women of Sierra Linda. Without a doubt, students found the experiences of visiting the community of La Vereda and meeting Jovita and other women who even in 2012 participate in her group the most inspiring part of the course. Although Julieta and Andrea traveled to Texas during those days, Julieta remained the point of contact for the trip, and it was she and her daughter who worked with Jovita to welcome the group.

Convivencia as methodology is significant in marginalized communities where members, especially women, have been completely ignored by those who frown upon women's activism and nontraditional roles outside the home. "Recall that what is key across feminist research and feminist ethnography is a commitment to studying the 'lived experience' of gender and its intersectionalities resulting in theory that is built from these lived experiences" (Pillow and Mayo 2007, 161). Because we are addressing the lived experiences of women who have historically been unheard, trust must be gained (Villenas 2000). Convivencia was necessary for gaining and building trust beyond the objectives of academic research. While our convivencia reconciled the purpose and potential of research outside of its colonizing history, it was only possible because a true relationship with participants required a reflexive process and vision (Pillow 2003; Villenas 1996, 2000). In the pages to come, especially those chapters that highlight Julieta, Andrea, Carolina, and Jovita, the reader is able to witness that convivencia as it transpired with all of the women in its many manifestations. Even in our convivencia, however, I remained cognizant of my multiple roles, responsibilities, and privilege.

Having visited the region a year earlier, I was keenly aware that my position as a U.S. citizen and daughter of Mexican immigrants would complicate the insider-outside binary (Behar 1993; Villenas 1996). The limitations of the binary were evoked while living in the region and becoming familiar with the migratory history of the area. The region's transmigration and its effects on the communities summoned memories of my parents' own migratory trajectory to the United States from the neighboring state of Zacatecas. My awareness of the plight leading so many men and women from these rural communities to the United States came from real familial experience. However, unlike many families in the area, my parents who settled and had children on the Ciudad Juárez–El Paso border migrated together, and so I have little recollection of my early years in Juárez. Growing up I often wondered what life might have been like in Juárez where my parents lived during the first two years of my life. I lamented during my years of identity development not living in Mexico, to eventually cherish my transborder reality and lived experiences (Trinidad Galván 2011). I consequently entered the field aware of the manner in which my U.S./Mexican-centered worldview and epistemological positioning could shape and impact my entrance into the field, relationship with the communities, and eventually the story I narrated (Delgado Bernal 1998; Elenes and Delgado Bernal 2010; Sánchez 2001; Sandoval 2000; Villenas 2012). The extent of all of this was unknown, however. Whether I would be accepted, if at all, rang hard in my heart for the first few months. Ultimately, taking seriously Mendez and Wolf's (2007, 658) idea that "researchers should approach the design of feminist methods as neither theory nor practice, but a strategy constructed out of political engagement within global and grounded, local contexts," I grappled with my researcher role during the extent of the research and even today as I write.*

In pursuit of a reflexive narrative and research, I tried to stay true to what Wanda Pillow (2003, 177) so eloquently describes as "critical to exposing the difficult and often uncomfortable task of leaving what is unfamiliar, unfamiliar." The hope is that in this attempt I have also moved from the superficial reflective nature of research that simply tries to "know the other," "know thyself," or "aims at truth" (Pillow 2003). If this journey taught me nothing else, it is the complexities of the worldviews and epistemologies that inform our research and of the lives we so humbly try to capture in our narrative. Julieta, Andrea, Carolina, Jovita, and all the women encountered during this journey are anything but monolithic. Their stories clearly challenge any interpretation of a single story, a single experience, or a single truth.

## Transborder Decolonial Feminisms

As a means to analyze and theorize campesinas' everyday conditions and teaching and learning (pedagogies), I draw on feminisms that attend to *transborder vivencias, decolonial projects,* and *spaces of praxis.*† Chandra Mohanty (2003) reminds us that for some women around the world borders

---

* See Borland 2007; Kim 2007; Mies 2007; Olesen 2003; Pascale 2011; Pillow 2003; Pillow and Mayo 2007; Villenas 2000.
† See Castellanos Llanos 2006; Castillo 1994; Castillo and Tabuenca Córdoba 2002; Collins 1991; Elenes 2011; Gargallo 2006; hooks 1999; Moraga 2000; Phillips 2006; Rojas 2009; Suárez Navaz and Hernández 2008; Villenas 2010.

are indeed real and can signify oppressive structures and/or decolonizing opportunities.

> Feminism without borders is not the same as "border-less" feminism. It acknowledges the fault lines, conflicts, differences, fears, and containment that borders represent. It acknowledges that there is no one sense of a border, that the lines between and through nations, races, classes, sexualities, religions, and disabilities, are real—and that a feminism without borders must envision change and social justice work across these lines of demarcation and division. (Mohanty 2003, 2)

In a similar vein, Saldívar-Hull's (2000) Chicana "feminism on the border" demands we address the multiple forms of domination women of color must confront every day. Feminism on the border "addresses the ways in which Chicana feminism participates on the 'border' between US feminism and Latin American feminism, and alongside the feminisms of other women of color in the United States" (Saldívar-Hull 2000, 56). This requires complicating, transcending, and working the borders in order to understand the manner in which our localities connect globally and our diverse subjectivities differentiate us as well as unite us (through notions of sameness and differences). Understanding women who stay behind in Mexico requires an analytic lens that acknowledges and works from a fluid sense of borders (transborder) and its personal and structural demarcations. It acknowledges that women who stay behind also contend with and transcend borders from their localized spaces and places. Indeed, recognizing and uncovering how transborderism functions reveals alternative realities (vivencias) and possibilities for transborder coalitions and supervivencias (Gargallo 2006; Suárez Navaz and Hernández 2008).

Decolonial feminisms also work to *decolonize* and challenge white supremacist heteronormative patriarchy (Fanon 1963; hooks 2013; Mignolo 2005; Mohanty 2003, 2008; Moraga and Anzaldúa 1981). The practice and work of decolonization requires a differential consciousness and a "self-reflexive collective practice . . . and political mobilization" (Mohanty 2003, 8). As Sandoval (1991, 15) suggests, "The differential mode of oppositional consciousness depends upon the ability to read the current situation of power and of self-consciously choosing and adopting the ideological form best suited to push against its configurations, a survival skill well known to oppressed peoples." Indeed, campesinas' struggles to push against certain configurations meant they had to read and adapt to the situation (Moraga 2000; Sandoval 1991). This ability to respond and change with the situation, however, required guidance. PLAMAC provided those tools by actively engaging women in consciousness-raising dialogue and teachings. Decolonial projects also work from the place of community knowledge by validating multiple ways of being and knowing. For instance, drawing on campesina spiritual epistemologies offers liberating sources of knowledge many times unexplored and invalidated. By presenting spiritual knowledge as valid and crucial, we reimagine the potential of race and culturally based knowledge to counter dominant epistemologies.

Historically marginalized communities in the United States and other parts of the world also create *third spaces of praxis* and possibility (Anzaldúa 1987; hooks 1999; Pérez 1999). This interstitial or third space is born of a cultural memory of colonization that seeks to advocate political projects and global perspectives (Elenes 2011; Pérez 1999; Phillips 2006; Stephen 2007; Suárez Navaz and Hernández 2008). Campesinas' multiple subjectivities are clearly linked and contingent on their relationships transnationally and similarly create third spaces of praxis and possibility. That is, as women who stay behind take on the responsibilities and leadership of their families and communities at home, they require spaces to build a critical consciousness and opportunities to reflect on their conditions and create change. The spaces and places of the SSGs represent one space of praxis, healing, and supervivencia. Like liberatory teaching and learning spaces, third spaces are intimately shaped by women's epistemologies. As hooks (1993, 13) posits, "The power of the group to transform one another's lives seemed to be determined by the intensity of each individual's desire to recover, to find a space within and without, where she could sustain the will to be well and create affirming habits of being." Similarly, campesinas required transformational spaces where convivencia prevails among women struggling with similar challenges but an intense desire to change their circumstances.

A transborder conceptualization also requires what Moraga (1981, 23) suggests is a *"theory of the flesh* . . . where the physical realities of our lives—our skin color, the land or concrete we grew up on, our sexual longings—all fuse to create a politic born out of necessity" (my emphasis). This "theory of the flesh" articulated by Moraga allows for that holistic theorizing of women's transborder existence. That is, a theory—founded on our knowledge, history, and struggles; a holistic approach to self; and the wholeness of our people—does not deny women's attachment and commitment to community nor does it negate the personal struggles and intersectionality women contend with. In previous work I used a womanist lens precisely because of its intersectionality, everyday situatedness (*en lo común*), vision of social change, and focus on wholeness—mind, body, and soul—(Trinidad Galván 2001). Phillips (2006, xx), for instance, describes womanist sensibilities as "a social change perspective rooted in Black women's and other women of color's everyday experiences and everyday methods of problem solving in everyday spaces, extended to the problem of ending all forms of oppression for all people, restoring the balance between people and the environment/ nature, and reconciling human life with the spiritual dimension." Clearly, this is seen in the women of Sierra Linda, who through their struggles, hopes, and visions attempt to move forward but not alone. They work in collective groups like the SSGs on communal issues, create women-centered spaces, and draw on their historical memory and cultural knowledge to attend to the needs of their family and community. Their pains and joy speak of communal and individual struggles. Their pedagogies and visions are about all of us—"committed to the survival and wholeness of entire people" (Walker 1983, xi).

## Looking Forward

As I got involved in the lives of the women of Sierra Linda, it became clear that their strength, while less overt, was inspiring. Uncovering their stories and supervivencia required more than first impressions or a number of encounters. As their individual chapters demonstrate, it took several months of mutual inadequacies and convivencia for the women and me to become close, friendly, and trusting of each other. Friendships organically emerged and with them complex, happy, and heart-wrenching stories. I initially relied on PLAMAC and its meetings to get acquainted with the women and their lives. Fascinating observations and field notes emerged from these meetings.

Yet it was not the women's interactions with PLAMAC but their teaching and learning in the SSGs and my interactions with them in their everyday lives that proved most insightful. In the SSGs I observed them fulfill PLAMAC's expectations by introducing some literacy activities or reflections. Even though PLAMAC had wide predetermined notions of what needs the SSGs should meet, the groups many times established their own needs, solutions, and unique engagements. The teaching and learning that took place in the SSGs were characterized by each animadora's strengths and insecurities and the group dynamics. Hence, the pedagogies enacted in the SSGs were filled with the complexities and contradictions of rural communities, living transborderly, patriarchal family and societal structures, and differing personalities. One could not decontextualize the meaning the women's teaching and learning had from its social, economic, and political meaning. As a result, three main ideas surfaced from the data that address women's survival. First, the *transmigration and transborder condition* of the region transformed community dynamics and social relations. Women and communities' transborder state required that women lead and attend to the needs and responsibilities of home and community. Second, women learned to manage and defy their new responsibilities by means of their participation in *a grassroots organization and community activism*. Part of women's response to the migration phenomenon was their integration in a grassroots organization that shaped their critical consciousness, activism, and community leadership. Third, women used their own (*lo propio*) cultural knowledge and ways of knowing to defy their transborder state. Campesinas drew on the cultural tradition of convivencia and their spirituality as sources of healing and supervivencia.

Although individual groups and women are highlighted in individual chapters, they are not my sole understanding of that phenomenon or situation. Rather, I came to understand these themes and their complexities from the lives and interactions of all the women I interacted with. Each animadora's unique leadership or molding of the group resulted in specific issues and ideas that broadly appeared in the data with all the women. Via narrative ethnography and life history interviews, I was able to chart four women's education, small savings group, and convivencia (Chase 2005). "Julieta: Wife of a Migrant Man" (chapter 1), "Andrea: Hesitant and Unappreciated Activist" (chapter 3), "Carolina: Devoted Mother and Community Leader" (chapter 5), and "Jovita: Caring and Humble Woman" (chapter 7) describe how we came to know each other—our convivencia. Our convivencia was not only a theme in the data (see chapter 6) but also what facilitated our coming to know each other and my portrayal of their narratives. Each chapter also describes the women's participation in the small savings group and an important theme from the data subsequently underscored in the chapter that follows. Migration, grassroots organizing, convivencia, and spirituality are themes discussed in the content chapters that follow each individual narrative.

Even though Julieta was not an animadora to any of the small savings groups, she is spotlighted in chapter 1, "Julieta: Wife of a Migrant Man." As one of many women contending with the incessant migration of her husband since the onset of their marriage, she most strongly spoke of her experience as a wife and sister who stayed behind. This chapter narrates Julieta's life, education, and work and serves to preface the migratory phenomenon in the chapter that follows.

The backdrop of women's supervivencia lies in the migration of loved ones and its consequences. Chapter 2, "Transmigration, Transborder Realities, and the Transformation of Women Who Stay Behind," explores from a global feminist perspective the manner in which women who stay behind are implicated in global processes and consequently survive these conditions using diverse social practices and relations. This chapter explores women's changing and contradictory ideologies and responses to the transmigration of their loved ones and the transborder condition of their community. In line with the overall concept of supervivencia, it examines the inequities migration causes that women who stay behind must contend with in order to survive. It sheds light on the migratory conditions of the region—a fact that lingers throughout the book—as women demonstrate their supervivencia in myriad ways. Women like Julieta who stay behind learn to survive economic and emotional limitations but also learn to organize and create new identities, coalitions, and spaces of self and communal empowerment.

Chapter 3 highlights Andrea, Julieta's older sister. "Andrea: Hesitant and Unappreciated Activist" underscores the trials and tribulations of grassroots organizing. Her narrative sets the stage for the upcoming discussion of activist work and globalizing from below as we learn of her leadership and the pains of community activism. Like each of the individual life history chapters, Andrea's chapter discusses her educational background, our convivencia, and her particular struggles. Her struggles with community organizing and SSG leadership introduce issues relevant to the chapter that follows.

Drawing on Andrea's narrative, the role of nongovernmental organizations (NGOs) in the construction and alteration of global/local processes comes alive. In chapter 4, "Globalizing from Below and the Work of Grassroots Organizations," Andrea's group and her narrative help to examine the difficult work of engaging in community activism. Through Andrea's work and doubts the reader comes to understand that "organizing from below" comes with struggle and pain. This chapter examines PLAMAC's work with the women of Sierra Linda and the visions, strategies, and forums they cultivate so as to counter the negative effects of global restructuring and ensure women's survival. The chapter argues NGOs combat "globalization from above" (e.g., corporate businesses, nation-states) by tapping into local knowledge and providing consciousness raising forums and reflections.

Chapter 5, "Carolina: Devoted Mother and Community Leader," highlights the eldest of the Acosta Valdéz sisters. Carolina's narrative underscores the significance of convivencia. Her story is about bringing women together to share and coexist and from there generate moments and opportunities of learning, healing, and supervivencia. An important testimonial is presented that demonstrates the group's convivencia and is later revisited in the following chapter as an example of communal healing and supervivencia.

Chapter 6, "Pedagogical Spaces of Convivencia and Healing," focuses on the significance of women-centered teaching and learning spaces that women can access, learn in, and share together. Carolina's group exemplifies such sharing and learning through convivencia, healing, and pedagogies of survival. This chapter examines women-centered spaces and their healing potential as alternative pedagogical forms. Like their decision to join PLAMAC to counter the negative effects of migration, poverty, and gender inequities, women rely on their own cultural traditions to survive. The chapter explores another form of human agency that Sierra Linda's women enact in defiance of the transmigration and transborder state of their communities. It presents their reliance on convivencia, as one cultural tradition, to resist material commodification and the division of communities as a result of the separation of families.

Jovita's narrative in chapter 7—"Jovita: Caring and Humble Woman"— exemplifies cultural epistemologies and the importance of spirituality in women's supervivencia. Jovita's story presents local cultural practices and traditions shaping women's teaching and learning spaces. Her story reflects the very intimate and personal knowledge that women hold and share with each other.

Through Julieta, Carolina, and Jovita's spiritual life histories, chapter 8 presents women's spirituality as an essential component in their lives, struggle for individual and communal change, and pedagogies of survival. "Campesina Epistemologies and Pedagogies of the Spirit" is about considering women's spiritual epistemologies—the source of their strength and ways of knowing and being in the world—as crucial in shaping the pedagogies enacted in their groups. It argues women's spiritual epistemologies are the means by which women self-define and remain whole, while operating within local, national, and global spheres. In women's educational and social spaces, their spiritual epistemologies inform the teaching and learning process by providing them individual and collective purpose. The book comes full circle in this last chapter as the notion of supervivencia comes alive through the women's reflections and spiritual sensibilities. It addresses the question of what social relations, cultural knowledge, and women-centered pedagogies sustain women's survival.

The conclusion summarizes the major findings and makes connections to larger discussions of transmigration and its implications for host and sending communities and education. The epilogue brings the women's stories back to the present and revisits where they are today after fourteen years. It reminds the reader of the trials and joys of rural life as well as the constant learning that takes place as women try to forge their own spaces of teaching and learning.

# CHAPTER ONE

# Julieta

## Wife of a Migrant Man

*Is solace anywhere more comforting than in the arms of a sister?*
—ALICE WALKER

Even though Julieta Acosta Valdéz was by far the woman I spent the most time with, I seldom recorded our interactions. Because our friendship developed almost exclusively outside the small savings groups, our interactions were many times not part of my field notes. At the time our convivencias were part of our everyday living and coming to know each other. We were either in her home during teachable moments, running errands, consulting traditional healers, at the church dispensary, or simply walking around Sierra Linda. I had not understood that those everyday interactions were not only part of our convivencia—as women, mothers, and friends—but also teaching and learning moments. Unlike her sisters Carolina and Andrea, Julieta was neither an animadora nor performed a leadership role in any of the small savings groups. Her participation, however, was significant in both her sisters' small savings groups. She participated in Andrea and Carolina's groups because she lived in town during the week and in their rural community on the weekends. Carolina's group in town was held on Monday afternoons and Andrea's group in La Vereda on Saturday afternoons. Her role in Andrea's group was much more prevalent as Andrea resisted her leadership role and often relied on Julieta's forthright personality, suggestions, and friendly nature to motivate the group. Julieta often helped Andrea feel confident about her own skills and on a few occasions convinced Andrea to share her expertise on alternative medicine and other topics.

Like Andrea, Julieta was also the wife of a migrant man. Manuel Alvarez, her husband, migrated to the United States years before their marriage and consequently had the opportunity to legalize his residency status.

Although Julieta and Manuel knew each other all their lives, it was during one of his visits back home in his early 20s that Julieta and he started dating. Only two weeks after their relationship began Julieta left with him, and they eventually married in 1985. As Julieta mentioned at a community meeting, "One gets married with the notion that one is going to marry and that they [husbands] will last two or three weeks, leave, and then come and go. They leave and won't return until December or others even longer. Some don't come during these days of the Christmas holidays or end of the year, and that's when we most feel their absence." Apart from his drinking, Manuel was a very responsible husband who always met his economic duties, and consequently the two were able to purchase property in La Vereda and Sierra Linda.

Like other women in her community, Julieta struggled to raise and educate their children and care for their home and land alone in the absence of her husband. Manuel's legal status in the United States—something uncommon for most migrants in the area—facilitated his returns an average of three times a year. As a result of his frequent returns I had the opportunity of interacting with Manuel during a couple of his visits. Theirs was the only transmigrant relationship I witnessed, and from it I partially understand the role and responsibilities of families who stay behind. During one of his visits, I witnessed the couple's opposing worldviews and the manner in which Manuel's new ideas from *el norte* (the North) were introduced into their home. One afternoon as we sat around the living room, Manuel asked Julieta to try on the outfit he brought her from the United States. Coy and unwilling to show off her outfit in front of her family and mine, Manuel critiqued her way of thinking.

MANUEL: *Deberías de ser más como los americanos, ellos son bien positivos. No se hubieran fijado.*

JULIETA: *Pues yo no puedo ser como ellos porque yo no los conozco, no he vivido con americanos.*

MANUEL: *No se trata de eso [vivir con ellos], pero hay que ser como los americanos, siempre le ven lo positivio a las cosas, no lo negativo. . . . No me entiendes, yo sólo te digo que ya tenemos que progresar y ser más como los americanos.*

JULIETA: *Pues no, yo no puedo ser como alguien que no conozco.*

MANUEL: You should be more like the Americans [U.S.]; they are very positive. They wouldn't have minded.

JULIETA: Well I can't be like them because I don't know them; I have never lived with Americans.

MANUEL: It is not about that [living with them], but we need to be more
like the Americans, they always see the positive side of things, not
the negative. . . . You don't understand me; all I am saying is that we
need to progress and be more like the Americans.
JULIETA: Well not me, I can't be like someone I do not know.

Their conversation proved to be a snapshot of their opposing ideologies. In
this case their opposing views of progress were evident. For Manuel, progress consisted of a relative openness to new ideas and ways of being, while
maintaining a positive outlook on life. It meant not being coy, as Julieta
seemed to be, or close-minded. However, both Manuel and Julieta vacillated back and forth between what they considered "progress."

On that same evening and after Manuel's earlier discussion of progress,
we sat at the kitchen table and talked about Manuel's legal status and the
possibility of Julieta and the children traveling to the United States. After
asking him whether he had considered legalizing and migrating his family
to the United States, Manuel promptly answered that he thought about it
but quickly discarded the idea. His ultimate reasoning: women change too
much in the United States. "As soon as they go to the United States they
become liberated and leave you," he answered. Clearly his response completely contradicted his earlier idea of progress and Julieta's need to be
more like the "Americans." As the wife of a migrant man, Julieta struggled
daily with the added responsibilities Manuel's migration placed on her,
but most importantly with the emotional drain of not having a husband to
support her.

Manuel and Julieta had four children. The oldest, Miztli, was fourteen
and attended middle school in Sierra Linda where they lived during the
week. Julieta and Manuel also had three sons, ages four, seven, and ten.
While the four-year-old stayed at home, his brothers attended an elementary school downtown with Carolina's children. Both Julieta and Carolina
lived in a new neighborhood complex just south of the city and on the road
to their rural community of La Vereda. Since the neighborhood was fairly
new, Carolina and Julieta felt the schools in the city offered a better education, and all the children took public transportation to attend school
downtown.

Of her five sisters and two brothers, Julieta (fourth after Carolina, Imelda,
and Andrea) stood among those with the least formal schooling. While she
was not the oldest, like Carolina who received no schooling, her parents'
dire economic situation forced Julieta to abandon school early. Like her other
sisters and Jovita, Julieta missed school in order to look after the family's
farm animals that roamed freely on different plots of land on the outskirts

of their community. While her mother attended to the house chores and her father to the harvest, the responsibilities of the animals and lighter house and harvest chores were left to the girls. As a daughter, Julieta was forced to miss school in order to attend to these chores.

*Cuando empecé ir a la escuela, mi mamá y mi papá todavía querían que fuéramos pero a la vez no nos ponían atención—"Tu todavía no vas porque tienes que cuidar [los animales]." Yo faltaba mucho. Ahí fue donde yo no tuve consistencia. Cuando iba bien seguido, yo sentía que iba aprendiendo bien todo. Pero luego faltaba, me hacían faltar—"No vayas porque vas a cuidar." Notaba que ya no podía, porque iba unos días y después faltaba unos días o hasta semanas. Por eso nunca salía de primero. Yo si quería ir, pero porque tenía que atender el maíz ya sembrado y en aquel tiempo menos iba [durante esa temporada]. A la edad de catorce años me fui a un internado y ahí fue donde yo aprendí lo que se. Nada más. Cuando llegue allá pues me recibieron y entre a segundo y de ahí me brincaron porque si la hacía.*

When I started going to school my mother and my father wanted us to go, but at the same time they didn't pay much attention to us—"You still can't go because you have to take care [of the animals]." I missed a lot. I didn't have consistency. When I went often, I felt like I learned everything well. But then I'd miss, they'd make me miss—"Don't go because you're going to look after [the animals]." I noticed I couldn't [do the work], because I attended a few days and then missed another few days or weeks. That's why I never finished first grade. I wanted to go, but then [during the harvest season] I had to take care of the corn harvest and I went even less. At the age of fourteen I went to a boarding school, and that's where I learned what I know. That's all. When I got there they put me in second grade, and from there they jumped me around because I was doing well.

In her narrative she continued to explain how her family relied on all-girl government boarding schools for their education. Schooling was free, but families had to provide their daughters' school supplies and personal items. In Julieta's case even that was difficult.

*Andrea fue la primera que fue por una señora que conocíamos y después nos mandaron a las demás, pero no aguantábamos. En ése internado sólo nos daban de comer y donde dormir con cama y todo. También habían talleres de corte y bordar. Entonces nada más estábamos Sara y yo en un internado en Aguascalientes. Yo me sentía sola porque era la mayor. No tenían [sus padres] para darnos jabón para lavarnos, ni pasta. Como yo estaba grande me daba pena. Después me vine y también ella [Sara] se vino, pero después Sara siguió yendo y ella vino terminando en un internado en Guanajuato.*

Andrea was the first to attend a boarding school because we knew of a lady [that recommended her], and later they sent the rest of us, but we couldn't bear it. In that boarding school we were fed and given a place to sleep with a bed and all. There were also sewing and crochet workshops. During that time only Sara and I were in a boarding school in Aguascalientes. I felt real lonely because I was the oldest [of the two]. [My parents] didn't have enough to give us soap or toothpaste; since I was older I was embarrassed. Later I left and so did she [Sara], but later Sara continued and finished in a boarding school in Guanajuato.

Both of her sisters—Andrea and Sara—got the most from their boarding school education. They both finished middle school, while the rest of the girls in the family only finished grade school or less. Julieta often used her family's economic situation to educate her children about the wonderful opportunities they had to attend school and the material wealth they enjoyed. Julieta mentioned to me on several occasions that she remembered having only one dress when she was growing up. "If the dress had been of good fabric it might have lasted longer, but it was fabric from back then that if you washed it too much it disintegrated. Since I only had that one, I would go to the river, take it off and leave only my slip, and wash it. When I was done I'd put it back on wet or wait until it dried a little. Really we were in bad financial straits. Now I tell my children that we are in heaven. Now clothing lasts so long you throw them away instead."

Julieta was not well off by any means, but she was better off financially than any of her other sisters. Manuel's secure employment in the United States and Julieta's excellent financial management provided them two homes, two used vehicles, and land. Julieta felt very fortunate and actually only complained about Manuel's drinking, which she found very disconcerting. She was especially concerned not with the unnecessary spending but the example he conveyed and time he spent away from the children. She felt he spent the bulk of his visits drinking instead of talking or engaging with the children. She often complained to him that even though he visited more than other men in their community he was disconnected from their children.

## La Convivencia

Convivencias with Julieta were always jovial and inspirational even during difficult times. One afternoon in April was no exception as we started the day in her home with the weekly English language lesson and ended in Sierra Linda's Catholic Church dispensary where we often went together. For the last couple of months I provided Julieta's, Andrea's, and Carolina's daughters English lessons in Julieta's home. Miztli and Lorena, Julieta and Andrea's daughters respectively, were fourteen and attending middle school while Lupe, Carolina's sixteen-year-old daughter, attended high school. I gladly attended to this responsibility usually once or twice a week. Because at the time all three girls attended school during the afternoon session we usually met in the mornings for an hour and a half. Lupe, older, was very mature and took things seriously. Lorena, not as mature but equally responsible, also attended the lessons. Unfortunately, it was Miztli, Julieta's daughter, who mocked the process and posed a distraction to the other girls.

The English language class ended at noon, and the girls each went on their way to get ready for school. On that day, Julieta's older sister Imelda was visiting. Imelda was the only sister I did not interact with or get to know. She became pregnant at a young age and left her community to make her own life. According to Julieta, Imelda's life up to that point had been very difficult. Imelda's first relationship was unsuccessful, and feeling outcast from her home and community she moved to Sierra Linda where after many years of ill-fated relationships and having several children, she continued to struggle. Of all the Acosta Valdéz sisters, Imelda suffered the most economic hardship. Julieta, who lived comfortably by rural standards, often sought out Imelda and helped her as much as possible.

Because Julieta's mornings were always the most hectic as she fed, dressed, and set the children off to school by noon, I intended to finish the lesson and ascertain whether Julieta had time to convivir. Since the boys were off in the living room getting ready for school and Miztli prepared to leave, Julieta seemed eager to do something together. She proceeded to go into her room and brought back a folder of materials to share. Her folder was packed with leaflets and handouts she accumulated throughout the years from various alternative medicine, critical literacy, and nutrition workshops she attended. Imelda, Julieta, and I then sat in the kitchen, where Julieta proceeded to share several sheets with information on alternative medical treatments.

As we looked through the material I asked questions that Julieta felt she could not answer. She progressed to lament that Andrea was not present to teach us and address my many questions. According to Julieta, Andrea was the most knowledgeable of her sisters. I couldn't help but show my surprise since I often witnessed Andrea's insecurities in her SSG and little willingness to share her knowledge or lead the group in discussions. It also demonstrated how little I had gotten to know Andrea even at such a late date in our relationship. Although we had become friends, she was not the kind of person to brag about what she knew. It would be Julieta in the months to come that pressed Andrea to lead activities in her SSG.

Julieta felt that apart from not being schooled, she had also not taken advantage of many workshops and programs offered in her community. While living in La Vereda and next door to her in-laws' home, she was always under the watchful eye and control of her husband's family. Because his family, like the rest of her rural community, criticized and looked down upon women who spent time away from home, Julieta stayed indoors and tried to stay away from rumors. Later in the day she described the ill treatment she received from her in-laws during her husband's absence and how that hindered her motivation to get ahead. As we all realized the time, Julieta, who had already prepared lunch, called the children to eat. After eating together, Julieta suggested we leave the girls at school and continue talking in the dispensary. The girls, Imelda, Julieta, Julieta's small son, my daughter Anayansi, and I all jumped in my minivan and went to the dispensary.

The *dispensario* (alternative medicine dispensary) was a small room behind the town's cathedral. The dispensary, like other church-related programs, provided alternative medical consultations at low cost. It offered a number of treatments, such as chiropractic massages, acupuncture-type treatments on the earlobe (*auriculoterapia*—auricular therapy) using mustard seeds, and herbal medication (*microdosis*). Each of us attended to our individual needs while my daughter and Julieta's son played by the entrance. Julieta placed seeds on her earlobes and purchased herbal medications for her mother-in-law, while Imelda consulted the woman behind the counter about her lungs. Imelda worked in the ceramic industry in town, which at times did not adhere to good working conditions. For instance, employees were not advised or given protective gear against dust and lead poisoning. After Imelda described her symptoms, the woman also recommended she see a doctor to have her lungs x-rayed for more serious problems.

Once we were done we decided to have a snack across the street. Directly in front of the dispensary was a health food store and restaurant. For a small city, Sierra Linda had several of these natural food businesses

and alternative health practitioners. After ordering, the three of us and the
two young children sat at one small table.

> RUTH (AUTHOR): *¿Esas microdosis las compro para su suegra?*
> JULIETA: *Sí. Mis hermanas dicen que yo quiero más a mi suegra que a mi
> mamá porque siempre estoy allá con ella. Pero si las quiero igual. O sea
> que siento lo mismo a pesar que me trato muy mal mi suegra al prin-
> cipio. Si realmente ella me empezó a querer desde que me vine para acá
> [Sierra Linda].*
> IMELDA: *Hasta se la cacheteaba.*
> RUTH: *Ayy apoco.*
> JULIETA: *Sí. Un día llegaron ella y sus hijas para darme.*
> RUTH: *¿Y todavía así la quiere como a su mamá?*
> JULIETA: *Sí. ¿Me paso de buena, verdad?*
> RUTH: *No. Es bueno que pueda perdonar.*

> RUTH: Did you buy those herbal medications for your mother-in-law?
> JULIETA: Yes. My sisters say I love my mother-in-law more than my own
> mother, because I am always at her place. But I love them the same.
> Rather, I feel the same, even though my mother-in-law treated me
> badly at first. Actually she only started to like me since I moved here
> [to Sierra Linda].
> IMELDA: She even slapped her around.
> RUTH: Really?
> JULIETA: Yes. One day her and her daughters came over [to hit me].
> RUTH: And you still love her like your own mother?
> JULIETA: Yes. I am too nice, huh?
> RUTH: No. It's great that you can forgive.

On this occasion she did not share what problems transpired between her
and her husband's family. It was clear, however, that she got along well and
cared for her mother-in-law even though she had mistreated her. Since it
is customary in many rural communities in Mexico for married women to
move into their in-laws' home when their husbands leave for el norte,
those first years of marriage were especially difficult since she did not have
the protection of her husband and her mother-in-law was stringent and
controlling.

Besides caring for home, children, and land, women who stay behind
struggle with community gender-specific norms that restrict their movement and opportunities. Because women's reputations are scrutinized when

their husbands are absent, patriarchal families work to ensure women stay respectable (Stephen 2007). Even though Julieta only lived with her in-laws during the first years of marriage, her own home was close enough to theirs that she felt equally confined. Actually it was probably her in-laws' proximity that allowed her to stay alone in her own home in her rural community even after her husband left for the United States. Since Julieta lived alone with her children in their rural home and in Sierra Linda during Manuel's migration that gave her freedom that her mother-in-law and sisters-in-law initially criticized. After all that transpired and not without great effort, Julieta felt she changed tremendously after leaving her rural community and her husband's family. In an interview I conducted in her home, she shared her limitations and initial struggles.

*La familia de mi esposo siempre me estaban molestando o no dejaban de criticarme. Y yo pues quería quedar bien [no salía] y como quiera ni quedaba bien [seguían criticándola]. Me molestaban y no me dejaban tranquila—me decían cosas. A mi siempre me ha interesado aprender cosas, como cuando había un taller, una reunión o algo, pero como que me tenían cohibida. Cuando me vine para acá dije, "No pues hora sí." Yo decía, "Me voy a sentir mas liberada de ellos, ya voy a poder hacer lo que yo quiera." Claro, siempre y cuando esté bien. Y cuando llegue a la vez se me hacía imposible. Carolina me decía, "Hay una reunión, vamos." Yo siempre estaba mentalizada que había que ir, pero siempre se me hacía imposible. Batalle para salir.*

My husband's family was always bothering me or didn't stop criticizing me. I also wanted to please them [and didn't go out], even though I never did [please them]. They bothered me and didn't leave me alone—they said things to me. I have always been interested in learning, like when there were workshops, meetings, or something, but somehow they made me coy. So when I came over here [to town] I said, "Now I will." I said, "I am going to feel liberated from them, I will be able to do what I want." Of course, always doing what is correct. And when I came here I felt like it was impossible. Carolina would say to me, "There's a meeting, let's go." I was always mentally trained that I should go but still felt that it was impossible. I struggled to get out.

Even though Julieta found herself far away from her in-laws' influence, she struggled to be free from their norms and criticism. According to her, her state of mind was not prepared to be free from the ideas that controlled her for so many years. She knew that attending workshops would be educational, but she still felt restricted by her community's ideals of women's place in the home, her devotion to her husband, and maintaining her honor as a respectable married woman (Villenas and Moreno 2001). She also mentioned being so used to home life in her rural community that although she was "free" in town she felt lost and confined. It was after over a year of living in Sierra Linda that she began to be more active. Not until she regularly participated in her local church, where Carolina was active, did she inquire about educational opportunities. As is evident in the following chapter, women like Julieta who stay behind must contend with gender-specific norms that stifle their social and educational opportunities and ability to lead in the absence of their husbands (Hondagneu-Sotelo 1992).

## The Small Savings Groups

Julieta did not lead any of the SSGs she participated in but played a crucial role. In her rural community Julieta was not afraid to speak out and urge Andrea to motivate the group by presenting different activities or sharing what Andrea knew about nutrition and alternative medicine. Julieta, and her youngest sister Sandra, expressed in the SSG what Andrea out of fear of further criticism abstained from voicing herself. This, of course, did not mean Andrea remained silent throughout the meeting, but rather there existed an almost unspoken agreement that Julieta and Sandra would confront or suggest controversial ideas. In the following SSG, for example, it was Julieta who pushed Jovita to reconsider succumbing to the community's plans for an end-of-the-school-year celebration that placed some families in economic straits.

As part of Jovita's daughter's birthday celebration, Andrea's SSG took place in Jovita's home one Saturday afternoon. Throughout the year and as part of their endeavor to convivir, the group celebrated each member's birthday every month. It was customary to have these birthday celebrations in Julieta's home because she had enough space and all the necessary utensils. However, this also meant the mess and cleanup was left to one person every time. In an earlier meeting the group decided to celebrate each member's birthday in his or her home.

On the way to La Vereda I stopped to pick up Julieta and Sandra, who were still preparing their dishes. We arrived at La Vereda a few minutes after four. Since Jovita's husband had decided not to migrate to the United States, Jovita was happy and welcomed the group. We laid our food items on a table she placed on one side of her large courtyard and moved about for some time until the meeting started. Karina, the birthday girl, together with all of Jovita's family, was present. All of the small savings group members were present, including Julieta and sisters Andrea, Sara, and Sandra, Julieta's brother Miguel and his wife Elena, Julieta's sister-in-law Zoraida, and three other members that were not part of the family.

After everyone arrived we immediately proceeded to eat. Jovita also made certain to serve everyone a slice of cake and a shot of liquor after the meal. Once done, we all made a toast to Karina's well-being and more birthdays to come. After the food and cake, the men stood by one of the tables drinking what was left of the liquor while the rest of us crowded around the other table. The conversations that followed touched on various topics. Andrea began by expressing that these birthday celebrations might serve to motivate the group. Because Alma—Jovita's sister-in-law—and Jovita both had elementary school children, the conversation shifted to the school's end-of-the-year celebrations. Both women had large families with multiple children in elementary and middle school. Jovita had nine children and Alma twelve. Since several of their children were finishing elementary or middle school, the activities required the families to spend money on the children's end-of-the-year activities.

JOVITA: I have two children that will finish middle school.
ALMA: And I have one that finishes kindergarten and another elementary.
JOVITA: I don't know how we are going to do it. The kids say that in the middle school they want them to wear a smoking jacket. I don't even know what that is.
JULIETA: What is that for?
JOVITA: Well, for the end of the year.
JULIETA: Why so much? In Sierra Linda they don't ask for so much. When Juan [her son] finished they only asked that he wear a white shirt, a red bow waistband, and ten pesos for the mass. They asked for very little. Here they ask for too much. People here are in bad shape [economically] but try to impress everyone.
JOVITA: Yes, but we don't have an option.
ALMA: One doesn't even find the means to do it all. I have two; we will see how we do it.
JULIETA: You should complain.
JOVITA: Are you kidding, if one dares to say something the other mothers immediately attack you.

ANDREA: Oh yeah, they immediately start—"What lazy women, don't you love your child, why did you have him? This is only once."

JULIETA: What do they think, that these kinds of things only happen once?

JOVITA: Those of us that have lots of children can't even open our mouths because they criticize us for having so many. Like if they were financially supporting them. The burden is on me not them.

ALMA: And since I have twelve what can I say? I just follow.

JULIETA: You should get together with other women you confide in and protest. If there are more of you they'll listen. Because really those who have a lot [of money] they can do it, but the ones who don't, just can't. When Miztli finished everyone used his or her uniform real nice and pressed. And then everyone was the same.

SANDRA: They should have a party for the poor and another for the rich.

JOVITA: You even get into debt, and later when you have some money you can't use it to buy food but rather to pay what you owe.

RUTH: What is it that you have to do that's so much?

JULIETA: Wow, you have to make food for everyone, give money for the mass and for the dress and the godparent.

ANDREA: All you do is waste a lot of food that ends up in the trash.

JULIETA: All the mothers are there—"Teacher, taste mine." They are all trying to impress the teacher, but how is he going to taste all of that food? That's why Manuel always says that we Mexicans are in bad shape, because we want to make a party for every occasion. That's why we don't progress.

Everyone laughs and agrees with Julieta's comments that in rural communities in order to show status you have to splurge during these types of activities. It seemed that even those with the least, like Jovita and Alma, fell prey to community competition. While Jovita might have liked to dispute the needless spending she did feel that other mothers felt the occasion merited some sacrifice. After the conversation ended and we conversed for a few more minutes the celebration concluded.

Julieta's newly acquired freedom and self-confidence, like that of the rest of her active sisters, was very promising. She had enough self-esteem, experience, and knowledge to search for programs and educational experiences that would cultivate her inquisitive mind and desire to learn. For instance, as a young woman she volunteered to be trained on nutrition and health issues. She took those consciousness-raising experiences and in turn educated various communities in the area. It was from this experience that she acquired a wealth of knowledge on nutrition and the processing and preparation of soybeans. Her preparation started at an even earlier age than Carolina and Andrea. She was only eighteen when she participated in this training.

*Un padre que celebraba misa ahí en La Vereda anunció que necesitaba tres personas de cada comunidad para aprender sobre la nutrición y después enseñarle a los demás. Entonces fuimos Leila, mi tía, y yo. Fíjate que yo si aprendí y participaba. Por eso yo a veces digo, "¿Dónde estoy ahora?" Porque éramos un grupo, estábamos en una casa, y aprendiendo todo lo que era de soya y lo concientizaban a uno. Decían, "Tienen que aprender bien porque van enseñar esto a La Vereda y a La Laguna y a otros ranchos que están más adentro." Me sentía que si podía.*

A priest in La Vereda announced one day that they needed three people of every community to learn about nutrition to later share with others. Leila, my aunt, and I went. I learned and participated. That is why I sometimes say, "Where am I now?" Because we were a group that worked in a house learning everything about the soybean, and they would do some consciousness-raising with us. They would say, "You've got to learn this well because you are going to go out and teach this to La Vereda and La Laguna and other communities that are farther." I really felt like I could do it.

When Julieta spoke of these experiences and the strides she was making, she lamented not having continued that path. She would further beat herself for allowing others, like her in-laws, to determine her future by putting her down and demoralizing what were genuinely good intentions. Like her sisters—who struggled to acquire knowledge—she too came upon many barriers that impeded her progress as a woman who stayed behind. With her, as with Andrea, rural community cultural beliefs that defined women's place in the home restrained them from participating in different programs and furthering their education. She felt it was not until recently that she was ridding herself of those sexist cultural impositions (Hurtado 2003). As a young woman, a few years before she married Manuel, she had become an adult literacy instructor of surrounding communities. However, gossip and cultural values that demeaned women as only responsible for and allocated to the private sphere extinguished her very young fire (Villenas and Moreno 2001).

*Llegó un muchacho con un programa para enseñar a leer y escribir. Y como yo si sabía poquito me preguntó si me gustaría enseñarle a la gente.*

*Yo acepté. Y me fui a cada rancho. Los que eran grandes como de mi edad más o menos si aprendieron a leer y escribir. Y luego me decían maestra. Me daba bien harta vergüenza. Traía una cartilla, así como ustedes, y nos daban nuevas palabras, ya hasta recortadas en cartulina. Yo tenía unos alumnos bien aplicados. Nombre hasta me querían ganar después. Pero hubieras visto como me afecto eso. Yo estaba muy a gusto porque allá me encontré un muchacho que era bien mi amigo, que yo lo quise mucho como amigo nada más, no otra cosa. Aquella gente [de aquel rancho] eran muy aventados a pesar de que no sabían y tenían el modo muy bonito. Pero los de La Laguna nos sacaron muchos cuentos. Que fue lo que me hizo a mi arrepentirme. Porque decían [de ella y la otra maestra] que ya no servíamos, ya no éramos unas señoritas, ya nos acostábamos con quien fuera allá por el cerro. Hubieras visto. Pero bueno a pesar de todos los rumores así me quisieron.*

A young man came [to the community] with a reading and writing program, and since I knew a little he asked me if I wanted to teach people. I accepted and went to the different communities. The older people, like my age, they did learn to read and write. They would call me teacher and I would get really embarrassed. I carried a literacy booklet, like the one you bring, and they would give us new words already cut out on poster paper. I had some serious students. Boy, they almost wanted to outdo me. But you should have seen how that affected me. I was very comfortable because I found a [male] friend there who became a really good friend and I really cared for him like a friend, nothing else. The people from that [rural community] were real diligent even though they didn't know much and had real nice personalities, but the people from La Laguna invented stories about us. That's what caused me to regret [being involved] because they would say [about her and the other teacher] that we weren't any good anymore, we weren't virgins anymore, and we slept with anyone over by the hill. You should have heard what they said. Well, in spite of all the rumors he [her husband] still wanted me.

After that episode she felt truly demoralized and worried that no man would want her. Like Hurtado (2003, 15) suggests, "According to Chicana feminists, Marianismo and Malinchismo dichotomized women's womanhood into the 'good woman' and the 'bad woman' according to their sexuality." It's very telling that Julieta's final comment coincides with this notion of the "bad woman" as she recollected that in spite of all the rumors her husband still wanted her. Ultimately, Julieta had to overcome the trauma created about women's roles and sexuality and initiate new opportunities to learn and serve (González 2005). She was fortunate to have an outgoing personality that drew people to her for advice or to suggest programs. It was not surprising to hear her speak of women who often sought her for company or information. For instance, during those days when we spent time in her home, it was not unusual to have other women knock at her door and visit.

The responsibility of her home, land, and children, like with Andrea, Carolina, and Jovita, also took its toll, and so she often needed someone to whom she could express her loneliness and frustrations. At times, days would go by when I would not see or hear from her. During those occasions, the responsibilities of being a woman who stayed behind without her husband extinguished her spunk and she preferred the isolation of her home. When she was finally ready she would share these dilemmas and attend *curanderas* (traditional healers) or the dispensary, which she felt eased the physical ailments incurred on her body (Finkler 1994). She also relied heavily on cultural and spiritual knowledge in order to attend to her physical and emotional wounds and *supervivencia*.

In the following chapter, I continue to journey through the everyday lives of Julieta and other women as they are enmeshed with those of their husbands and loved ones abroad. I argue that migration of primarily men creates conditions that shape the economic, cultural, and ideological positions of those who stay. Julieta's story is spotlighted as one example of women's transborder relationships with their husbands and the accommodations, resistance, and transformations of women who stay behind.

# CHAPTER TWO

# Transmigration, Transborder Realities, and the Transformation of Women Who Stay Behind

*How does that saying go? "Cry in poverty but don't cry alone." That's the way it is. What good is it to live in a palace if you are not happy? But one also cannot live happily in poverty. . . . So the husband says, "You know what? I am leaving [to the United States] to make at least enough for a small room. . . ." But after all of the years gone by and all of the situations endured one is still unhappy because we miss our husband.*

—ANDREA ACOSTA VALDÉZ

The numerous stories of migration and struggle by many of Sierra Linda's women draw attention to the migratory state of these rural communities and of the supervivencia of those who stay behind. Andrea's quote poignantly exemplifies the paradox of attempting to reach happiness through the economic benefits migration can afford but then realizing life away from her spouse is not happiness at all. This chapter explores women's changing and contradictory ideologies and responses to the transmigration of their loved ones and the transborder condition of their community. In line with the overall concept of supervivencia, it examines the inequities that migration causes and campesinas must contend with in order to survive. It sheds light on the migratory conditions of the region—a fact that lingers throughout the book—as women demonstrate their supervivencia in myriad ways. Women who stay behind learn to survive economic and emotional

Portions of this chapter appeared in the journal *Globalizations* (Trinidad Galván 2008).

limitations but also to organize and create new identities, coalitions, and spaces of self and communal empowerment.

Sierra Linda's rural communities mirror many peasant communities across Mexico that traditionally subsisted from an agricultural economy. Since the implementation of NAFTA (North American Free Trade Agreement) in 1994 and other neoliberal policies, rural communities turned to out-migration for economic survival. Indeed, no single factor in the last three decades has affected these communities more than the constant exodus and movement of its members. Andrea, whose husband lived and worked in the United States during most of their fifteen years of marriage, reveals the ecological and economic changes occurring in the area that have partially contributed to the migration phenomenon in her community. She states, "Before it rained, and people would harvest and have corn and beans, but now with the drought, now it has left us without food . . . but also one needs not only to eat, one needs shoes, clothing, all of that, so what do people do . . . leave." As Andrea's words confirm, men and women incessantly attempt to survive and provide for their families through their movement and the opportunities it might offer.

During the period of study, the state of Guanajuato led the country in the number of migrants to the United States. It was ranked first in out-migration among Mexican states, with over 366,000 migrants coming to the United States from 1997 to 2002. Those that followed in descending order were the neighboring states of Jalisco, Michoacán, San Luis Potosí, and Zacatecas (see figure 2) (Consejo Nacional de Población n.d.). As Patricia Arias's (2004, 182–83) quantitative research in Guanajuato reveals,

> The state of Guanajuato has experienced an unusually intense and diverse process of economic change in both rural and urban settings. Some of these changes have clearly produced increasing hardship, social marginalization, and the exclusion of local actors and local knowledge from broader economic activities. At the same time, however, these changes have thrust Guanajuato and its people into the front line, the vanguard, of globalization and development, especially in the agricultural and manufacturing sectors. . . . In all sectors, international migration, embedded as it is in the historical memory of the people and constantly expressed in everyday life, represents a key resource that households can draw upon as they adapt to change. Migration to "el otro lado" has been, and continues to be, the means by which Guanajuatenses confront and resolve the successive, uncontrollable, and incomprehensible transitions to which

their lives and work have been subjected through the workings of the global economy.

Indeed, the constant transmigration of people from Guanajuato means those who stay behind are required to confront and resolve what is left of their home and community infrastructure. Because men make up a greater portion of those migrating back and forth, this pervasive transmigration greatly affects the women who stay behind to assume all of the duties of home and community. Migration was inevitably one of the most common themes of discussion among the women of Sierra Linda during any meeting, gathering, or interview. With the exception of a handful of studies,* there is little known of how families, and women in particular, respond to the changes they and their communities face when loved ones migrate. Even more importantly, Sierra Linda's women represent those who stay behind to care not only for the home but also lead community projects and engage in activist work (Dyrness 2011). Hence, "looking at gender as a constitutive element of [migration]," transnational ties, and identities even among those not migrating is crucial to this work (Hondagneu-Sotelo 2000, 117). In my presentation of campesinas' responses to their loved ones' migration, I draw on the work of transborder feminists and feminists of migration studies in order to genderize my analysis of the migratory phenomenon of the area and its effects on those who stay behind (Pessar and Mahler 2003; Salazar Parreñas 2009; Silvey 2004).

## Transborder Feminism and Transmigration

*Making explicit global-local connections in women's lives "allows for the subversive possibility of women seeing beyond the local to the global."*
—MENDEZ AND WOLF 2007, 656

Women who stay behind apply a face, an intimate view, to global structures and transmigration, a view that extends beyond an economic phenomenon that subsequently dismisses the incessant exchange of ideas and stories encountered in "power-filled social relations," such as those experienced by many campesino men and women (Brah, Hickman, and Mac an Ghaill 1999, 8). I find it important to consider that when issues surrounding global

---

* Durand and Massey 2006; Hirsch 2007; Kearney 2000; Salazar Parreñas 2005; Stephen 2007; Wilkerson, Yamawaki, and Downs 2009.

restructuring and transmigration are seen as all-engulfing large-scale events, the mundane daily occurrences and the portraits of resistance and resilience are overlooked. This resiliency is clearly expressed by some of Sierra Linda's women. Hence as Mendez and Wolf (2007) suggest, understanding the dialectics of global and local relations brings women who stay behind to the center of migration studies. In the same way, Salazar Parreñas (2009, 6) reminds us that "feminist migration scholars have the responsibility of identifying and documenting the ways that gender inequalities shape people's experiences of migration whether men or women." I would also add that considering the transborder reality of migratory communities and families, we should be cognizant not only of "people's experiences *of* migration" but also people's experience *with* migration. Considering that it is primarily women who bear the brunt of the migration at home, acknowledging their experiences is fundamental to foregrounding the gender inequities they must contend with. A transborder feminist approach to migration and the global-local (glocal) connections communities maintain through this transmigration provides a helpful analytic framework for centering women and families left behind. That is, what this book provides is a gendered look at those impacted by the migration phenomenon and their response to their transborder realities.

The transmigration of the region—the result of the movement of spouses to and from the United States—introduces new ideas, capital, bodies, and information and alters the roles and perspectives of women who stay behind (Massey 1994). As Stephen (2007) suggests, the reality of these communities is more than simply transnational or transmigrant since movement between nations is only part of the story. She suggests the term "transborder rather than simply transnational . . . [because] the borders they cross are ethnic, class, cultural, colonial, and state borders within Mexico as well as the U.S.-Mexico border" (Stephen 2007, 6). Much like Anzaldúa's concept of *nepantla* as the "in-between space [that] facilitates transformation; as the boundaries break down, the identity categories that before were so comfortable—so natural, as it were—no longer work; they dissolve, compelling us to find new ways to define ourselves" (Keating 2000, 5). Women who stay behind are precisely in these "in-between" spaces of struggle and transformation as they confront changing family and community dynamics and find new ways to define themselves and survive.

How can we best understand the landscape of women who stay behind? Feminist theories and accounts of global restructuring and power relations across space and time contribute an important dimension to a transborder feminist framework (Massey 1994). For instance, although it is evident from

Julieta's transborder relations described in chapter 1 that women who stay behind are indeed implicated in global relations, women's position in this process continues to be understudied. Consequently feminist scholars in this area continue to criticize global migration studies for ignoring gender relations.* As with many other issues, women are affected differently and influence circumstances in particular ways. Because global restructuring continues to emphasize First World, capitalist, and Western views, there must exist a deliberate focus on poor racialized women and other marginalized groups. While I discuss the manner in which gender is absent from discussions of global restructuring, I must stress that campesinas' rural demarcation is never detached from their ethnic, racial, and class status (Anzaldúa 1987; Hurtado 1999; Pérez 1999). In Mexico's context the mere marker of campesina suggests rurality, hence, indigenous, racialized, brown, and poor (Batalla 2009).

Runyan and Marchand (2000, 225) point out that "feminist accounts . . . reveal more clearly the broad range of power sources at work in global restructuring by examining cultural and social forces. They also stress multiple forms of human agency in terms of both the construction of and resistance of global restructuring." Feminist accounts shed light on the power relations, complexity, and interconnectedness of these relations. This interconnectedness requires understanding genderized social relations of power, as women traditionally thought of as confined to private-realm spaces or as nontravelers are excluded from transborder or migration discussions. Feminist researchers acknowledge the interlocking of social and power relations across various spaces (nations, communities) and levels (global, local) (Massey 1994; Salazar Parreñas 2009). Transborder social and power relations demonstrate campesinas' implication in these glocal, social, and power relations because the movement of loved ones and other disjunctures alters their ideas, roles, and positions in the community. A "focus on women . . . notes the multiple social relations they maintain with not only men but also other women. In other words, we need not engage in a comparative view when we only focus on women but could instead embark on a comprehensive account of gender in the study of migration" (Salazar Parreñas 2009, 5). In this case, women who stay behind must confront community antagonism from both men and women and contend with community and familial responsibilities they are unprepared to

* See Alexander and Mohanty 1997; Glick Schiller, Bash, and Blanc-Szanton 1992; Hondagneu-Sotelo 1994; Karpinski 1999; Marchand and Runyan 2000; Pessar and Mahler 2003; Salazar Parreñas 2009.

assume. These contentions are clearly linked to women's unequal position in society (Pessar 2003). These transborder gendered relations point to the numerous power relations women straddle locally through their husbands' movement.

The translocality and consequent changing ideologies of women who stay behind can best be understood through a transborder feminist lens that points to the numerous power relations women straddle locally and abroad. Locally, as will be evident shortly, they must contend with power struggles that hinder leadership, educational, and employment opportunities. Nationally, their campesina demarcation also forces them to contend with class, race, and ethnic discrimination. As alluded to earlier,

> Feminist views of identity and subjectivity turn migration studies towards an understanding of the migrant [or transborder] self as constituted through a range of intersecting, sometimes competing, forces and processes, and as playing agentic roles in these processes. They take seriously the experiences and narratives of migrants' interpretive voices as a lens onto the ways in which broader-scale structures are represented, understood, mediated and funneled into particular understandings of self and agency. (Silvey 2004, 499)

In the section to follow, we see women's agency and responses to their transborder condition and, as Silvey (2004) suggests, the competing forces and agentic roles they play as they face new roles and responsibilities.

## Women Who Stay Behind

*Their social relationships and their varying and multiple identities [are] generated from their simultaneous positioning in several social locations both to accommodate to and to resist the difficult circumstances and the dominant ideologies they encounter in their transnational fields.*
                                        —GLICK SCHILLER ET AL. 1992, 4

As the preceding Glick Schiller et al. quote suggests, rural Mexico's transborder character drives both migrants and those remaining to creatively survive their changing condition. An examination of transborder communities, such as this one, demonstrates quite dramatically the complexity engrossed in the movement, integration, struggle, and resistance of travelers and stayers. Women who stay behind, for instance, have to survive economic constraints and emotional heartache but also learn to organize and create new identities, coalitions, and spaces of self and communal empowerment. Within a single community, women and their families respond differently and in contradictory ways to their transborder state and *supervivencia*. Women's narratives express the manner in which they accommodate to, contest, and transcend their condition.

## Accommodation

As women stay behind without their husbands, brothers, and sons, they learn to accommodate to their newfound roles and responsibilities (González 2005; Hirsch 2007; Stephen 2007). Their accommodation comes as a result of the many responsibilities they have to assume in their home and community, which, as PLAMAC codirector Guillermina López Bravo suggests, drives them to "struggle and not stand back waiting." Women who stay behind endure more responsibilities both at home and in their communities. The larger workload women assume in the absence of their spouses and loved ones requires an extensive amount of time and energy and a shift in gender roles. On many occasions Julieta complained about the amount of responsibilities she alone had to endure: "Here I have to take care of the children, feed them, clothe them, and also worry about our plot of land." Jovita also recounted how during her husband's yearlong stay in the United States she was responsible for the duties of the home and harvesting of the land: "And I remember that in all that time during the rainy season, when I had to feed everyone, I had to work a lot. Since he left me the [agricultural] lot, I had to work hard irrigating our harvest." Although *campesinas* are always at the center of the agricultural harvest of their land, the absence of men in the family means they alone must contend with this role.

In addition, most women feel a tremendous responsibility imposed on them from faraway spouses and community members to perform all of their tasks quietly and without bitterness. While family networks act as intimate moral support and not just transmigrant economic and cultural networks, they can also work against women's accommodation and transformation. Transmigrant communities literally live beyond their borders, and men are kept current on family occurrences and in turn exercise their power or judgment (Hirsch 2007; Ojeda de la Peña 2007; Stephen 2007). This was the case for Julieta during the initial years of her marriage when her in-laws kept a strong hold on her and monitored her every move. Although her husband wasn't vigilant regarding her whereabouts, her mother-in-law took on the patriarchal role of maintaining women in the family in their place. This isn't different from claims made about the role that women can play in maintaining and reproducing patriarchy (hooks 1990; Moraga 2000). Julieta eventually resisted her in-laws' controlling manner by moving to Sierra Linda and there accommodating to her new independence. As she states, "[When I left] I told myself, I believe I will be free. And now I can do what I want. Of course, always doing the correct thing."

Other women, like Andrea, learned to accommodate to the community's patriarchal judgment and control by altering their beliefs on men's role in the family and strategically using family networks when handling family troubles. Although Andrea's husband was controlling, his lack of communication and attention to family matters meant Andrea had the freedom and support of her extended family network to rely on and make changes in her life. As Andrea states in her life history interview, "I got tired of the chores of the house. I'd rather choose to know the outside world. When I can I focus and move forward." After becoming actively involved with PLAMAC, Andrea did not resist any opportunity the organization provided to the community in order to move forward. Andrea was by far the most active woman in her community and family. Precisely because she chose to participate in grassroots organizations and lead community projects, more gender-traditional women criticized her.

In Andrea's case, community support and social networks also included grassroots organizations, such as PLAMAC, that assist women in their accommodation. PLAMAC provided economic and social support for its members as well as new perspectives on the migration phenomenon and women's roles in it. Guillermina López Bravo worked closely with several groups of women in Sierra Linda. From her direction, the groups spent time reflecting on the social and economic problems of their communities. During one meeting Guillermina reflected on the situation of women who stay behind and stated the following:

*Yo digo que para las mujeres que tienen hermanos, niños o esposos en el norte no pueden estar esperanzadas en el dinero. Porque como puede llegar [el dinero], no puede y que van hacer. Los hombres están allá en peligro y un mes mandan y otro a la mejor no. No pueden estar con los brazos cruzados esperando que les caiga. Como mujeres podemos hacer lo nuestro. Pero hasta lo que esté en nuestras posibilidades aquí. Lo que se pueda. Pero por lo menos luchamos, no nos quedamos sólo esperando.*

I say that for women who have brothers, sons, or husbands in the North [United States] they can't be dependent on the money. Because like it may arrive [the money], it may not and then what are you going to do.

The men over there are in danger, and one month they may send and another they may not. You can't have your arms crossed waiting for it to fall on you. As women we can do something. But depending on what is at our disposal here. What we can do. But at least we struggle and don't stand back waiting.

Guillermina often spoke strongly about the need for women who stay behind to lead in the development of their community, since most men's undocumented status in the United States could not assure them their job, residence, or income. She argued that the economic subsistence of men, women, and entire families was frequently at the disposal of unjust U.S. government policies and employers that could deport men at any time. Therefore, Guillermina felt it was partially PLAMAC's duty to uncover these tribulations, expose a different lived experience, and provide the tools to make it a reality. That is to say, if families found themselves without the income of migrating family members, as often occurred, there were other possibilities for subsistence.

Women like Carolina and Andrea accommodated to their circumstances by leading community groups, opening their own small businesses, and engaging in personal development activities. Although it was Carolina's eldest son who migrated, she sought every community opportunity to provide financially and holistically for her family. Of all the women, Carolina made all the necessary accommodations to bring women together to learn. Even though she initially struggled because she felt that she did not have the necessary skills or knowledge, women consistently followed her. "All the women of the community have followed me, even the older women who tell me, 'You know how, you tell us and do as you wish,'" Carolina said. Similarly, as a result of Andrea's leadership role and participation in PLAMAC's community groups, she—with the help and support of her sisters and family network—initiated several community projects and was even nominated for local office. Antiquated ideas that women were not made for politics or must resign themselves to a life without their husbands were quickly being challenged.

## Contestation

Women who stay behind learned, with the help of loved ones and community organizations, to accommodate to their new situation and responsibilities. However, many of the same women also resisted their transborder state. Many realized they could not resign themselves to the permanent migration of their loved ones. Some of the women struggled with both their aversion to the migration of the men and their need for economic remittances. Consequently, some women in transmigrant communities find migration favorable, others unfavorable, and still others are caught between the two. In an interview, Julieta spoke to migration's economic benefits but was also weary of the disintegration and breakdown of the family. She says migration both benefits and complicates their lives. "In some cases it benefits us [migration] and in others it harms us. Economically probably. But I also say that maybe living together as a couple, as a family and resolving our problems together, good or bad as they may be, is better, because with sacrifices one can advance."

As the spouse of a migrant man, Julieta depended on Manuel's remittances to financially survive, but his absence also produced physical and emotional sorrow. I listened to narratives of—and from our close relationship witnessed—physical ailments that she related to the excessive responsibilities of being a single parent. The physical and emotional drain placed on women should come as no surprise. Wilkerson et al.'s (2009, 623) study, also conducted in rural Mexico, on the mental health of women left behind concluded that "the migration of husbands had a significant effect on the mental health of wives in that the separation produced a decrease in wives' mental health." Unlike those in Wilkerson et al.'s (2009) study, women in Sierra Linda—as will be made evident—had the support of social organizations, extended family, and their spirituality to address their emotional and physical ailments.

Jovita also expressed the huge emotional drain her husband's migration caused her during that short period. Although her economic situation was the most precarious, she was more concerned with the emotional state of her family than living in abundance. Jovita's narrative clearly stresses that the migration of loved ones, and the financial security it may provide, does not sufficiently make up for the loss of emotional and familial support.

> *Horita que me atacan [la comunidad], que me echan habladas yo lo soportó, yo lo soportó porque lo tenge a él [a su esposo con ella]. Él es el único apoyo que tengo. Yo me siento muy contenta que esté él . . . y yo le digo, "Yo lo siento mucho pero yo prefiero pedir limosna pero no estar lejos de ti." Porque si iba estar sola [sin pareja] pues mejor me hubiera estado en mi casa [con sus padres].*

Right now that I am attacked [by the community] and they talk about me I can endure it because I have him [her husband with her]. He is the only support I have. I feel really happy that he is here with me . . . and I tell him, "I am very sorry, but I would rather beg in the streets than be far away from you." Because if I was meant to be alone [without a partner] then I would have stayed at home [with her parents].

Jovita's family represented for her not only economic remittances but also the love, support, and strength women possess against the many struggles they face. She felt she could neither accommodate nor resign herself to such a situation. When women are at the center of research, an array of ideologies emerges about what's important to the family. Jovita's dissenting voice is a perfect example. She resisted both the effects of migration on family structures and women and families' decisions to give up family unity for a few pesos. She reiterated her resistance by stating, "I'm sorry, but I do not want [migration]. I prefer that if we have one tortilla that we eat it between the two of us. I searched for a husband, I didn't look for money." Even Julieta, who vacillated back and forth, expressed, "I have lived all my life like this [without her husband by her side], and I don't have a full stomach. Sometimes we do, but other times one feels alone and with no one to share what little we do have, just alone. In those cases one doesn't even eat." In addition many women resisted not only the separation of families and lack of support that migration produced but the lack of recognition they received for their work.

It must be acknowledged that entire households are responsible for the mobilization of remittances and resources, and consequently campesinas who stay behind call for recognition for their share of these responsibilities. Julieta, for example, recognizes the crucial role she plays in her husband's contributions. At one point she expressed this insight to Manuel after he complained (by phone) that she was not properly caring for their children.

*Sí, es cierto que no les di [desayuno esa mañana que él habló con los niños]. Pero tú tampoco, por lo menos yo de ves en cuando, pero tú nunca porque no estás. ¿Tu crees que con sólo mandar dinero eres padre? Pues no, el dinero no se mueve sólo, aquí yo tengo que moverlo.*

Yes, it's true I didn't give them any [breakfast the morning he called and spoke to the children]. But you also don't give them, at least I do now and then, but you never do, because you aren't here. You think that by merely sending money you're a father? Well, you're wrong, money doesn't move on its own; here I have to make it work.

Indeed, many women who stay behind oppose and resist the migration of their loved ones because they find it socially costly in enforcing strict gender roles. While women are asked to take on added roles that go unrecognized, the same does not occur for men. For instance, Salazar Parreñas (2005, 47) notes in her study on Filipino migrant women that "the expansion of mothering duties in transnational families increases the work of women, in the same way that the narrow construction of fathering limits the responsibilities of men. I found that fathers left behind get away with having far fewer responsibilities than the mothers left behind." Undeniably, many of Sierra Linda's women show feelings of opposition and resentment, as they understand migration to be only one answer to family survival. Women, however, are not resigning themselves to this situation and instead question, like Andrea, when their family will finally be reunited.

> *Cuando uno se casa y forma la pareja, vive muy poco tiempo como pareja. Unos a los días agarran y se van y hasta los años vienen y otra vez se van. Así se va uno año por año. Yo a veces le decía [a su esposo], "¿Cuando iremos a estar juntos? ¿Será hasta que ya estemos viejos, que ya no sirvamos para nada?"*

> When one gets married and becomes a couple, one lives very little as a couple. Some leave days after [they are married] and don't come back for years and then leave again. And that is how one lives year after year. Sometimes I would tell him [her husband], "When are we going to be together? Will it be until we are old and good for nothing?"

Clearly, many women cannot resign themselves to a solitary life and the added responsibilities that come with it. Instead, Julieta, Andrea, Jovita, and many other women convey feelings of resentment and alienation. Hondagneu-Sotelo's (1992) work with women also demonstrates a degree of household discord with regard to the issue of migration. She recommends a closer look at the "power relations operating within the family or household unit" so as to ascertain the kind of contention and family decision making transpiring (395–96). Julieta and Andrea's mother Chuy's wishes, for instance, to report her son's irregular stay in the United States to the *migra* (ICE) so as to force his return home demonstrates the extent to which families diverge in opinion. The contention and power dynamics of the family unit demonstrate difference in opinion (or choice) on the matter of migration.

Statewide grassroots organizations also choose to change community perceptions about the need to migrate and leave their communities. One woman put it well when she stated,

*Alguien un día dijo que en México no hay pobreza sólo migración, pero nosotros como mujeres tenemos que enseñarles a nuestros hombres que aquí si se puede. Para que no tengan que ir a otro país que no es el nuestro y no perder nuestras culturas y tradiciones. Porque de allá sólo vienen muertos, esposos e hijos.*

One day someone said that in Mexico there is no poverty, only migration, but women like us must show our men that they can do it here. So that they don't have to leave to another country that is not ours and lose our culture and traditions. Because from there they just return dead, husbands and sons.

Indeed, those who stay behind must also contend with the grief that accompanies the permanent loss of a loved one. Many women must also endure the hardship that some men and women do not return, either because they have found permanency and a new family in a distant country or because they departed this life in their attempts for better opportunities.

During this research, Julieta's husband Manuel died of a cerebral hemorrhage in Houston, Texas, at the young age of forty-seven. Fortunately and without due notice, his last days were actually spent with Julieta, who only three months before his death in 2006 crossed the border to be with her husband. Although they spent his last living moments together, she struggled for years with U.S. and Mexican authorities to claim his rightful retirement funds. It is only since 2010 that she has finally been able to obtain a visa and make all legal arrangements to claim his retirement funds and visit her eldest son. Indeed, the migration of loved ones has real repercussions on women and families, as Julieta and Manuel's story illustrates. Their marriage of over twenty years was always a transborder relationship. Julieta's dream to eventually live together was short-lived. Instead, Manuel's untimely death was another reminder of the efforts women, like Julieta, make to transcend the negative effects of their loved ones' transmigration.

## Transcendence

Many of the women who stay behind also find ways to transcend community ideologies and conditions. Although the absence of men calls on women to assume men's roles, such as that of community leaders and heads of household, socially and culturally the community is unwilling to accept women in these roles. Hence, women must also contend with not only added responsibilities and the loss of loved ones but gender-specific attitudes of women's role in society (Espiritu 2003; López 2002; Salazar Parreñas 2005). Even with the absence of many community members, women are continually antagonized for their participation in public community affairs and their "negligence" in the home (González 2005; Villenas and Moreno 2001).

Andrea, for instance, who often struggled to encourage women to join community projects, stressed that women did not participate in community projects or PLAMAC because they were afraid of not only their husbands' criticism but the community's in general.

> *Tienen miedo hacer un proyecto . . . [Dicen], "No, yo no me quiero meter en problemas, yo no quiero que hablen de mi y que digan que yo hice esto . . . " Ellas tienen un miedo, que . . . la gente hable de ellas. Por ejemplo, a nosotros nos dicen mujeres huevonas sin quehacer. No lo han dicho en nuestras caras. Pero yo pienso que mas que nada es un proceso. Un proceso del que primero hasta no ver no creer. O sea cuando ellas se asesoren de que esto es algo bueno y se les quite la superstición [que las mujeres no deben participar en asuntos públicos].*

> They are scared to work on a community project . . . [They'll say], "No, I don't want to get into problems; I don't want them to talk about me and say I did that. . . ." They are scared . . . people will talk about them. For example, they tell us we are lazy women who have nothing better to do. They have said this to our faces. But I think that it is more than anything a process. A process that entails seeing is believing. That is, until they take stock that this is something beneficial and they rid themselves of the superstition [that women should not participate in public matters].

Women's ability to transcend these cultural and androcentric ideologies often means making sense of the contradictions of womanhood, since many times it is other women who critique them for being actively involved in community projects (Salazar Parreñas 2009). Sofía Villenas and Melissa Moreno's (2001) examination of *mujer*-oriented mother-daughter pedagogies suggests that women's teachings include the contradictory and often complex expectations of being a *mujer del hogar* (woman of the home) and one who knows how to *valerse por si misma* (make it on your own). Julieta and Andrea's discussion of other women's perceptions of a mujer del hogar follows a similar vein to what Villenas and Moreno (2001, 677) describe as a gender socialization founded on a "Spanish colonial legacy of *honor y vergüenza* (honor and shame)." Upon deeper examination they find that women's *vergüenza* comes as a result of not "fully" contributing to their household (economically). Hence, women in those cases embrace *el hogar* (the home) so as to equally contribute to the household. Transborder feminists capture this contradiction and complicity because they focus on the manner in which heteronormative patriarchal and white supremacist structures bind individuals and keep these contradictions hidden (Elenes 2011; hooks 2013; Salazar Parreñas 2009). Chicana feminists, for instance, address the manner in which female images work to reproduce and also break from heteronormative patriarchal norms, like that of Malintzin, La Llorona, and the Virgin of Guadalupe, to demonstrate how stringent gender roles are created and challenged (Anzaldúa 1987; Elenes 2011; Hurtado 2003).

As discussed previously with regard to women's participation in community projects, women did find ways of contributing to their households by establishing small family businesses or learning a trade (e.g., seamstress) that could eventually provide an income. Women like Andrea and Julieta who engaged in community projects were coming to terms with not only their newfound responsibilities as *jefas del hogar* (head of the household) but also proactive ways of minimizing the future migration of their children. Because they were trying to create livable conditions at home, they did not question their contribution to the household. Indeed, many of the women felt their contribution to the household far outweighed that of their absent husbands.

Interestingly enough, it is also the absence of men that gave these women greater flexibility to maneuver their chores and time away from home, because even though male dominance is still present, community needs forced women to transcend and alter this cultural norm. Similarly, in Hondagneu-Sotelo's (1994, 65) study of women and families who migrated to the United States from Mexico, the migration of men "enables them [women], indeed requires them, to act decisively and autonomously." In fact, it became a joke around women's community reunions to respond, "*Es que tengo el gobierno en la casa*" (The government awaits at home) when women could not participate for more than several minutes. Women learned to joke about the inflated power given to men in their communities, since they were keenly aware that due to the absence of men they had the opportunity to participate in PLAMAC's community groups.

Although at times emotionally affected by their community's perceptions of women's place in society, women like Julieta, Carolina, Andrea, and Jovita transcended these ideals because their own ideologies changed. The men's absence essentially forced them to attend to public matters that eventually also shaped their perceptions (Hirsch 2007). Their incorporation and work in PLAMAC, for instance, proved a determining factor. Andrea and

Julieta, who both participated actively in PLAMAC's work, expressed their need to do something more than care for home and children.

> **Andrea**: *Mas que nada para mi yo lo entiendo como la superación de una persona, uno trata de superarse. Ellas están en una rutina diaria, haciendo lo mismo, su quehacer. No les interesa mas que su puro quehacer, lavar, planchar, ver sus hijos. Yo no siento que le estamos faltando al marido ni nada por el estilo. . . . [Queremos] también ver cosas nuevas . . . superarse, salir.*

> More than anything I see it as the self-improvement of a person. That one tries to self-improve. They [women who stay home] are in a daily routine of chores, doing the same thing. They are not interested in anything else than their chores, wash, iron, look after their children. I do not feel that just because one wants to advance that we are disrespecting our husband or anything of that nature. . . . [We] also want to see new things . . . advance, get out.

> **Julieta**: *No es tanto que yo siento que me aburra [de los quehaceres] pero como que yo siento la necesidad de buscar la manera de superarme un poco mas. Yo se que no va ser todo lo que yo quisiera, pero también pienso que si uno le hace la lucha no se va quedar así. Disfrutar algo mas de la vida.*

> It is not so much that I get bored [of house chores] but rather that I feel the need to find a way to advance a little more. I know that I won't change as much as I would like, but I do believe that if one tries you are bound not to stay the same. Enjoy life more.

Clearly the temporary absence of men, the incorporation of women into the labor market, and/or the integration of men into a country that debilitates men's power position result in changes in gender relations (González Pérez 2011; Hondagneu-Sotelo 1994). While women find they can assume more control or negotiate household authority and transcend traditional gender roles, this is not always the case. Salazar Parreñas's (2005) study of families in the Philippines where it is primarily children who are left behind suggests that men's roles are rarely altered and that in lieu of the mother's absence other female family members take over the care of the children and not the father who is present. "Indeed, transnational families are significant because they pose a challenge to the maintenance of the ideology of separate spheres as well as the traditional gender division of labor in the . . . family" and the enactment of gender roles (Salazar Parreñas 2005, 6).

Hondagneu-Sotelo (1994, 65–66) suggests a woman's newly acquired leadership opportunities and capabilities result in an increase in "her sense of self-esteem as a good wife who then eventually identifies as a *mujer fuerte* [strong woman]." However, this work demonstrates that taking the "reins" (*tomar la rienda*), as Hondagneu-Sotelo and others suggest, comes at a high cost for women if they are not supported. It is through painful experience and time that women transcend gender-specific cultural norms and come to be accepted, valued, and appreciated for being mujeres fuertes. Even though most of the women are already strong in their own way, it is through their public participation that they learn the hardships of being assertive. In the case of the women of Sierra Linda it was their active participation in PLAMAC, which introduced skills, critical consciousness, and a transformative perspective, that enabled them to confront their new roles as strong women and survive their conditions (Dyrness 2011). PLAMAC's role is a critical piece to the overall story of these women's transformation and missing in many other studies of women and families left behind (Salazar Parreñas 2005; Stephen 2007). In other words, transnational communities require support in confronting the changes, challenges, and transformative possibilities of their transborder state.

The narratives heard here are stories of supervivencia and resiliency in the face of hardship, mourning, and accomplishments among campesinas who stay behind and assume the care and responsibility of their children, farm, and overall community. This chapter helps to situate the women among current feminist discussions on global migration, revealing how the high incidence of migration from the area changed community dynamics and imposed greater responsibilities on women. Women responded to these changes by accommodating, contesting, or transforming their ideologies and response to their transborder state. We see that women respond differently and in contradictory ways to their newfound positions and responsibilities. With the help of extended family and PLAMAC women are able to accommodate their roles and responsibilities to meet their needs. Many of the same women also resist their new roles because they find them socially costly. They find that the emotional cost or loss to the family far exceeds the financial benefits. Still others learn to transcend their transborder state by changing their ideologies and, in many cases, those of the community (Vila 2000). With the help of PLAMAC, women's views and skills are altered and with them their family structure.

These stories of migration provide the backdrop for women's supervivencia throughout the book. How rural community dynamics change in the midst of transmigration and transborderism is essential to understanding women's responses and supervivencia. In the rest of the book I discuss how women use grassroots organizations and their own cultural knowledge to survive their conditions. In turn, Andrea Acosta Valdéz's life history to follow and the crucial work of grassroots organizing and community activism demonstrate the personal and collective development of transborder communities and the ideas, skills, and knowledge that ensure women's supervivencia.

# CHAPTER THREE

# *Andrea*

## Hesitant and Unappreciated Activist

*Though we tremble before uncertain futures may we meet illness, death
and adversity with strength may we dance in the face of our fears.*
—ANZALDÚA 2009, 205

Upon meeting Andrea I could not foresee how much I would appreciate
her strong commitment and hard work. Although she was the first woman
I met and spent months interacting with, there was much she did not
share. It would take almost the extent of the research to get to know her.
Actually, our friendship did not flourish until I became close to her
younger sister Julieta. It was then that she began to disclose her history in
the community and reveal her insecurities, introverted spirit, and hesitant
nature.

The first two weeks in the area were spent looking for a possible home
for my family and me. During one of those summer days, Guillermina,
PLAMAC's codirector, with whom my family and I were staying for the
time being, stopped to speak to Andrea on our way to town. Andrea was
the animadora of one of the two small savings groups in her rural community of La Vereda and the first community member we met and approached
on that day. A small woman standing about five feet tall, in her midthirties,
she was petite even at five months pregnant and expecting her third child.
She had two daughters, ages fourteen and six, whom she raised with the
help of her parents and sisters. Her eldest daughter Lorena, for example,
had begun middle school a year and a half before and was living with
Julieta in Sierra Linda. That left Andrea to care for her younger daughter,
Mayela, who attended elementary school in their rural community, and wait
for the arrival of her third child. Because Andrea and Mayela were alone
during the week, Andrea spent most of her day in her parents' home or store
in the company of her younger sisters. She also frequently spent nights in

her parents' home where she felt safer and supported by family. This was especially true during the birth of her son in November when she needed special attention and care. As a single mother, her family's assistance was especially crucial, since it freed her from the children momentarily and allowed her to attend PLAMAC's meetings or other workshops and lead her SSG.

Andrea's husband, Juan Martinez, migrated to the United States and had traveled occasionally back and forth during the last thirteen years. He chose a life away from his family after numerous attempts to work locally and in other parts of the country. However, unlike other men in the community who lived together in the same city in the United States, Juan resided elsewhere and did not contribute to household expenses or communicate regularly. His undocumented status in the United States resulted in unstable job opportunities and few and far between visits. As a matter of fact, he left just months before the birth of his son, and when I returned after the child's first birthday he had not yet returned. Without spousal economic and emotional support, Andrea and her children were forced to rely heavily on her extended family to *sobrevivir* (survive). During one community meeting, Andrea expressed,

> At least you [referring to the women she was talking to at the time] have your husband here and share with him what you have, what little you have. But here one is alone and worse off, because one is alone and the little we do have, or the little they do send, we owe. Things get paid off and again we are left in a bad situation, worse off than women who have their husbands. Because one is alone morally, but you're with your husband and know that if you can't make it [financially] at least you are together. I think that being together changes things.

Andrea's rural community was off the main road to Sierra Linda. Unlike other neighboring communities, La Vereda was fortunate to have direct access to the main road even if it became muddy during the rainy season. This meant La Vereda was rarely ever completely disconnected from town and its resources. It was approximately a three-mile drive from the main road to her community, where besides the *huisaches* (Nahuatl word for small thorny trees), *nopales* (prickly pear cactus), and an occasional animal, the rest was vast bare hillside. At the entrance of Andrea's community, humble and elaborate homes sat on both sides of the road. Five hundred yards from the entrance was the main plaza and community chapel. Directly in front of the main plaza were Andrea's parents' small store and phone service as well as other homes. Andrea's parents' small store, a communal site taken over by her parents several years ago, was the only local store (others sold fewer items directly from their home). The room where the store functioned was actually communal property that many community members labored to build. Her mother and younger sister, Sandra, sold an array of items, from dairy products to household detergent, sugar treats, and refreshments. On many weekends their store served as the site for the purchase and consumption of alcoholic beverages where men lingered late into the evening drinking, listening to music from their vehicles, and speaking loudly about their adventures in el norte.

As an ejidatario (communal landholder) and community commissioner, Andrea's father Alberto knew a lot about land rights and community politics. Andrea once expressed to me that her father also had contact with people *en la presidencia de Sierra Linda* (in the local government of Sierra Linda), and it was from his *palancas* (political connections) that she and her family found out about different social programs. Precisely because Andrea's family led various community projects they also exposed themselves to community critique. Andrea would often share the pain and turmoil of leading community projects and the criticism she endured. In the same breath, however, Andrea also voiced how difficult it was to motivate her community to participate in or lead any of these community projects themselves. She felt that her family initiated projects not out of a profound desire to lead the community but rather from the lack of incentive of other members. For instance, Andrea and her family initiated important and necessary community projects like the implementation of a water system only to be criticized once it was done. In an interview I conducted in Julieta's home, she described how they worked to implement the water system and the hostility they received. At her sister's kitchen table, she voiced her frustration while Julieta sporadically commented in agreement. "We [her family and she] contributed with the construction of a water system. We worked a lot, a whole lot. We went and talked to people and took them out of their homes. 'Come, let's go work, and let's go do the furrows.' Because we made the furrows to put the pipes. For what? So that ultimately they criticized us. So that the entire community turned against us."

At a public meeting in the chapel courtyard, Andrea and her family were removed as directors of the water system project and verbally attacked. After calling the community to a meeting, several members of Andrea's community accused her and her family of keeping some of the money for the project. At the meeting they voted to remove Andrea and her family and established a new board of directors. In Andrea's interview she described that meeting and her reaction to the accusations:

*[La gente gritaba], "¡No ustedes andan por delante porque les queda, les queda dinero. Y ahora se los vamos a quitar!" Y les contesté, "¿Ustedes lo quieren? No crean que tengo mucho interés en quedarme, en quedarnos adelante como representantes de un comité. No me interesa. Yo ya estoy harta de robarles. Porque ustedes dicen que les robo. Y voy a quedar bien rica con todo lo que ustedes me dieron." Y ya nomás se quedaron pensado. Y luego les dije, "Si hay gente que deberás con toda voluntad cooperaron para que el servicio del agua se realizara. Yo se que ustedes no me van a dar las gracias, ni tampoco se las estoy pidiendo, pero yo si quiero darle las gracias a todos ustedes que confiaron en nosotros y gracias a ustedes se hizo la obra. Porque si son gente razonable, que aunque no se meten a sacar una comunidad adelante si dan su cooperación." Si tú hubieras estado en esa reunión—haz de cuenta que éramos unos criminales. Todos contra nosotros—"Que eres una sin vergüenza, eres una quien sabe que." Bendito sea Dios después de todo nosotros salimos bien. Salimos adelante con los informes, porque vinieron a ver los de la presidencia. Dijeron [la comunidad], "Estos nos están robando." Y nos quitaron de la delantera. O sea, ahora ya están otros. Nos quitaron el plato, según ellos.*

[The people yelled], "You are leading this because you get something out of it, you get money. Now we are going to take it away from you!" And I answered, "You want it? Don't think I have a lot of interest in staying and leading this as a committee representative. I'm not interested. I am sick and tired of stealing from all of you, because that is what you say I am doing to you. I am going to end up real wealthy with all you have given me." And they kind of stepped back and thought. And then I told them, "There are people that wholeheartedly cooperated with the water system so it could become a reality. I know all of you are not going to thank me, I am certainly not asking you to, but I do want to thank all of you that believed in us, because it was thanks to you that the project became a reality. Because you are reasonable people, and even though you don't stand at the forefront of a community project you do collaborate." If you had been at that meeting—it was as if we were criminals. Everyone was against us—"You have no morals, you are God knows what." Thank God we came out all right. We came out all right with all the paperwork. Because people from the town presidency came. They [the community] said, "These people are stealing from us." And they removed us from the leadership. So others are in charge now. According to them they took our plate away.

The episode in and of itself brought her great turmoil but was also a reminder of the history between her family and the community. Andrea not only helped lead the water system project in her community but also participated in other projects like rebuilding the church tower, placing concrete on the church courtyard, directing the cultural center, and representing her community in other state programs. The rebuilding of the church tower, for example, was another project people convinced her to lead. Because Andrea was sometimes active and vocal, people in the community assumed she wanted to be involved in everything. As an active community member she was used when there was a need to get something done. In turn, she was criticized if things did not go as other nonparticipating members anticipated.

During one rainy evening many years ago, lightning struck one of the church towers and dismantled it. She described how the community "brainwashed" her into thinking she should take on the task of obtaining the funds for the reconstruction of the tower, but once she did she was criticized.

*Ellas [algunas mujeres de la comunidad] agarran y me lavan el cerebro, pero yo no me la creí. Dije, "Bueno por la iglesia y por la comunidad, y para ponerle otra torre a la iglesia que no tenía, yo sí lo hago." Pero [viéndolo bien] lo de involucrarse en eso de la comunidad esta difícil. Uno se trauma. Y yo digo que a veces ando de mal humor por lo mismo, que me haiga quedado eso [la angustia de saber que no agradecen]. Que yo tenia la buena intención.*

They [some of the women of the community] take me and try to brainwash me, but I don't believe them. I said, "Well I'll do it for the church and for the community, and to place another tower on the church that didn't have one, I'll do it." But [in retrospect] being involved in things of the community is difficult. One becomes traumatized. That's why I say I'm in a bad mood sometimes, because I was left with that [anguish of knowing they weren't grateful]. That I had all good intentions.

She clearly had the desire and willingness to work for the good of everyone but felt demoralized by people's apathetic feelings and cleverness in evading responsibility. Hence, her responsibility as the animadora of her small savings group stemmed from these same feelings of being placed at the forefront because others did not want to be in a position that required direct social responsibilities. Andrea did not choose to be the animadora of the first small savings group in her community but was again placed in a position no one else wanted. When asked how she got involved with the small savings group, this was her response.

> People here are not interested in those things [community projects]. The only thing they want is what's related to their work in the home, their chores, make tortillas, wash and all that. And they don't like to engage in what they call problems. Because, well, they say that they are not lazy women who just run around inventing things to do. So they said, "Let it be her [Andrea]." Really what they want is to rid themselves of that [any community responsibility], so that they are not referred to as women with nothing better to do, lazy, lacking sense [*mujeres desjuiciadas*].
>
> I went around asking everyone [if they wanted to join the SSG]—"Well no not me, and no not me." And no one wanted to. Then Guillermina would come often and say, "What happened?" "Well, no one wants to [join the SSG]. I already asked everyone and no one wants to." She'd say, "Well ask them again, that is precisely the job of an animadora." And from there I was named the animadora of the group. But that's because my people are difficult. There is a person here in the community who says, "Excuse me, but you can't get people in rural communities to do anything." He meant that even when you give them something, like when you say, "Hey, if you come to this, I'll give you something," they won't go even out of interest.

Being referred to as *mujeres desjuiciadas*—lazy women who have nothing better to do—was a recurring theme in her and her sister Julieta's interviews. Both women were cognizant that their community looked down on women who deviated from women's "traditional" place in the home (Trinidad Galván 2001). All four women struggled to strike a balance between caring for their home and children, as they certainly took pride in that, and educating themselves and playing some type of critical social or political role in society.

Andrea felt her role as animadora was to somehow bridge the disparity between what women could and could not do. For that she wanted motivation, ideas, and support on how to motivate her group, alter women's and men's perceptions of each other, and mobilize her community. A number of times she asked Guillermina to come and talk to her group and asked me to engage the group in critical activities around gender issues and literacy. When she voiced, *"Quizás ustedes sí pueden motivar al grupo"* (Maybe you can motivate the group), it came from the insecurity that she was not in a position or did not possess the tools to motivate others. Indeed, Andrea most clearly embodied the difficult task of working for a common cause and the discord and conflicts women endured. In addition, her narrative reveals that activism and community organizing is messy and unstable (Dyrness 2011).

## La Convivencia

Those first months with Andrea were awkward. Her quiet nature kept her from opening up. Consequently, she relied heavily on the presence of others like her sister Julieta and her aunt Jovita to create moments of conversation. In her community, she was usually the contact person since most of the meetings and training sessions were held in her parents' home or small business. Upon my arrival to La Vereda in early December, Guillermina had not arrived yet to give the sewing class. I found Andrea in her parents' home with her infant son as her sister-in-law, Elena, came in and out. It was 11:30 in the morning when I arrived at Chuy's home. On this day our small talk revealed some important facts, even though we continued to feel uncomfortable without Guillermina and Jovita's presence among us. I took the first silent opportunity to ask Andrea about her incorporation into PLAMAC to break the ice and formally hear her side of the story.

Andrea proceeded to share how Dulce [Guillermina's niece and member of the PLAMAC team] came looking for the community commissioner or another leader and only found Andrea. Since Andrea's father held the post of commissioner, she replied, "Well, he isn't here, but if you want to leave the commissioner a message he is my father and I will make sure he gets it." Since PLAMAC's intentions were to assemble the community for a meeting, Andrea agreed to communicate their wishes to her father. Andrea relayed:

> And so then I told my father and even forgot that they would be coming. After some time Silvia and Guillermina show up to a community meeting and talked to everyone about the SSGs. Once they were done Guillermina asked who could be in charge of putting a list of interested people together. Well, since no one was interested they said, "Let Andrea do it." So I was given the task of jotting down who wanted to be in the groups. But no one wanted to. No one was interested.

Clearly this disinterest and immediate transfer of responsibility to Andrea was a concern and a recurring theme for her. Her community's disinterest in any social or political organizing was to her a real problem and one she constantly tackled, especially as the daughter of the community's commissioner and niece to the *delegado* (delegate—Jovita's husband). Indeed, her family's leadership roles in the community almost by default came to rest on Andrea, who was not always willing to accept some of those responsibilities. Consequently, she seemed to initially resist any involvement with PLAMAC since that entailed being at the forefront of another community project.

> *Pues pasó el tiempo y llegó otra vez Guillermina y me pregunta, "¿Ya tienes la lista de personas?" Y yo le decía, "No todavía no." Y ella volvía a venir y me preguntaba de la lista y me invitaba a las reuniones de La Laguna y yo no iba. Hasta que después hasta me dio pena que venía y yo nada. Y me invitó a otra reunión y le dije, "Si voy a ir." Y no fui, así que a la siguiente dije que sí porque ya me daba pena que me decía y decía y yo no quería. Me daba flojera. Hasta hice la lista. Pero ninguna de las mujeres que estaban en ésa lista están en mi grupo hoy. Nomás dijeron que querían y a la hora de la hora ni participaron.*

> Time went by and Guillermina comes back and asks me, "Do you have the list of people?" And I answered, "No, not yet." And then she would come back again and ask me for the list and invite me to different meetings in La Laguna that I wouldn't attend. Until I started to get embarrassed that she continued to come and I did nothing. She invited me to another meeting and I told her, "I'll go." And I didn't go, so the next one she invited me to I did go, because frankly I was embarrassed that she would tell me and tell me and I didn't want to go. I was lazy. I even made the list she wanted. But none of the women on that list are in my group today. They just said they wanted to join, but when it came down to it they didn't participate.

Elena, Andrea's sister-in-law, who had been coming and going during our conversation, was now also listening to Andrea retell her story.

RUTH (AUTHOR): How did you get the women who you have now to join your SSG?

ANDREA: Well, I told Jovita that we should start a group. And I also told some women who had jobs, and they wanted to do it until they got off work. I would tell them that I was inviting them to this and explained it, and they would say yes. And now it is the ones that I didn't invite that stayed. This is why sometimes I tell my mother, "I don't know, we don't learn. We have to start with ourselves. They say we should set the example."

RUTH: Later they were motivated, weren't they?

ANDREA: Yes, some of them [pause]. Actually no, not really. And then Jovita said she wanted to open her own [SSG]. She wanted to be daring and open one separately. She said, "What do you think?" Then Guillermina told her that in La Mesa there were two or three groups. She told her, "If you want to, then start one. Get your people together." And so she did.

Andrea seemed proud that she carried out Guillermina's instructions, albeit with hesitation. This hesitation stemmed from that family history she carried and the group's apathetic attitude. Her comment that one must start with oneself rang hard, because she felt she needed to be motivated and willing to do things in order to set an example for others. Too many damaging experiences with her community negatively affected her persona and caused her to have feelings of failure and isolation. She also took PLAMAC's suggestions, during many animadora meetings, to heart. Namely, that motivation and passion need to start within oneself in order to model and encourage others (hooks 1993). I initially failed to understand the emotive and pessimistic tone with which she spoke about community participation. I did not realize then that it came from real experience. I also initially underestimated her desire to change things for herself, her loved ones, and her community.

As the conversation unwound and we stood in silence with only short phrases about how the year would end and the level of motivation of the group, Andrea began to inquire about Jovita. Clearly, silences bothered both of us. When I volunteered that I was surprised Jovita was not working in her garden, Andrea seemed surprised I knew this. I often noticed that women made indirect remarks to each other about who Guillermina and I spent the most time with. Before I really decided to attend Andrea and Jovita's small savings groups regularly, and when I still visited La Laguna's group, they often asked whose group I visited the most.

As we ended the conversation and stood in silence, Andrea attempted to keep us entertained by inquiring about the end-of-the-year festivities. All the small savings groups in the area were going to come together for an end-of-the-year convivencia. Because I missed Guillermina's last visit, I did not receive information about what this entailed. Andrea then filled me in on the date and time. I, however, would not attend that convivencia. The sudden death of my maternal and only grandfather kept me from joining the groups on that occasion. Andrea, then, without any prompting from me, shared her desire to learn and grow.

*Yo me acuerdo que antes cuando yo estaba soltera yo salía mucho, mucho salía a Sierra Linda. Yo tenía la sala de la cultura. Como tipo información y eso. Y ahí le hablaban a uno y como que iba aprendiendo, pero después la deje [cuando se caso]. Y poquito antes de que llegará Guillermina con PLAMAC yo decía, "Para que dejé mi sala, yo todavía la tuviera." Yo a veces digo, "Aay no, ya perdí la noción de lo que es dedicarse, de andar con la gente, de oír otras cosas, de oír cosas buenas, cosas positivas." Ahora nomás metida aquí en el rancho, ni pa'allá ni pa'acá. Ya como que no me está gustando. A veces que le digo a las muchachas [hija y sobrinas], "Puede que todavía me meta a la escuela." Me dicen, "Tú estas bien locata." Pero no, loca no, porque hay que morir aprendiendo.*

I remember when I was single I would go out frequently; I would go out a lot to Sierra Linda. I was in charge of the cultural center. Like an information center. There they trained us, and I felt like I learned things, but then I had to leave it [when she married]. Just before Guillermina arrived with PLAMAC I used to say, "Why did I leave my center; I could still be in charge." I sometimes say, "Oh no, I have lost all notion of what it's like to be committed, to work with people, to listen to other things, to hear good things, positive things." Now I am just stuck here in the community, not there or here. I am really not liking this. Sometimes I tell the girls [her daughter and nieces], "I might just go back to school." They tell me, "You're really crazy." But not really, because we have to die learning.

Andrea really did yearn to be in a positive and supportive environment that she could feed off of and not feel so lonely and beaten for her desire to be politically or socially active. She was also thirsty for knowledge— knowledge she could gain and share. Even though she mentioned feeling disconnected from others because she was stuck in her community, she and her sisters actively sought educational projects and opportunities. In town, Andrea had two sisters, Julieta and Carolina, to inform her of opportunities and information shared by their local parish. Andrea could have had more opportunities if she and Carolina had interacted more. Because Carolina had lived in Sierra Linda for so long, she was somewhat disconnected from

La Vereda and her family. During our last good-byes, Andrea expressed to me how unwise they were for not relying more on me as a resource. *"Podríamos haber aprendido mucho de ti y no tomamos la oportunidad hasta ya muy tarde"* (We could have learned a lot from you, but we didn't take advantage until it was too late). Because of my relationship with PLAMAC, they continued to perceive me as a teacher. As much as I attempted to assure them that what they were teaching me was immensely valuable, I do not believe they were ever really convinced of it.

Andrea also longed to further her formal education. Of her seven brothers and sisters, she and her sister Sara had the most formal schooling. Andrea had actually, with the help of a family friend, attended some of her elementary- and middle-school years in a government-subsidized boarding school for girls like Julieta. Despite the fact that it was a really disturbing experience, because she left her family, she thanked her parents for the opportunity to attend school. Her educational opportunity did not come without costs. She missed her family desperately and cried herself to sleep for some time. Because Andrea attended school, she sidestepped caring for the family's farm animals like Julieta. Since her family lacked the financial means, the opportunity for even those initial primary grades was limited. However, Andrea felt her education allotted her other ways of thinking and a desire to learn. She finally returned home after her family could no longer afford her stay precisely when she finally adapted to the situation and was learning a lot. She stated, "Had I stayed I would have learned a lot more."

We then began to move to the far tree and fence that bordered Jovita's house. The backside of Jovita's home was directly connected to Chuy's courtyard where Andrea and I stood taking in the warm sun. It had been almost an hour, and again we wondered whether Guillermina would show. We also wondered why Jovita was not around. Andrea then yelled out to Jovita, who finally responded that she would be over momentarily. It was when we proceeded to one of the bedrooms to wait for Jovita that I shared an outfit I had begun to sew for my eldest daughter's dance performance. In the next week, my daughter's school was commemorating Our Lady of Guadalupe's apparition, and she was required to wear a special outfit. I brought it both to get some help putting it together and to use their communal sewing machine. Andrea encouraged me not to wait anymore and start it. It was not much longer when Jovita walked in and spread her hellos and kisses and immediately changed the conversation to schools and teachers. Schools were a common theme among the women's conversations. As on other occasions, they criticized the quality of education their children were receiving and the inconsistency and quality of the teachers. I volunteered to bring some literacy material from home and work with their first-grade daughters. They accepted immediately, and a month later I had an informal literacy session with their daughters in Andrea's home.

Our convivencia and normal interactions were less a part of the everydayness of Andrea's life away from PLAMAC than was the case with Jovita, Carolina, and Julieta. I believe that had I become close with her younger sister Julieta earlier on, my relationship with Andrea would have been different. Unlike this December interaction, in our last months together Andrea and I took trips and were comfortable in each other's company without others. We also picked up where we left off when I returned six months later and throughout my numerous visits during the last fourteen years. Andrea's story, however, provides an essential component to women's struggle for supervivencia—the activist's story.

## The Small Savings Group

Andrea's small savings group took place in her parents' store, directly across from Jovita's home and on the corner of the main square. It was very convenient for her parents and sister Sandra, who attended to customers, but not equally comfortable for the group that conversed, wrote, or participated in various activities while customers came and went. The group's location also hindered real dialogue among the group's participants who felt uncomfortable with the presence of others not in the group. This was a concern Jovita voiced to me during her interview. Jovita felt it was difficult to interact and participate in the store. Also, the space where the women interacted was small because there was a counter and merchandise to contend with.

The counter stood in the middle of the room so as to separate these kinds of gatherings, which took place any time more than two or three family members were present, from the rest of the store. Her father, a member of the group and the only male, usually stood behind the counter ready to engage or intrude on the women's conversation. From the left wall hung racks holding an assortment of potato chips and snacks that a traveling company filled periodically. Self-made shelves were also placed on that wall where household detergents and creams were located. The counter and a nearby table were filled with candy, *pan dulce* (sweetbread), and the ingredients for make-it-yourself tostadas with pig's feet and *cueritos* (pig's skin preserve). Two windows on the right wall looked out to the chapel, plaza, and passersby.

During one small savings group reunion, Andrea started her meeting with a booklet PLAMAC provided to all the animadoras. With the help of a fellow grassroots organizer from northern Mexico, who educated PLAMAC about the SSGs, PLAMAC helped put together an elaborate booklet with the women's quotes and songs. On this occasion Andrea was not without ideas and commenced her meeting by presenting and discussing the booklet and encouraging the women to compose their own songs to include in the next booklet. Her lively manner and smile were evidence of the pride she felt that one of her songs was in the booklet. It was actually her younger sister Sandra who composed new lyrics to two José Alfredo Jimenez songs. Since he was Mexico's legendary composer and a native of Sierra Linda, the people of these communities took great pride in his songs. Both of Sandra's new lyrics appeared in the booklet, and one had Andrea's name on it. However, like other SSGs and regardless of the day's activity, some women were uninterested in the conversations or lessons presented by Andrea. On this occasion it was her sister-in-law Elena who was eager to quickly distribute members' money bags and leave. As treasurer Elena was responsible for the box and only awaited the vigilanta, in charge of the key, to open the box. Elena expressed her desire to open the box and leave immediately after. She asserted that the arrival of her husband from the United States created an obstacle for her, and so she did not want to stay for the discussion.

During the meeting and after saving their money, Elena's predicament led the group's discussion. Women tried to convince Elena of not succumbing to her husband's wishes. It was mainly her husband's sisters—Andrea, Sandra, and Julieta—who argued she should ignore him and stay. Eventually Elena left and the conversation changed to birthday celebrations. Part of the group's activities was celebrating all member birthdays. On this occasion Jovita sat on the cement floor, knitting furiously without maintaining eye contact with anyone, while the group considered her daughter's upcoming birthday celebration.

ANDREA: I was thinking that it would be a good idea to celebrate each person's birthday in their home, so that the mess isn't always left to one person. Then, Karina's is the next birthday so we would have it in Jovita's home.

JOVITA: Well I don't know, I don't want to clean, and I don't have dishes either. It's best not to celebrate it; she hasn't been coming for weeks. I am going to bring it [the cake] according to my taste, because I can only bring what I have the means for. But if you are going to criticize me I'd rather not bring anything.

ANDREA: Don't be difficult.

SANDRA: Boy, so many problems just to come to an agreement.

The group continued their plans, everyone discussing what food item to bring to the birthday celebration, while Jovita commented on her lack of utensils and sitting accommodations, the untidiness of her home, and her unwillingness to tidy up for the group. The women sarcastically responded that they did not care about the mess and would bring their own stools, plates, and utensils.

Even though Jovita felt comfortable voicing her opinions, I had never seen her react in this manner. After Jovita left the group, the women briefly commented that Jovita's grumpiness really stemmed from her husband's wishes to travel to the United States for work. As clearly expressed in chapter 2, Jovita was able to withstand all of life's hardships and sobrevivir, because, unlike other women whose husbands were gone, she had her husband at her side. For Jovita this was no overreaction; she really did not want to be alone. A week later, the group celebrated Karina's birthday in Jovita's home. It was a jovial convivencia and one the entire group enjoyed, including Jovita. Since by the time the birthday celebration took place, her husband had decided not to migrate north, Jovita was her usual cheery self.

Andrea's story exemplifies a genuine struggle to develop and bring changes to her community. Consequently, it reveals the effects community resistance and ambivalence can have on someone who truly wishes to educate and guide others. Her personal evolution, self-assurance, and sense of womanhood (lo que es ser mujer) were deeply denigrated. Andrea felt she needed to get away from her home and community, both to escape the trials of community politics and gossip and to grow as a woman outside such stringent definitions of womanhood. Andrea's story throughout the book, but in the chapter to follow in particular, illustrates her continued struggle to respond to her community's needs and merit the same level of respect afforded to women who chose the somber "quiet" of their home. Even though she spoke negatively about women who chose to be uninvolved in community projects and dedicated to the chores of their home, Andrea could not easily dismiss their criticism. Even as she disclosed other women's criticism nonchalantly, she was clearly wounded by their words. In a society where women's worth is measured by the tidiness of their homes, the cleanliness of their children, and their savory dishes, being referred to as a "lazy woman who has nothing better to do" is quite condescending. Indeed, Andrea and other socially active women were strapped into "controlling images" of womanhood that they were desperately trying to break from (Collins 1991; Dyrness 2011).

While Andrea probably had more schooling than many of the women of her community, she felt boxed into definitions of womanhood that, according to her, women who "did not know better" constructed. In a second interview conducted in my kitchen close to the end of the year—and in the presence of her sisters Julieta, Sara, and Sandra—Andrea criticized her community's apathy toward communal projects and concern with gossip.

> Si tú te fijas, como que la gente, cuando se refiere a preparación o las elecciones crees que le tomarían interés. Ni le toman. Si la gente se preparara, tuviera interés, tuviera tantas ideas para sacar a la comunidad adelante. Y si llegarán los proyectos [podrían decir], "Yo me encabezo no me interesa que digan lo que digan, al fin de acabo a la gente nunca se le da gusto." ¡Pero, ah no, es preferible estar metida en su casa, que ver que la gente las critiquen! Dicen, "Fíjense que fulana y fíjense que zutana." Para eso si están bien listas. Pero no para sacar un problema en beneficio a la comunidad. Ahí si no hay quien quiera. Por eso nosotros sí nos han señalado fuertemente. Yo fui a la escuela, si no no hubiera salido de cuidar chivas, si así soy ignorante a la realidad, estuviera peor. Porque uno crece entre ése ambiente. Nomás como animales, vamos, que come y bebe y lo demás. Y hasta ahí nomás. Lo demás que se quede. Porque la comunidad no agradece.

If you notice, you would think people might be interested in preparing themselves or [understanding] the election process, but they don't. If people prepared themselves, had an interest, they would come up with so many ideas about how to improve the community. And if the programs came, [they could say], "I'll do it. I don't care if they say what they say. You can't satisfy people anyway." But, oh no, they prefer to be stuck in their homes than have people criticize them! They say, "Look at so and so, and so and so." For that they are really smart. But put through a project that benefits the community, there you don't find anyone. That is why we [she and her family] have been seriously criticized. I went to school, if not I would still be looking after goats—as it is, I'm ignorant to many things, I'd be worse off. Because one grows among that environment. Just like animals, in a sense that just eat, drink, and all that. And that's it. The rest is unimportant. Because the community is ungrateful.

Here again we can see the anguish of one woman's struggle with gender-specific roles that try to box her in and keep her in "her place." Andrea's narrative is a plea for additional gender-specific analyses of rural women's struggles with activism and community organizing (Cervone 2002; Dandavati 1996; Dyrness 2011; Hurtig, Montoya, and Frazier 2002).

Clearly Andrea struggled with her anger and disillusion but also did not lose faith. Although she involved herself in the community and was subject to criticism, she continued to partake and search for ventures that might empower her and give her the tools to get in touch with her community as well as sobrevivir. The words she expresses here are words of hope.

> *Fíjate que un día yo me puse a pensar, y dije, "Dios mío yo quisiera que Tú me dieras sabiduría. No para mí sino para poder darles un consejo, y decirles, 'No, estamos mal, estamos actuando mal. Mira sal adelante, deja ésas ideas que no lo llevan a uno a nada bueno.'" Porque [esas ideas] para hacer una obra o para involucrarse en algo no sirven, porque éstamos con ideas ya antiguas.*

> One day I started to think and said to myself, "Oh God, I wish You would give me wisdom, not so much for my sake, rather to give advice and tell others, 'No, we are wrong, we are doing things wrong. Look, try to get ahead, leave those ideas that don't lead to anything good.'" Because [those ideas] don't work when you try and create a project or become involved, because we are [working] with ancient ideas.

Her faith rested in eventually being able to gain the "right" knowledge, skills, and motivation to inform her community. And so her struggle continued. Hence, upon first meeting Andrea, I could not foresee the real struggle within. It took the extent of our initial eighteen-month relationship and the next few years to see beyond her introverted and at times pessimistic nature and uncover her insecurities as well as her hopes and dreams. She was actually a formidable woman. She was a conscious and experienced activist who was not appreciated. She also, it must be noted, did all of this alone—as the sole provider and caregiver of her family—and while struggling with poverty and her husband's absence. As Anzaldúa's (2009) quote at the beginning of this chapter so eloquently conveys, Andrea met these adversities with strength and danced in the face of her fears. The following chapter shows how Andrea, like other women of her community, uses PLAMAC's guidance to gain a new perspective and the skills and tools to lead her community and sobrevivir.

# CHAPTER FOUR

# Globalizing from Below and the Work of Grassroots Organizations

*I sometimes think that I know things, but at the same time one feels unsure, and at times all you need is the support of another person.*
— JULIETA ACOSTA VALDÉZ

In March 2000 eight women met in La Vereda's community store to *convivir* and explore community problems. As on other occasions, the women sat near the store entrance on benches or milk cartons while they worked out of their literacy manuals and conversed. As they worked, Andrea, *animadora* of the small savings group, turned to me and asked if I brought anything to share. I took out a clipping I recently found in one of Mexico's national newspapers. I handed it to Sara, Andrea's younger sister, who proceeded to read the article "En la Tierra del Machismo las Cosas Cambian" (In the Land of Male Chauvinism Things Change). Based on lived experiences and community knowledge, they immediately called attention to the title's inaccuracy. The women countered that machismo in the area had changed very little and that the community's response to Andrea's recent nomination to local politics was an example of its persistent presence in their community. What follows is the group's discussion, characterized by their astonishment at their community's reaction to the unheard of nomination of a woman.

> RUTH (AUTHOR): *¿Qué podemos decir del titulo del articulo, "En la Tierra del Machismo las Cosas Cambian"?*
> ANDREA: *Aquí no.*

Portions of this chapter appeared in the *Journal of Latinos and Education* (Trinidad Galván 2005).

JULIETA: *Aquí más bien florece.*

ANDREA: *Si, como el arguende y los chismes que empezaron después de que me propuso Jovita para delegada. Ahí empezó un arguende, "Cómo se me ocurría, una vieja de delegada, que esperanzas."*

SANDRA: *Quedaron hasta espantados al pensar que una mujer puede llegar a ser delegada.*

ANDREA: *Hasta salí yo bien criticada, porque como podía hasta pensarlo.*

ALMA: *Hasta dijeron ahí unos señores, "Ni que una mujer pudiera andar a las dos de la mañana resolviendo algún asunto."*

JULIETA: *Claro que podemos. Cuando me iba aliviar era la una y ahí andaba yo.*

ANDREA: *Claro, yo también a las dos de la mañana andaba buscando quien me llevara [al hospital] para aliviarme. Nadie se espanto entonces, ni dijeron, "No, usted no vaya, dejé que yo vaya ha buscar."*

RUTH: What's your opinion on the article's title, "In the Land of Male Chauvinism Things Change"?

ANDREA: Not here.

JULIETA: Rather, it blossoms here.

ANDREA: Yes, like the scandal and the gossip that started after Jovita nominated me for mayor. The scandal began, "How could I even think that an old bag could be mayor, unheard of."

SANDRA: They were frightened by the sheer thought of possibly having a woman in office.

ANDREA: I was seriously criticized, because how could I even conceive of that.

ALMA: Some of the men even said, "It's not like a woman can go around at two o'clock in the morning resolving a matter."

JULIETA: Of course we can. When I was going to deliver my baby it was one o'clock in the morning, and there I was.

ANDREA: Of course, I also ran around at two o'clock in the morning looking for someone to take me [to the hospital]. Nobody was shocked or frightened then, nor did they say, "No, don't go, let me go find someone."

Although the article commented on what appeared to be real societal changes, the group did not agree. Andrea and the rest of the group took the opportunity to discuss what men in the community saw as the audacious acts and thoughts of a few women. Because a woman had never been considered or nominated for office in La Vereda, the community could not conceive of such a thing. The women, on the other hand, were not only able to consider the nomination but also could relate their experiences as women and delivering a child in a rural community to the obligations expected of a mayor. They found men's critiques unwarranted and distorted and felt their obligations as women were equally significant to those of the community mayor. As Andrea mentions, no one in the community finds it daunting to hear of an expectant woman searching late at night for a ride to the town hospital. It was impossible, however, to conceive of that same woman inquiring about or mending a political dispute. Patriarchal norms of women's place and responsibilities created the illusion that mayoral obligations of serving the public good were separate and more significant than the private-sphere obligations of campesinas (Pessar and Mahler 2003).

They ended the discussion by examining how men's narrow views of womanhood ultimately shape men's expectations of them and consequently hinder women's personal growth and that of the entire community (Collins 1991). For example, a woman's choice to work outside her home, according to some community members, reflects badly on her husband, whose manhood is questioned. This is especially true for husbands living in the United States, who from their distance cannot "control" their wives. It also reflects badly on women, since they are judged as "women who have nothing better to do than think up ways to get out of the house." Due to lack of employment opportunities, more men and women leave rural communities than ever before. This not only signifies a change in family and community dynamics (women are left alone) but a desperate need to prepare women who stay behind to assume many of the responsibilities left by the men and also create local opportunities that can impede further migration. Popular education and grassroots organizing are ways of preparing women to assume leadership positions and impede the migration of further community members (Cervone 2002).

This meeting was a result of PLAMAC's work, whose aim in its various projects was the improvement and education of poor rural communities and their residents. Their wide view of education covered critical literacy, personal growth, leadership and technical skills, and critical consciousness. The small savings groups and meetings organized or supported by PLAMAC attempted to incorporate all these forms of education in order to prepare participants to assume leadership roles in their communities. This chapter documents the manner in which these communities resorted to regional grassroots organizations, such as PLAMAC, to counter the negative effects of migration, poverty, and gender inequities and expectations. It explores one of the many forms of human agency that Sierra Linda's women enacted in defiance of global restructuring and transmigration. In other words, how are grassroots organizations, like PLAMAC, engaging transborder communities in their resistance to glocal processes? Even though globalization contributes to the stagnation of rural communities—by expecting developing countries to technologically compete in the world market, escalating unemployment, and impelling the emigration of campesinos and working-class people—nongovernmental organizations (NGOs) are able to counter community stagnation by introducing community activism and consciousness-raising spaces and praxis.

## Globalizing from Below

Women's attempts at confronting the transmigration of their community influenced their participation in grassroots organizations and community activism. As Mendez and Wolf (2007, 654) posit,

> The uneven expansion of global capitalism has brought with it new contradictions and interactions among capitalist, nationalist/racist, and patriarchal systems of domination, reconfiguring preexisting power structures and giving rise to new dimensions and scales of power. And yet globalization also has brought about some new and exciting possibilities for unsettling systems of domination. . . . The explosion of nongovernmental organizations (NGOs) onto the political stage represents an important element of this process.

Similarly, Appadurai (2000) argues for the importance of new social forms that "globalize from below" and combat the negative effects of globalization. He describes grassroots organizations and their work as a "series of social forms [that] emerged to contest, interrogate, and reverse these developments and to create forms of *knowledge transfer* and *social mobilization* that proceed independently of the actions of corporate capital and the nation-state system (and its international affiliates and guarantors). These social forms rely on *strategies, visions,* and *horizons* for globalization on behalf of the poor that can be characterized as 'grassroots globalization'" (my emphasis) (Appadurai 2000, 3). Discussions surrounding the migration of community members, the reasons behind it, and its effects on the entire community allude to a global-local connection.

What Appadurai (2000, 15) suggests is that NGOs historically concerned with "matters of equity, access, justice, and redistribution," like PLAMAC, are now becoming "global in their concerns and their strategies. These emergent social forms—part movements, part networks, part organizations . . . are the crucibles and institutional instruments of most serious efforts to globalize from below." Grassroots organizations dedicated to issues of social justice use strategies, such as the dissemination of knowledge, to mobilize groups. Indeed, the kind of knowledge transfer and social mobilization Appadurai alludes to is key to my discussion of PLAMAC and the SSGs. Through PLAMAC's work, such as the SSGs, it was able to contest and influence the knowledge, beliefs, and values disseminated from beyond borders (such as community members in the United States) and within communities.

The small savings groups were one vehicle for the introduction of consciousness-raising forums and reflections like those presented at the beginning of this chapter. Through their work, PLAMAC provided the strategies (SSGs) and visions (through consciousness-raising reflections) with which to alter the negative effects of globalization. Indeed, PLAMAC's visions aspire to stimulate personal and communal wholeness, which actually goes beyond the creation of "knowledge transfer and social mobilization that proceed independently of the actions of corporate capital and the nation-state system" (Appadurai 2000, 3). Instead PLAMAC is interested in addressing the emotional upheaval that global economies create with the disruption of family units and the creation of transborder communities. Campesinas' subordinate place in society required that PLAMAC also create opportunities of feminist practice and praxis to confront, for instance, the kind of antagonism and marginalization experienced by women like Andrea.

Works surrounding social mobilization (Appadurai 2000), feminist practice within popular education (Manicom and Walters 2012a), and differential consciousness are crucial concepts used in this chapter for understanding campesina community work (Sandoval 1991). According to Manicom and Walters (2012b, 3), feminist practice and popular education both "subscribe to a conception of pedagogy as decidedly not just a set of neutral teaching methods used to convey prescribed content, but rather a guided and unfolding process that involves learners actively in exploring new ways of thinking about and relating to their particular situations as they conceive themselves as subjects." Likewise the intersection of gender, class, race, sexuality, and citizenship representative of a differential consciousness was also an important component of women's community participation and praxis (Sandoval 1991). In what follows, I discuss the basis of PLAMAC's vision

and work and explore its use of educational spaces to construct and dis-
seminate knowledge (knowledge transfer), engage in reflections that ultimately lead to social action (social mobilization), and undermine some of
the negative effects of "globalizing from above."

## Popular Visions of Social Justice and Wholeness

### A Vision of Social Justice

*Primarily, I say that people should get ahead . . . create fair conditions.
That, for example, all the rights that we have, they should become real. If
we have the right to good housing, a job, good health, they should be real,
in other words, not just on this paper. Help them to become conscious that
it can change, that reality can change.*

—GUILLERMINA LÓPEZ BRAVO, CODIRECTOR OF PLAMAC

PLAMAC began its work in the state of Guanajuato in 1987. Both Guillermina and Silvia López Bravo, codirectors of PLAMAC, dedicated their
lives to educating and organizing others. As Guillermina's statement reveals, they aim to raise individuals' level of consciousness. According to
Guillermina, this vision was influenced by their commitment to their religious beliefs and accompanying social agenda and their philosophy of
popular education. I use *popular education* as that described by Manicom
and Walters (2012b, 3):

> Popular education—participatory, dialogical, inventive, and community-
> oriented pedagogical practice—[that] fosters critical consciousness (*"con-
> scientización"*) and the collective production of emancipatory knowledge
> and praxis—that is, ways of understanding "the world" and self that iden-
> tify, demystify, and challenge prevailing relations of domination to open
> up new possibilities for engagement and incite collective action for
> change.

Indeed, every aspect described by Manicom and Walters was evident in
PLAMAC's vision of social justice and community work. Guillermina further describes that "our objective is to help people gain consciousness that
things can change, that their reality can change . . . and we use literacy as
a tool."

Initially, PLAMAC's vision and part of its work was born out of its association with and commitment to the Catholic Church. It would not be

until later that its vision was also informed by the work of a literacy organization. Historically, the Catholic Church had direct links to social work, grassroots organizations, and the "development of 'people's theology'" (Naples 1998, 91). It is from a spiritual vision of social justice and equality, as partially informed by priests' interpretations of the Gospels and liberation theology, that the link emerged (Burdick 1992; Gutiérrez 1991; Stephen 1997). Comunidades Eclesiales de Base (CEB—Christian Based Communities) became a means for the creation of NGOs. Within this desire for social justice and equality lies the Church's work and advocacy for historically marginalized communities (Naples 1998). For instance, in the United States, "churches provided the primary sites for soup kitchens, literacy training, childcare programs, and collection of clothing and monetary contributions after poor communities lost government funding" (Naples 1998, 98). Naples (1998, 90) documents how women's involvement in their respective churches and the Church's "preferential option for the poor" served as women's initiation into community work.

It was through a spiritual vision of social justice that many grassroots organizations and women's involvement in community work were born. As discussed by Stephen (1997, 34), with regard to the Church in El Salvador, the "popular Catholic church, following liberation theology, was an important political actor" during the 1960s, such that

> the progressive Salvadoran Catholic church began to define poverty and oppression of the masses as a sin. . . . The organization of hundreds of Christian base communities that discussed and organized around the problems of poverty in relation to biblical teaching politicized both the rural and the urban poor.

As Dandavati (1996, 53) mentions, "The church was . . . the first to show how NGOs could function in opposition to the state." Many organizations, however, in either amicable or disagreeable terms, broke off their direct affiliation with the church and formed community-based NGOs. Most disaffiliations came after the degree of political involvement or ideology of the organization became too radical for the Church (Dandavati 1996). For instance, Guillermina noted that "Dr. Laubach was a very spiritual person and carried a very strong religious motivation. And we here, the different groups—literacy projects, popular savings banks, rural development—all came out of the movement of the 1960s."

PLAMAC's vision of social justice and equality, in turn, questions and attempts to reverse the negative effects migration has on rural communities. PLAMAC works with poor communities independently of the state, which is often invested in international corporations that exploit the working poor. For instance, although the Mexican government often expresses concern over the migration of so many *paisanos* (conationals), its reliance on their economic remittances militates against any political and economic ventures to create conditions that ensure opportunities at home. PLAMAC, on the other hand, attempts to fill that void by creating opportunities for self-awareness, employment, and small business ventures. As Guillermina further suggests,

> *Los Pequeños Grupos de Ahorro funcionan para convocar a participar de manera sencilla en el proceso organizativo. Esta experiencia contribuye a que las personas, principalmente las mujeres, vayan apropiándose de su historia, de su realidad y problemática, particularmente a las mujeres jóvenes, que en ocasiones parecen estar muy dependientes de los "dólares" que envían sus padres, hermanos o esposos. La experiencia de confianza en sí mismas y de organización que son los PGA, les ayuda a despertar hacia un compromiso de formarse como mujeres no dependientes, que se rebelan ante lo sencillo y cómodo de "no salgo a estudiar ni trabajar porque no me hace falta, ya llegará el dinero," "no sé . . . no puedo."*

> The small savings groups function to promote simple participation in the organizing process. This experience contributes to people's, primarily women's, appropriation of their history, their reality and problems, especially young women who on occasion seem to be very dependent on the "dollars" that their fathers, brothers, or husbands send them. The self-worth they experience and organizing they do in the SSGs help them wake up to a new commitment and formation of nondependent women that rebel against the simplicity and comfort of "No, I don't go out and study or work because I don't need to, the money will arrive," "I don't know how . . . I can't."

Just like PLAMAC's vision for social justice informed its work in communities across the state, so did the idea of wholeness. The critical literacy method that eventually became the nexus of its work was founded on a vision of communal and individual wholeness.

## A Vision of Wholeness

*[Our objective] is to promote education, but an education that increases the capabilities of the participants and their whole development. Education as a medium to the full development of the human being. Our work*

*lies in the operational end. We want to foster through education the act of saving, self-employment, and work training, but towards that end [full development of the human being]. That people begin to organize themselves, begin to learn to talk, to word things—all depending on the particular needs of each community, of each group.*
—SILVIA LÓPEZ BRAVO, CODIRECTOR OF PLAMAC

Guillermina and Silvia's literacy work, philosophy of popular education, and organizing experience also stem from their training in the Laubach method. The method, based on the vision and work of Dr. Frank C. Laubach, affords PLAMAC the vision and tools with which to engage groups of people in consciousness-raising themes, reflections, and literacy training (Laubach 1999). Indeed, as Silvia's statement reveals, PLAMAC's objective is to educate and develop the whole person. Because the organization wanted to ensure the complete formation of the whole person, it turned to a context-embedded philosophy of education. Its goals went from merely teaching to read and write to the "full development of the human being . . . all depending on the particular needs of each community, of each group." This vision of individual and communal wholeness is quite remarkable in that it recognizes that people's needs go beyond basic survival. Like Plantenga (2012, 30) suggests, PLAMAC tried to "engage learners as a whole person. . . . What enables us to work together for social change is not merely belonging to specific social categories, but our shared values and the responsibility each one of us is willing to take for those values. Thus justice should be done to the notion that people are much more than the sum total of their various social identities."

This vision of wholeness moves past Appadurai's idea of new social forms (e.g., grassroots organizations) combating the negative effects of globalization through only ideological (knowledge transfer) and societal (social mobilization) movements by also nurturing people's spirit and in so doing ensuring their survival. Supervivencia goes beyond responding to the global political economy to also include everyday cherished interactions. This is where Chela Sandoval's work and idea of differential consciousness interacts with women's special mode of survival. "The differential mode of oppositional consciousness depends upon the ability to read the current situation of power and of self-consciously choosing and adopting the ideological form best suited to push against its configurations, a survival skill well known to oppressed peoples" (Sandoval 1991, 15). This vision allows for women's needs, interests, and forms of remaining whole to materialize. Because the Laubach method is context-driven—its philosophy is couched in the experiences and conditions of people—there exists a place for cultural traditions and beliefs to emerge, be validated, and be used as educational tools (Laubach 1999; Trinidad Galván 2001). As stated in the Laubach manual, the method seeks to increase participants' literacy skills, critical vision, and desire for change.

> It [the organization—Laubach Popular Literacy Projects in Mexico, Civil Association] does not look solely, through a technique, to teach to read and write. Its objective is much wider, it looks to teach the adult, understood as a permanent process that will promote the conditions with which the participant will reach: a personal realization, a critical vision of reality and participation in his/her community in order that s/he will achieve a community transformation. (translated from the original Spanish text, Alfabetización Laubach Mexicana 1976)

This permanent process, couched in the social, emotional, and material conditions of participants' experiences, seeks through a critical vision and the construction and dissemination of knowledge to transform their present reality. Guillermina described the literacy work of PLAMAC this way: "We have a wide concept of literacy, because we have to learn to defend our rights, to organize, and that in itself is learning. And it's our responsibility to help people discover their potential, so they can organize and strive to resolve things." Communities are encouraged to become coinvestigators and actors so that they can define their problems and solutions (Clover 2012; Dyrness 2011; Jacobi 2012; Plantenga 2012). For example, months before I arrived in the area, Guillermina inserviced the animadoras on the instruction of the literacy method. Subsequent visits resulted in the creation of the community's own literacy manual, which women used occasionally. Figure 3 is taken from the literacy booklet made by a group of women of the different rural communities of Sierra Linda. The example highlights the community's need for a direct and functional road between the town and surrounding communities.

Although not an exact match, the Laubach method has affinities with some of Freire's popular education concepts. Like Freire's (1998) notion of praxis—action and reflection—the Laubach method works from the idea that people need to understand their reality in order to act on it and change it. As seen in figure 3, Sierra Linda's literacy manual identifies the community's lack of roads, its right to have them, and the action taken. Like Freire's generative themes, which arise from people's experiences, worldviews, and needs, the Laubach method also works thematically. Even though

| | gusano | | La <u>cuenca</u> <u>del</u> gusano <u>no</u> <u>tiene</u> <u>camino.</u> |
|---|---|---|---|
| | no | | La cuenca del gusano <u>se</u> <u>une.</u> |
| | no | No | La gente <u>de</u> la cuenca del gusano <u>pide</u> camino. |
| | gu  sa  no<br>go  se  ne<br>ga  si  na<br>     so  nu<br>     su  ni | | gana      gallo      goce<br><br>nace      necesita<br><br>La cuenca del gusano tiene <u>derecho</u> a <u>tener</u> camino. |

*Figure* 3. A sample page of Sierra Linda's literacy manual. This page identifies the community's need for roads and the action taken to establish roads: 1) The Gusano Valley does not have roads; 2) The Gusano Valley unites; 3) The people of the Gusano Valley ask for roads; 4) The Gusano Valley has a right to have roads.

the areas identified by the manual are wide (e.g., family, culture, economy, politics, religion, recreation), from these topics surface concrete local themes like road accessibility.

To return to Appadurai's (2000) discussion of "globalization from below," the *concientización* and praxis the Laubach literacy method promotes and PLAMAC uses contribute to new epistemologies and pedagogies for change. Andrea's nomination for office and women's critical engagement with men's responses to her nomination are excellent examples of women's differential consciousness and critical vision (Sandoval 2000). Women's critical discussion of the events of the nomination clearly underscored a deeper understanding of their intersecting subjectivities and not the strict gender roles ascribed to them by the men and patriarchal system of their community (Collins 1991; Gargallo 2006; Pérez 1999).

Even though globalization has contributed to the stagnation of rural communities—by expecting developing countries to technologically compete in the world market, escalating unemployment, and impelling the emigration of campesinos and working-class people—NGOs are able to counter community stagnation by fostering a differential consciousness and ways of conceiving different lived experiences. The following discussion situates

PLAMAC's vision amid tactics it uses to transform women's visions into reality and ensure their *supervivencia*.

## Forums for Knowledge Creation, Consciousness-Raising, and Praxis

### Knowledge Creation

Appadurai's idea of knowledge transfer and my idea of knowledge creation were evident in various settings, such as the small savings groups, animadora meetings, and group workshops. For instance, the exchange of experiences and knowledge new and older members of PLAMAC engaged in took place in a workshop titled *Compartiendo Experiencias* (sharing of experiences). In these workshops new members were exposed to novel ideas from the experiences and accomplishments of older members. Andrea's nomination by Jovita is one example of the social mobilization triggered by the dissemination of knowledge. What inspired Jovita to nominate Andrea for local office was the knowledge created and transferred in various PLAMAC meetings.

The women of Sierra Linda were involved in the sharing of experiences on at least four occasions during the year. Older members, like those from La Casita—a community that worked with PLAMAC for over eight years—shared their experiences and accomplishments with newer members, like those from Sierra Linda. As the women of Sierra Linda listened to real-life accounts of successful projects and community work, they received ideas and encouragement. At one meeting in particular, women from various PLAMAC projects and other organizations met in PLAMAC's office and shared the work they did in their respective communities. The knowledge transfer that took place played a determining role in Jovita and Andrea's launch into local politics.

From Sierra Linda, eight community members, my family, and I piled into our small minivan and drove for two hours to PLAMAC's office in Irapuato. During the meeting, twenty-two women and one man (Jovita's husband) gathered in PLAMAC's largest room. The women of Sierra Linda and La Casita shared their work in the SSGs, and the women of Cocinando en Común* (Cooking Together) shared their experiences as small en-

---

* Cocinando en Común (Cooking Together) is another project widely used throughout Mexico and other Latin American countries (see Dandavati [1996] for similar projects in Chile;

trepreneurs, cooks, and community organizers. This meeting, which took place in November 1999, was the first sharing of experiences the women of Sierra Linda attended. As we sat around the room, each woman took the opportunity to speak about her experiences in her respective group. Aurora and Araceli Pérez from La Casita spoke first. Part of that mutual teaching and learning experience occurred as follows:

> **Aurora (La Casita):** I am the educator/motivator of a savings group. We started after Salinas [Mexico's ex-president] and we were in bad shape [economically]. PLAMAC has given us information on various topics, like domestic violence, and in the group we help each other. I was dominated by my husband who mistreated me, but now I don't allow it. Also the community judged us crazy when we tried to organize our September 15 celebration. I was the one that gave it [yelled the famous words]. Even though the community has criticized us, because they say that our husbands don't have their pants on, we have accomplished a lot.

> **Araceli (La Casita):** I have been with [the directors of PLAMAC] for eight years. I really like politics and they prepared me. So now no man of my community shows off in front of me or shuts me up. I know my rights. I ran for local office but lost. But I lost because the mayor gave the people a kilo of tortillas.

It was from these moments of knowledge transfer by experienced women like Aurora and Araceli that the women of Sierra Linda gained ammunition in the form of confidence, ideas, and knowledge. That is, the knowledge shared revealed possibilities and ideas for personal growth and social mobilization. Since Araceli and Aurora shared both their sacrifices, as objects of community gossip, and their accomplishments, as candidates for local office and organizers of a national holiday, Jovita and Andrea explored the possibility of running for office even at the expense of community antagonism. In spite of Andrea's eventual political defeat, Sierra Linda's accomplishments should be commended. This initial sharing of experiences

---

Stephen [1997] for other regions in Mexico; and Acosta-Belén and Bose [1995] for Latin America and the Caribbean). It is a collective endeavor to provide local families' daily meals. A group of local women invest, shop, cook, converse, and clean together. The work is equally shared. Shopping and cooking together reduces costs and lessens women's preoccupation with the kitchen and cooking. By sharing these chores women spend more time with family and less time in mundane chores. Because women also share time together, a space/place is created from which to discuss personal and collective issues.

took place in November, and it was in March of the following year, at a community hearing, that Jovita nominated Andrea for office. Amazingly enough, even if they were unsuccessful, it took the women of Sierra Linda only four months to take the knowledge shared by others, envision it for themselves, and act on it (praxis). In a matter of months this group of campesinas took action. Soon it was these women who were sharing similar experiences of empowerment at other meetings.

In March 2000, PLAMAC organized another sharing-of-experiences meeting in a different city in the state. The small community was located approximately forty kilometers southeast of Sierra Linda. As with other events held in different cities, this was also an opportunity for women to visit other parts of Guanajuato for the first time. I drove four women and their children from Sierra Linda, and Guillermina picked up women from La Mesa and La Casita. Present were women from La Casita, La Mesa, Sierra Linda, the local community, and community organizers from around the state with close ties to PLAMAC. Approximately twenty-five people gathered in the large courtyard of a community member's home. La Casita's women began the meeting by standing in the middle of the courtyard and sharing their experience as leaders and organizers of their community. La Casita's women were again serving as role models for other women. They shared once more their initiation into local politics, personal liberation, and community accomplishments. Sierra Linda's women were asked to speak next. It was then that Andrea, even though her words expressed insecurities and humility, stated:

> *Hace poco se hizo cambió de delegado y nosotros participamos. Dice mi compañera Jovita, "Que sea Andrea." Yo me sentí mal, porque no estaba preparada. Después le dije, "Por lo menos nos hubiéramos preparado." A mi realmente me da vergüenza platicarlo porque no hicimos nada, pero ya nos quedo la espina.*

> Just recently there was a change in local office and we participated. My colleague Jovita said, "Let it be Andrea." I felt bad, because I wasn't prepared. I told her later, "At least we should have prepared ourselves." I am really embarrassed to even talk about it because we didn't do anything, but it left us that itch.

It is clear from Andrea's words that Sierra Linda's women were starting to share experiences of pioneering leadership never before seen in La Vereda and surrounding communities, as well as the trials that came with such endeavors. As Andrea expressed, "It left us that itch," and that was a big step in their initiation not only into local politics but social action as well. Only months after I left, the women of La Vereda organized their own 15 de septiembre celebration. As with their idea to run for local office, Jovita, Andrea, and her sisters took on the ideas shared by women in the sharing-of-experiences workshop and acted on them. Like Sampaio's (2004, 197) work in Chiapas, these "critical spaces enabled the development of women's political consciousness rooted in particular communities, [and] asserted an 'oppositional' political subjectivity that challenged discourses marginalizing women and racial minorities." The critical spaces PLAMAC created enabled women's critical consciousness and desire for change. Women learned to reject the bystander mentality for a differential consciousness.

Sandoval's (1991) differential consciousness is clearly evident. Campesinas contend with gender, race, and class oppression in and outside their communities and constantly mold their actions and tactical positions (like guerillas). While they began to push against heteronormative patriarchal structures of leadership in their community, it was only possible because their differential consciousness recognized and drew on "allies, country-women and men of the same psychic terrain" (Sandoval 1991, 15). Freire's idea of praxis is also evident here. For example, the sharing-of-experiences forum was itself a reflection and dissemination of knowledge and experiences by Aurora and Araceli. Moreover, Jovita further reflected on these new ideas and acted on them by nominating Andrea. After her defeat Andrea's SSG also took the opportunity to reflect on what had gone wrong and how they might approach local politics in the future. The sharing of knowledge and experiences resulted in the political and social mobilization of Andrea and Jovita, which they were subsequently able to further explore in Andrea's SSG. The following section explores how these spaces functioned and provided campesinas a space and place for the engagement of consciousness-raising reflections as part of PLAMAC's idea of praxis.

## Consciousness-Raising and Praxis

PLAMAC was certainly committed to the idea of praxis—"the action and reflection of men and women upon their world in order to transform it" (Freire 1998, 60)—and the spaces in which alliances can be formed (Mohanty 2008; Sandoval 1991; Suárez Navaz 2008). With feminist praxis "comes a realization of the need to understand better, in a more nuanced way, the processes of learning that are inherent to expanding autonomy and claiming agency, to mobilizing and organizing" (Manicom and Walters 2012b, 2). Most of PLAMAC's workshops and animadora meetings included some type of reflexive discussion tied to organizing and action. Although PLAMAC helped begin the SSGs, its work was rarely directed to the groups. Both distance and lack of resources hindered PLAMAC's full integration into the small savings groups. Their work was directed at the animadoras of the groups who were then responsible for disseminating the information (knowledge transfer) and essentially initiating their own projects (social action). As Andrea's narrative suggests, this was a difficult task for the women but necessary if the community was to become truly emancipated. The dialogue and reflections taking place in the animadora meetings aimed to prepare the women to initiate their own group reflections and projects. Silvia acknowledged this in her interview.

> We aim to help people start to recognize that they are capable of organizing themselves, that they are capable of speaking, that they are capable of proposing things, that they are capable of doing collective work. And there is where our education work lies. That people get the picture. That they say, "Ahhh, I know how to organize, I just didn't know it was community organizing [the term]." For example, the small savings groups, when people administer their resources, when people decide what they want to do, then the people are learning to organize themselves. Our work is helping them see what they are doing is community organizing. They organize to save, coordinate their festivities, and organize for any activity. They can organize to solve problems they have in common, to solve problems that affect a lot of people of their community.

During one of the first animadora workshops I attended the group engaged in a thoughtful discussion while receiving cooking and sewing lessons. After their discussion and while the food was cooking Silvia took the opportunity to discuss the results of an assignment the SSGs recently produced. Their assignment was an attempt to recover some of the history of their community by either writing what they knew themselves or interviewing elders. As only one of many group projects PLAMAC engaged communities in, history recovery was intended as both a reflexive mechanism and an attempt to recover and record the history and knowledge of communities. History and experience revival was also an endeavor PLAMAC and other NGOs employed to record community approaches to cultural and economic wholeness in the midst of rising transnational businesses and communities throughout Mexico. Some key questions this history revival endeavored to answer included these: What are rural communities' greatest obstacles? How do rural communities continue to survive and thrive?

For this project, some women turned in essays on local community incidents and responses during the Mexican Revolution. Silvia read out loud what women turned in and encouraged them to discuss survival accommodations women made during the revolution while men left to fight the war. For instance, two women shared how women altered their appearance or hid from revolutionaries to survive the war. Women were forced to adapt so as not to be kidnapped or raped by revolutionaries or soldiers during the war. From the connections made to the community's war history, this assignment and reflection urged campesinas affected by the migration phenomenon and living in transborder communities to act on their reality and advance changes. It helped women further understand how the migration of community leaders (mainly men) affected them and the need to assume roles left behind. Silvia encouraged women in the SSGs to reconsider ways in which their community adapted in the past and could potentially respond to new challenges. As Silvia stated, "Do what's necessary to change what you think is wrong with your situation." Silvia further stressed the issue of social action by concluding the meeting with a reflection that pressed the need to act on these thoughts. This was the story:

Paso que empezó un gran incendio en un enorme bosque. De inmediato todos los animales empezaron a salir y correr para escaparse y salvarse de las llamas. Por supuesto los más grandes salieron primero, porque eran más veloz y tenían las patas más grandes para correr más rápido. De los pocos animales pequeños que pudieron salir fue un colibrí. Pero en cuanto salió a salvó se devolvió y regresaba de nuevo y se volvía ir. Los animales más grandes se burlaban y decían, "¿Que colibrí tan tonto, porque se regresa?" Después de un rato el colibrí ya bien cansado de ir y venir, le pregunta un venado, "¿Porqué vienes y vas, exponiéndote a las llamas?" El colibrí le contesta, "Todos hacemos lo que podemos." Resulta que el colibrí cada vez que iba hacia el incendio llevaba una gota de agua en su piquito para tratar de apagar el incendio.

It happened that a great fire began in a huge forest. Immediately all the animals started to run out and save themselves from the flames. Certainly the larger animals got out first, because they had larger feet with which to run faster. One of the few small animals that got out was a hummingbird. But as soon as he was safe he returned and would return again and again. The larger animals would make fun and say, "What a dumb hummingbird, why does he return?" After a while, the humming-bird was very tired of coming and going. A deer asked him, "Why do you come and go and expose yourself to the flames?" The hummingbird an-swered, "We all do what we can." It turns out that every time he would come and go toward the fire, the hummingbird took a small drop of water in his beak to put out the fire.

Silvia concludes, "Realize what the hummingbird was trying to do. Simi-larly we should all try to do what we can. We need to start by changing things from the inside. From our own home."

There was a fairly long silence as women continued to reflect, eat, and move about cleaning. Finally a couple of women connected the narrative to changes they were endeavoring to make in their homes. Both women discussed placing larger household chores on their sons, normally some-thing they would not do if their husbands were present. With the absence of their husbands in the United States they now had the freedom to mold their sons differently and in the process raise men who were not afraid to work around the house or honorably support a spouse's wish to work out-side her home. Women felt it necessary to teach their sons the value of housework as future husbands or single workers in the United States who would have to do for themselves. The women interpreted their effort as one more drop in the fire but one that could possibly make a spouse's job and relationship much easier. Campesinas were desperately trying to change the terrain of the household and community while learning and drawing from the tactics of allies like Silvia and Guillermina (Hondagneu-Sotelo 1994; López 2002; Sandoval 1991).

Like similar grassroots organizations described by others, PLAMAC not only attempted to meet the basic needs of community members but also engage them in reflections that could increase people's critical conscious-ness and sense of wholeness (Dyrness 2011; Manicom and Walters 2012a; Naples 1998; Sampaio 2004). In this case, women's dire economic need, as they await monetary remittances from their absent husbands, is addressed in Silvia's use of the community's main source of food (maize). Furthermore, engaging the group in reflections like the example of the hummingbird nar-rative is a call for praxis as described by Freire (1998, 60)—"the action and reflection of men and women upon their world in order to transform it." In the same way, the Laubach method considers reflection as "the most im-portant vehicle that we have to walk towards that being more every day, which is the vocation of every man [and woman]" (Alfabetización Laubach Mexicana 1976, 49).

From these reflections, the method proposes that people analyze their everyday activities by (a) examining their reality; (b) investigating and understanding the "why" of things; (c) understanding the causes and consequences of their lives in the economic, social, political, and other realms; (d) constantly questioning what they think and do; and (e) not accepting their first response but rather continuing to search for the causes that provoke their actions (Alfabetización Laubach Mexicana 1976, 49). This process of reflection draws people, through the act of questioning, to actively confront their needs or problems. This is certainly evident in community history and experience revival activities and the hummingbird reflection. PLAMAC situates its work around these reflections and consciousness-raising discussions to provide people with working options and the potential to change what they identify as wrong with their current situation. These options help communities counter the negative effects of globalization by acting on conditions left behind by migrating community members, confronting their transborder state, and challenging patriarchal beliefs.

The significance of PLAMAC's work in Sierra Linda's rural communities rests on its ability to globalize from below and halt the negative outcomes of global restructuring. This chapter discussed PLAMAC's role in engaging campesinas and preparing them for leadership roles and community organizing. PLAMAC used the small savings groups and other meetings as spaces from which to increase group consciousness, meet basic needs, create subsistence opportunities, and contribute to the wholeness of members. From its work in Sierra Linda, PLAMAC was inadvertently addressing the migration problem of the area because it brought groups of people together to reflect and act on their reality. From the SSGs and other meetings PLAMAC was able to create moments of knowledge transfer, consciousness-raising, and praxis that eventually led campesinas to act and lead community projects. Andrea and Jovita's introduction to local politics, for instance, reflects the knowledge transfer, social mobilization, and differential consciousness of women engaged in reflexive practice. From their participation with PLAMAC, Sierra Linda's women were gaining a differential consciousness and learning to organize and lead their community.

Women, however, also had their own intentions and made use of the SSGs and their newly acquired tactics and beliefs in cultural ways and for personal benefits. Campesinas appropriated and used the SSGs as spaces for their own healing and learning. Jovita and Carolina's life histories and the chapters that follow address these very local and intimate expressions of their spirituality, folk healing, and convivencia to ensure their supervivencia.

# CHAPTER FIVE

# Carolina

## Devoted Mother and Community Leader

*Committed to survival and wholeness of entire people.*

—WALKER 1983, XI

My first encounter with Carolina Acosta Valdéz took place after meeting her sister Andrea, who guided Guillermina, my family, and me to Carolina's home in the hopes of finding housing in Sierra Linda. She invited us upstairs where she offered us lemonade and told us the home she inquired about had since been occupied. After a few minutes, Carolina summoned Marisol, the person in charge of the key of her SSG, who had insight into vacant homes in the neighborhood. Together with Marisol we walked down several streets. After discarding two possibilities, we returned to Carolina's home where she offered to vacate her home and move into her mother-in-law's home next door. We thanked her for her generosity but said we would continue looking. After that encounter Carolina continued to be my point of reference as I repeatedly went to her for guidance and suggestions as to where else to look. She informed me of schools in town that her children attended and on many occasions showed us around town and talked to people.

At the time she had seven children, two boys and five girls. Her eldest son, only eighteen, had worked in the United States for over a year. Her second child, daughter Lupe, was a sixteen-year-old high school student. Her third child, a daughter, attended middle school, and her other three attended elementary school while the youngest stayed at home. From the outset Carolina and her husband expressed a strong commitment to alternative medicine, nutritious foods, and in the case of Carolina, strong spiritual devotion. Her participation and training in numerous workshops on alternative medicine and natural healing not only cemented her ideals and the purpose of her small savings group but also afforded her a degree of self-esteem, knowledge, and experience evident in her interactions with others.

The family's livelihood consisted of a family mill that either her husband Agusto or daughter Lupe ran early in the mornings and the income from his traveling sales business. While Agusto spent most of the day on his bicycle selling alternative medicine around town, Carolina contributed to both businesses by at times tending the mill, consulting patients, and selling alternative medicine from home. Agusto was rarely around and at the time lived next door in his mother's home, while Carolina and the children lived in their home. Carolina expressed in an interview—as the two of us sat at my kitchen table after running errands in the plaza of Sierra Linda—that she did not receive help with the children. "Although he is the one that brings home the money, when it comes to the children, I have to raise them alone," she said. His business responsibilities and distance from the family meant Carolina was home alone tending to all of the duties of the household and the children.

While all four women's narratives exemplify the strong commitment they had to their families' economic, educational, and spiritual well-being, Carolina was the most proactive and stouthearted about seeking programs for her and her family's survival. Hence, it was not surprising to learn that her small savings group consisted of women she led in other church-related programs. Carolina's small savings group was an offshoot of the honoraria group—a devotional group that prayed to Jesus Christ while He is present in the Eucharist. The same group of women also participated in the pastoral social (a church group whose mission is serving the community). This group of women participated in all three groups out of their commitment and Carolina's advisement. The women considered Carolina a strong and worthy leader and followed her, even during her struggles and insecurities. She expressed to me early on how difficult it was initially for her to be at the forefront of these church-related groups.

> A veces es tan difícil, pero tan difícil, porque yo no era capaz ni de hablar con nadie. Me costó mucho hablar, aprender hablar delante de los demás. Te juro que lagrimas me costaron, porque no sabía hablar. La primera vez que intente, dije, "Pero si yo no entonces quien lo va hacer." Y forme ese grupo [honorarias], y era un trabajo en el que tenia que hablarles.

> Sometimes it is so difficult, but so difficult, because I wasn't even capable of talking with anyone. It cost me a lot to talk, to learn to talk in front

of others. I swear that it cost me tears, because I didn't know how to talk. The first time I tried, I said, "But if I don't do it then who will." So I formed this group [honorarias], and it was a job where I had to talk to them.

Although those initial insecurities were behind her, she still worked arduously to keep the women engaged and committed to the various groups she led. While it was her son and not her husband who migrated to the United States, she was still solely responsible for the upbringing and education of her children. That task in and of itself was a tremendous drain on her day and her ability to engage fully in the SSG and other community groups.

As with her sisters and her aunt Jovita, it was from our daily interactions and everyday living that I began to know her, become close, and build a friendship. That initial interaction with Carolina and Guillermina was the first and last instance in which I affiliated Carolina with PLAMAC. Instead our friendship grew directly from our interactions with each other as PLAMAC never attended or guided her group. This disassociation both facilitated and hindered our interactions as I did not depend from the onset, as in rural communities, on my relationship with PLAMAC to visit or interact with Carolina.

## La Convivencia

As friends we found mutual interests and a resource in each other. Her knowledge of alternative medicine, nutritious lifestyle, involvement in the church, and clear desire to transform her family and community's values intrigued me and catered to my own interests. Her words on the first day I attended her SSG revealed her commitment and service orientation.

> *Del grupo de la parroquia yo quería que nos juntáramos para conocernos y aprender de nosotros. Mis hermanas que ya estaban en un grupo de ahorro, allá en el rancho, me invitaron a ahorrar. Les dije que me ayudaran hacer mi grupo aquí. Y así empezamos aquí. Yo les rogaba y les decía [a las mujeres de la parroquia], "Miren hay que entrar en esté grupo de ahorro."*

I wanted the parish group to come together to get to know and learn from each other. My sisters who live in a rural community and were already in a savings group invited me to save with them. Instead I asked them to help me start my group here. And that is how we started here. I would ask and tell them [the women of the parish], "Look, let's start this savings group."

Her words and actions also revealed her desire to learn and share with others. Even with all the responsibilities of a large family, she was by far the most socially active and informed of the three sisters. In her neighborhood, parish, and medicinal circle, people knew her and of her. Her desire to involve herself in different activities and her housework, children, and family business meant she was always busy attending to her responsibilities.

Carolina's heavy schedule undoubtedly affected her small savings group meetings. After several visits to her SSG, my initial reaction was that she was not performing well her role as the educator/motivator of the group. A number of times I arrived and found the small savings group members waiting outside her home. On one occasion I found the sliding door to the ground floor locked. As I waited, Marisol arrived and was also surprised to find the door locked: "I really think they aren't here, otherwise her door wouldn't be locked. She also forgot two weeks ago." Her voice expressed irritation that this was not the first time, and as Marisol expressed at other SSGs, these outings were a break from her busy schedule. Marisol then suggested, "Why don't I go and see if she's at her sister's [house]; sometimes she's there, and that way we aren't waiting." I did not know it at the time, but she was referring to her sister Julieta, who played an important role in my relationship with Carolina's sisters and other women.

Thirty minutes later—after a number of other women arrived and waited—Carolina appeared and quickly opened the door and welcomed us. Marisol hastily opened the box and the women began to take their bags. Carolina apologized for being late and then realized that there was also a church meeting in just a few minutes. Most of the women were simply passing through, saving, and leaving the meeting. Carolina further apologized to me as I had planned an activity for that day.

As we interacted and came to know each other in the months to follow, I found out how busy Carolina's life really was and how this affected her SSG. During that occasion and others when she arrived late, it was her commitment to her children's nutrition that kept her away. Instead of allowing her children to spend money on unhealthy food outside the school during dinner (they attended school during the afternoon session), she fetched a bus into town and took them home-cooked meals. Consequently, during our visits I made sure to stay open to how or where our visits went, and so many times visits became trips together. Those moments of real interaction and learning took place in the sheer moments of living, spending time together, and being each other's ears and companion.

During these initial months—when the group was not fully participating because of the inconsistency of the meetings and lack of time—there were days when Carolina and I were left to talk privately. After Carolina's continued lateness, the group opted to change the time to one hour later. However, that did not solve the absenteeism problem, because now Carolina was there, but few women attended. At one particular meeting in October, my mother and I arrived to find only Carolina and three other women present. I was prepared to make a cream of broccoli soup and cheesecake but quickly became discouraged by the numbers. Carolina also did not look well that day. On that occasion she walked carefully, almost fragilely around the room. She remained physically and emotionally detached from the group as she stood in the back and did not make comments. Shortly thereafter, she was notified through the neighborhood phone booth about a telephone call from her son in the United States. During her absence the women discussed the low attendance of the group. In particular, Marisol expressed, "I believe they got tired of coming and finding no one here. All of them are very busy, and they became disillusioned when the little time they have to get out they have to spend waiting."

As the women spoke, I prepared the cream of broccoli soup. Once the soup was ready, each woman took a cup and proceeded to leave the meeting, promising to attend the next meeting at which time we would make the cheesecake. Soon my mother, Carolina, and I were left alone while I cleaned up and prepared to leave. Carolina still seemed disconcerted and tired. Our real conversation and *convivencia* commenced then:

RUTH: *¿Está bien Carolina? Parece cansada.*

CAROLINA: *Me estoy recuperando de un accidente. Por eso no platique mucho hoy. Hace dos noches tuve un accidente. No se como fue que el perro se desato y ataco a uno de los puercos. Estaba bien oscuro y yo estaba sola cuando escuche los chillidos y baje a ver que pasaba. El perro tenía al puerco agarrado del cuello y no lo soltaba. Yo jalaba y jalaba al perro para que lo soltará y nada. Por fin como pude quite el perro. Creo que con la fuerza que hice me lastime porque cuando subí me empecé a sentir muy mal. Me sentí morir. Me sentía tan mal y no había nadie que me ayudara. Yo deberás pensaba que me iba morir. Fue en los siguientes minutos o horas que perdí el bebe. Ya tenía dos meses [de embarazada]. Me he estado curando con puros productos naturales. He estado en cama varios días. Hoy es el primer día que me levanto.*

*No quise ir al doctor porque la otra vez, como le hacen lavado a uno, lo dejan bien adolorido, peor creo yo. Está vez me dio miedo ir.*

RUTH: *Carolina mejor se hubiera quedado en cama a reposar. Nos hubiera dicho para no tener la reunión. Usted todavía está muy delicada y debería estar recuperándose no atendiendo al grupo.*

CAROLINA: *No ya me tenía que levantar.*

RUTH: Are you okay, Carolina? You look tired.

CAROLINA: I am recovering from an accident. That's why I didn't talk very much today. A couple of nights ago, the dog somehow got loose and attacked one of the pigs. It was very dark and I was alone when I heard the pig shrieking, and I went down to see what was happening. The dog had the pig by the neck and wouldn't let him go. I pulled and pulled to get the dog off, but nothing. Finally I was able to get the dog off. With all that exertion I must have hurt myself because as soon as I went back up I began to feel terrible. I felt like I was dying. I felt so horrible, and there was nobody there to help me. I really thought I was going to die. It was sometime during those next few minutes or hours that I lost the baby. I was already two months [pregnant]. I have been curing myself with natural products and have been bedridden for several days. Today is the first day I am up. I didn't want to go to the doctor, because the last time, since they cleanse you, they leave you feeling worse. This time I was simply scared to go.

RUTH: Carolina, you should have stayed in bed and rested. You should've told us so we wouldn't have had the meeting. You are still very fragile and should be recovering, not meeting with the group.

CAROLINA: No, I needed to get up.

Important conversations, such as these, that revealed not only her strength but also her frailty were usually discussed after the SSGs or during walks or rides together. Furthermore, only after sharing her miscarriage after the meeting did she discuss it with the group at the next meeting. Her miscarriage was worrisome and forced me to ask more questions, such as why she found herself alone during a time of need. Had her husband cared for her up to that point? Was the SSG one more added chore that she could do without? How could the group's responsibilities be better coordinated? Clearly even though she was a remarkable woman with lots of energy and knowledge, her well-being was in question. A year after this meeting she gave birth to her eighth child and suffered a severe nervous breakdown that I am unsure she fully recovered from. In fact, during subsequent visits over the past fourteen years, my interactions with her dwindled. Her responsibilities at home overwhelmed her, and she interacted little with her sisters and me when I visited. However, during the twelve months of our convivencia her experience and knowledge brought me well-being, rekindled my spiritual beliefs, and taught me the pleasures of everyday teaching and learning.

In the next SSG meeting when Carolina shared her miscarriage, I noticed a dramatic change in the group. Somehow Carolina's miscarriage united the group. During this November meeting, I came prepared with a recipe and reflection. I brought all the necessary ingredients to make a cheesecake with a recipe PLAMAC taught the women of Sierra Linda's rural communities months before. Only a few women were present when I arrived, including Carolina's younger sister Julieta who attended for the first time. Because Julieta and one other woman were new, introductions were in order. I immediately noticed Carolina's sister for only that reason.

I proceeded to place the cheesecake and cream of broccoli recipes on the wall and started the cake while women continued to arrive. On this occasion I also brought with me a reflection from a book an aunt recommended. I remember that I chose the story because it helped one reflect on the everyday (*lo cotidiano*). Once the pie was in the oven I began to read the short story. However, as the women listened attentively I found the language difficult to understand and the message hard to tease out. After reading it, I asked:

RUTH: What do we understand from this small message?
CAROLINA: I didn't understand anything.
CELINA: I understood that we need to value what we see, like the sun. That is what I understood.
GUEST: Yes, like when you see things for the first time.

Carolina took the liberty of rereading the message to the group. It was from Celina's words and after listening to it again that the message materialized. Celina interpreted it this way:

*A mi lo que me llamo la atención fue—el distanciarse de las cosas. Como que al distanciarse las ves diferente. El árbol ya no es sólo el árbol que ignoramos cuando vamos al mandado. Lo podemos ver como algo vivo, que vive junto con nosotros. Hay que reflexionar sobre lo cotidiano, sobre lo que hacemos todos los días pero que le da significado a nuestras vidas. Lo que nos parece costumbre.*

What I found most intriguing was the need to distance ourselves from things, because when you distance yourself from things you see them differently. The tree is not just the tree we ignore on our way to buy groceries. We can see that it is a living thing that lives together with us. Let us reflect on the everyday, on what we do every day that gives our lives meaning. What seems routine.

The story was an attempt to reflect on and discuss the manner in which our everyday chores of home and work shape, restrain, or relieve us. Carolina then interjected and shared her miscarriage with the group. It was truly a moment of coming together and convivencia. Carolina was not only talkative and charming, but her voice and mannerisms—gentle and spoken from the heart—moved the group. She spoke of her miscarriage like a calling from God, as she felt near death but not quite ready to leave. As she voiced her experience she clenched her chest and signaled to her heart.

> CAROLINA: I was really sick, and the only thing I thought of was that I was going to die alone. How could it be possible that I was going to die alone even though I always have gatherings with other women. I told God, "Lord please don't take me. I haven't realized all I want to do, there is still so much to correct."
>
> CELINA: Lack of communication. Someone should have been there.
>
> CAROLINA: One needs to live every day as if it were the last. The importance of these meetings is not just the saving, it is the sharing.
>
> LEONOR: But the saving part brings us together.
>
> CELINA: Still, we need to help each other so that no one is alone during a time of need like Carolina.
>
> CAROLINA: We need to have more trust in one another, because why didn't I call you when I felt so bad? Let's see each other as sisters.
>
> CELINA: Yes, we need to have more trust so that we can speak to others about our problems.
>
> CAROLINA: You also could have helped me with a remedy.
>
> IMELDA: The same thing happened to me. I got really sick once and instead of telling someone I withstood the pain. I finally went to the doctor, who gave me something that didn't work, and when my family found out they said, "Why didn't you tell us? We could have given you a remedy. That doctor just made you worse.

After this conversation the group expressed their willingness to continue meeting and sharing. Carolina and I were left again to reflect and share with one another. She mostly expressed feelings of discontent with her present life, as she had not fulfilled what she set out to accomplish as a young woman. Her aspiration had been to go to school and become educated. She certainly had not counted on so many children and a husband she felt was not supportive. She sensed the years passed, and she mainly dedicated her life to her home and children. Really she underestimated how educated and knowledgeable she was about so many things. I made sure to mention these thoughts and how much I admired her accomplishments both at home and in the community.

Unlike Andrea's narrative that expressed her struggles with the tensions of leading community projects, Carolina's reflected a yearning for the time and skills to lead. Both, however, were constrained by gender norms that defined and constrained women in the role of mother and housewife (Collins 1991; Elenes 2011). Like Chicana feminist discussions of the limited roles women are boxed into, the traditional maternal image of Our Lady of Guadalupe reflects the constraints and challenges of breaking from patriarchal perceptions and expectations (Anzaldúa 1987; Castillo 1996; Elenes 2011; Hurtado 2003; Saldívar-Hull 2000). In particular, Carolina and Andrea embodied the struggles of breaking free of gender norms expressed by their husbands and, in the case of Andrea, from the community as well.

## The Small Savings Group

Carolina's in-town small savings group took place in her home in a fairly new neighborhood on the outskirts of Sierra Linda. The neighborhood, only in existence twenty-five years, recently had its main street paved, while most homes were surrounded by dirt roads. Like most of Sierra Linda, this neighborhood had no vegetation and also yearned for the days when trees filled the area and the community counted on a nearby river. In her small savings group, Carolina's role was twofold: she engaged the group (animadora) and kept the box in her home (tesorera). Since distance hindered PLAMAC's ability to consult the group or help run its meetings, Carolina relied on her sisters Andrea and Julieta for information. Because the group never received formal instruction, it lacked guidance. Consequently, this group desperately wanted a PLAMAC affiliate that could direct them and alleviate the animadora's workload and responsibilities. I, in turn, spent a significant amount of time in this SSG because of its nearby location and my close relationship with Carolina.

Carolina's group was at times disinterested because women's daily activities in town were more structured. Women in town did not seem to lack motivation but rather time. The women of this group were consumed with housework, child care, and employment obligations. Afternoons were set aside for making dinner, attending church meetings, or caring for their families. Consequently some women attended the SSG with a sense of ambivalence toward any activity that required more time than that allotted for saving their money.

When I attended Carolina's SSG for the first time in August, a dozen women were in attendance. Women, most married, ranging from their midthirties to late sixties, sat on benches, chairs, and crates around the large bottom platform of Carolina's home. I immediately noticed a high anxiety to save and leave as some women entered and left throughout the meeting and others fidgeted around as other women and I spoke. The group used that first visit to articulate their individual needs and expectations of the group. Carolina initiated the discussion by stating I would be visiting and providing the group various workshops. Marisol set the stage by instructing the group to express their interests to me: "She is the project [SSG] representative and is here to help us. Introduce yourself and tell her why you joined the group and what you would like to learn."

Carolina proceeded to introduce herself and modeled for the other women an introduction that included their names, reasons for joining the small savings group, and what they would like to learn from the meetings. Carolina stated: "I would like to learn how to make new, nutritious, and economic foods. I want to make my money stretch while making nutritious foods for our families so that we don't give our children junk food. For example, learn to prepare soybeans and wheat, things like that. New and better ways to eat."

Reflecting back on her introduction and concerns, Carolina was more knowledgeable on her subjects of interest than any other woman in the room, especially me. It soon became obvious this group had clear objectives on the use and function of the SSG. Undoubtedly their experience in the church and church groups already provided them with a common interest and concern for alternative medicine and nutritious foods. My task then was to inquire with PLAMAC on how these needs could be met. Upon taking the group's concerns to Guillermina and realizing none of the projects was possible due to lack of personnel and time, I was suddenly left to discover what talent I possessed. I felt the need to take up any teachable role they wanted and needed. I concluded from their initial health-conscious description that they were interested in nutritious foods. I then attempted on various occasions to make yogurt or wheat bread and search for recipes of interest. My cooking inexperience and inability to provide other desired services (e.g., alternative medicine workshops) were clear.

Besides being very active in her church, Carolina was determined and knowledgeable. She took advantage of educational programs offered by the Catholic Church, the Mexican government, and private enterprises. Even though it meant a struggle with her husband at every turn while raising her children alone, she had done it for over fifteen years. Through her participation in the church, she acquired leadership skills, a critical consciousness, and an understanding of the environment, her body, and her well-being. The pastoral social, for example, shaped her service orientation by comparing her mission to the community to that of Jesus on Earth. This group also helped develop her public speaking and leadership skills. From the training she received in the pastoral social, she informed her neighborhood on the need to use the resources at their disposal and revive their ancestral traditions. Indeed, the pastoral social taught her to serve her community and search for answers and programs. At times that meant going outside the church. Because Carolina was not receiving direct guidance from PLAMAC, she turned to a government program for skill building. This program provided the small savings group a space in a home they were leasing and a staff knowledgeable about resources in the community. The women in Carolina's SSG began to receive baking, crocheting, and knitting instructions. However, the organization began to take over the SSG. I attended Carolina's group during this time and saw the dynamics of the group change.

When I returned for the holidays six months later, the group had changed dramatically. Internal disagreements with the government organization and personality conflicts among the group caused many members to leave, including Carolina. During that holiday visit, I attended the meeting, which Carolina was no longer a part of, because Julieta wanted me to see what happened to the group. Few of the original women were present at that meeting, and I could feel the tension in the room. Some women did not speak kindly to or of each other. Most of the tension surrounded who was in charge, who participated, and who contributed to the bakery cooperative. The bakery group had become a small enterprise with money involved. One of the government organization leaders with whom I kept in touch after returning to the United States was literally removed by the other organizers. After visiting the group and upon talking to Carolina, I found she started her SSG again in her home. As she stated, "We are happier here in my home." And sure enough, the women followed her again.

Indeed, Carolina's talkative and pleasant personality coupled with her ample experience as a leader in her church made it easy for other women to follow her. However, as was the case with Andrea and Jovita, leading others was never easy, and she contended with other women's busy schedules and concerns. Of course, there was also the matter of her husband and the gender roles she struggled to break away from. This also meant that, even though her husband was physically present in her life, she was still at the head of her family and the primary caregiver of her children. As will be evident in chapter 6, her spirituality and strong commitment to others kept her cemented and afforded her the strength and desire to continue.

# CHAPTER SIX

# Pedagogical Spaces of Convivencia and Healing

*Spending time with others (la convivencia) compels you to reflect, to be positive. It teaches you to be more social, to greet people and get to know them. It helps you be a better people . . . it calms the spirit.*

—ANDREA ACOSTA VALDÉZ

Carolina's small savings group centered on her extended knowledge of alternative medicine, involvement in the church, and desire to transform her family and community's values and nutrition. Her words on the first day I attended her SSG revealed her service orientation. She stated, "I wanted the parish group to come together to get to know and learn from each other. My sisters who live in a rural community and were already in a savings group invited me to save with them. Instead I asked them to help me start my group here. And that is how we started here." As mentioned in chapter 4, PLAMAC's work in these communities and with the introduction of the SSGs fulfilled three interwoven pedagogical practices. First, PLAMAC trained community educators to take on leadership roles through its leadership workshops and animadora meetings. Second, it used critical literacy activities and praxis to increase members' critical and differential consciousness and community activism. And third, it supported the convivencia that emerged from women's dialogue and collaboration. Indeed, all the women participating in the small savings groups shared that the opportunity to convivir and be with other women was the most important part of the meetings. This chapter explores another form of human agency that Sierra Linda's women enacted in defiance of the transmigration and transborder state of their communities. Like their decision to join PLAMAC to counter the

A version of this chapter appeared in the journal *Ethnography and Education* (Trinidad Galván 2010).

negative effects of migration, poverty, and gender inequities, women relied on their own cultural traditions to sobrevivir. This chapter presents campesinas' use of and reliance on the cultural tradition of convivencia as social relations of personal and communal healing.

While campesinas adjusted their identities as women who stay behind to their transmigrant state and learned new ideologies and skills from PLAMAC, they also derived great strength and sustenance from cultural knowledge and traditions. From women's differential consciousness, method of community organizing, and cultural knowledge, they transformed the SSGs into pedagogical spaces of convivencia and healing (hooks 2013). Carolina's life history and SSG underscored the importance of "living in the company of others" to create unique pedagogical opportunities for survival. Indeed, Carolina's epistemic position and the manner in which she led the SSG best embodied the concept of convivencia and, I argue, its relationship to supervivencia. What I present—through Carolina's narrative and SSG—is the agentic role campesinas also exercised through their implementation and use of ancestral cultural knowledge and traditions. My later discussion of spirituality is also relevant, but here I draw attention to the cultural tradition of convivencia as fundamental to campesinas' survival.

Spanish philosopher José Ortega y Gasset's (2007a; 2007b) notion of vivencia—to live and experience things—is crucial to my understanding of campesinas' desire to engage in each other's company and the link between convivencia and supervivencia. Since the SSGs were places where women lived and experienced things together, I see them as crucial spaces of healing and supervivencia. From hooks's (1993; 2013) idea that healing can only be found through collective sharing and testimony, for instance, I illustrate the manner in which women's convivencia fostered a collective sharing necessary for personal and communal healing and survival.

## Places of Social Relationships, Teaching, and Healing

During Carolina's miscarriage testimonial shared in chapter 5, her small savings group renewed their vow to support each other, foster a sense of sisterhood in the group, and share healing remedies. Even with the difficulties that the group presented, the fact that they came together created opportunities of support and sisterhood so essential for women's survival. While PLAMAC's leadership underscored the educational and collective organizing aspects of the SSGs, it also recognized the SSGs' multifarious objectives. Guillermina, for instance, described the SSGs' objectives this way: "We need to take care of three moments in the small savings groups, the savings, la convivencia—how we are going to help each other while we dialogue—and education." Consequently, it was not surprising to attend these meetings and have many of the women respond that the most important part of their meetings was the time they spent sharing with each other. As one woman stated, "We help each other thrive, we coexist. We create union among each other." My focus here on the sharing of lived experiences and cultural knowledge is evoked by the importance of the spatial dynamics and place of the SSGs. While PLAMAC provided training and a vision for collective organizing, the women used their own cultural knowledge and ways of knowing to combat the negative effects of transmigration and globalization. They drew from their cultural tradition of convivencia to resist material commodification and the division of communities that is a result of the separation of families.

An important component to address here is the intersection of space and place, because the SSGs were actual places where women engaged in social relations (convivencia) (Cervone 2002; Gruenewald 2003). Henri Lefebvre (1991), in his pivotal discussion of the social dimensions of space beyond just location, states that spaces inhabit social relationships, hence social practices. An examination of space uncovers the social relations it creates and the potential these social relations have for groups of people. I speak here of spaces and places, places as the connection of self with locations and beyond and in terms of spatiality, the "articulated moments in networks of social relations" (Massey 1994, 155). In this case both the relations and locations (spaces and places) played significant roles in women's teaching and learning, convivencias, and eventual supervivencia. The transmigrant and transborder state of these communities was in itself a play on space via faraway places and relations (Appadurai 1996; Kearney 1996; Stephen 2007). While campesinas' relations transcend borders and their immediate location, the intimate geographic locations they used for their SSGs were also significant and essential to their supervivencia.

Indeed, the place of the SSGs was a crucial "location" in an actual geographic place (Soja 1989; Tuan 1977). In this vein, I concur with scholars that advocate for the reunification of the social and cultural practices of places.* For instance, Casey (1997, ix) suggests, "To be at all—to exist in any way—is to be somewhere, and to be somewhere is to be in some kind

* See Callejo Pérez, Fain, and Slater 2004; Casey 1997; Gruenewald 2003; Lefebvre 1991; Low and Lawrence-Zúñiga 2003; Massey 1994; Rodman 2004; Soja 1989; Tuan 1977.

of place. Place is as requisite as the air we breathe, the ground on which we stand, the bodies we have." Indeed, "places are the ground of direct human experience" and provide meaning to the interactions and social relations that occur in them pedagogically and otherwise (Gruenewald 2003, 623).

To be sure, each small savings group was a social interaction somewhere. The SSGs were led by the animadora of the group who chose the location (place) of the meetings. As the only animadora of a group in a neighborhood of Sierra Linda, Carolina led meetings in her home. In most cases the identities of the SSGs and their inhabitants determined how these spaces and places functioned and the ideologies at work (Gruenewald 2003). Because Carolina's home epitomized nutritional and healthy living, the social relations of the group focused primarily on alternative medicine, organic food, and a nutritional diet. As will be clear shortly, because Carolina's group cared about the well-being of its members, the teaching and learning transpiring in the meetings were more than just the transmission of knowledge but included its potential to heal. This did not mean the social relations at play in these places remained the same, quite the contrary. The dynamics of the group were evidence of peoples' comfort (or lack of it) in their place, given that places can be safe or antagonistic. This was indeed the case for many women involved in the SSGs but was best illustrated in Andrea's SSG. She, like other women involved in the SSGs, was many times criticized and misunderstood. This misunderstanding by those outside the SSGs impacted the dynamics of the groups, which were often fraught with conflict and ambivalence (Gruenewald 2003). "For each inhabitant, a place has a unique reality, one in which meaning is shared with other people and places. The links of these chains of experienced places are forged of culture and history" (Rodman 2004, 208).

Bearing in mind that places are forged with all the history their inhabitants bring, it is also important to point out the difficulties these campesinas encountered among each other, their families, and their communities. Being referred to as mujeres desjuiciadas (wild and untamed women) by their community and criticized by their husbands and other women for participating in the SSGs affected the groups and the women participants (Trinidad Galván 2001). Julieta and Andrea spoke of the criticisms their communities expressed of their desire to get ahead and challenge traditional gender roles. Julieta recalls that other women criticized her for attending to public matters: "It's other women who believe that going out of the house is like not obeying their husbands. It's because they are submissive. They see leaving the house as bad. They say we boss our husbands around, and since they don't boss theirs they don't go out (of their home)." "How the family does gender," as López (2002, 113) suggests, insinuates a double standard prevalent in many Mexican and other Latino families that mark acceptable and stringent behavior for men and women.

Carolina didn't receive criticism from other women or community members but rather from her husband. Even her miscarriage testimonial hinted at severe marital discord and differences in how large a family they wanted. During an interview she poignantly revealed her long-standing desire to educate herself and others in light of her husband's domineering attitude.

*Primero estaba en el grupo de honorarias de adoración. Pero me zafe de eso y dejé a otra mesa directiva porque mi marido me sacaba, no me dejaba. Me costó mucho trabajo que me dejara. Iba y me sacaba de la iglesia. Le decía, "Mira me voy a ir una hora." Pues si me pasaba tantito o no le avisaba, iba y con el claxon sonaba ahí. Le decía [al sacerdote], "Hay padre me tengo que ir. Ya me hablan." Porque él [esposo] no me dejaba. Eso era pelearme cada vez que me iba. Cada mes echarnos un pleito.*

I was first involved in a devotional group, but I left it and established another board of directors because my husband would not let me [attend]. He would take me out. It cost me a lot of hard work to get his permission. He would go and get me out of the church. I would tell him, "Look I am going for an hour." Well, if I went over just a bit or I didn't inform him, he would go and honk there . . . I would tell [the priest], "Excuse me father I have to go." Because he [husband] didn't let me [participate]. We would fight every time I went. Every month we would argue about it.

She felt that her attempts at learning and teaching others were hindered by his compulsion to keep her at home and with the children. To some extent he accomplished that. Her mornings were work intensive and difficult. Feeding and preparing five children for school was an extremely heavy task. Carolina found it paradoxical that her marriage to Agusto—intended as an escape from poverty and an opportunity for an education—was now her biggest obstacle. She imagined that once married she would be free to go to school. Marriage placed her in greater economic destitution and created more work. Yet she never gave up faith. She searched in the church, where it was safest for women and where she could also find spiritual support.

Although her struggle was still difficult and she felt she learned very little, others recognized her tremendous efforts and acknowledged her wealth of knowledge. While Carolina spoke humbly about what she knew, her education was apparent in her demeanor and language. She stated, "I have been at it [participating in the church] for fifteen years and I still feel like I haven't progressed. But the other women have always followed me. I started fifteen years ago and they still follow me. Even the older women tell me, 'You know best, you take care of it as you wish.'" Indeed, the group kept with her during all the years she struggled to free herself and lead the SSG.

Since PLAMAC aimed to prepare groups to recognize and create changes in their communities, much of their work in these communities attempted to increase peoples' critical consciousness and communal relations through dialogue and reflection (Freire 1998). Every meeting worked to challenge the traditional notion of women's work and pressed women involved in the SSGs to create *sororidad* (women-centered alliances) in their groups. In that respect they reflected the affinity groups discussed by Ellsworth (1992, 109), namely, small-group dynamics that equalized power relations "based on shared oppressions, ideological analyses, or interests." Because the SSGs typified community and self-serving spaces, "they provided some participants with safer home bases from which they gained support, important understandings, and a language" for confronting circumstances outside the group (Ellsworth 1992, 109). Indeed, community criticisms and women's own relationships with spouses, such as Carolina's struggle with her husband, speak precisely to women's everyday struggles and the burgeoning need for pedagogical spaces of healing and survival.

## The Healing Nature of Convivencia

*And when we speak we are afraid our words will not be heard nor welcomed but when we are silent we are still afraid. So it is better to speak remembering we were never meant to survive.*
—AUDRE LORDE'S "LITANY FOR SURVIVAL" IN HOOKS 1993

Taking into account that the SSGs were spaces where women "lived in community" and shared their cultural knowledge and lived experiences, this togetherness led to pedagogies of survival (supervivencia). In attempting to make this connection, Black feminist critic bell hooks's and Spanish philosopher José Ortega y Gasset's work help tie convivencia to well-being and wholeness. Hooks (1993) claims the reason certain communities of color continue to survive is related to the spaces and ways of knowing that foster that existence. She tells us that in "the years before television, folks talked to one another. Conversations and story-telling were important locations for sharing information about the self, for healing" (hooks 1993, 16).

The healing that resulted from opportunities of sharing, according to hooks, occurred "through testimony, through gathering together everything available to you and reconciling it" (hooks 1993, 17). Similarly, Carolina's group used communal spaces (member homes), gatherings (SSGs), and knowledge sharing as forms of remaining whole and surviving the struggles they faced every day. The teaching and learning that transpired in Carolina's group consistently centered the well-being of each woman. Carolina and other women in the group shared this during the first meeting I attended.

CHUITA: *Yo vine al grupo porque Doña Carolina me invito, y yo le tengo confianza porque ella me curo mi pie. Y aunque yo no se leer ni escribir, y yo creo que ya no aprendí porque ya estoy muy vieja y mis ojos ya no me dan más, pues nomás vengo ahorrar y quiero aprender de comida integral.*

CECILIA: *Yo también en mi casa no puedo ahorrar así que mejor me integre al grupo. También quiero aprender hacer pan integral y me interesa un préstamo para empezar un pequeño negocio.*

IMELDA: *Lo que a mi más me sirve de esté grupo es que me salgo de la casa y me olvido de mis problemas y del problema que tengo de los nervios. Es que padezco mucho de los nervios y a veces estoy bien mala, pero aquí se me olvida. Lo que yo quisiera es que no fueran solamente una vez a la semana. Para mi no es suficiente porque cuando regreso a mi casa otra vez me vuelven los nervios y me pongo mala.*

CHUITA: I became part of the group because Carolina invited me, and I have a lot of trust in her because she cured my foot. And even though I don't know how to read and write, and I believe I am too old to learn, besides my eyes just won't give anymore, I come to save. And I would like to learn about wheat foods.

CECILIA: I also cannot save at home so I decided to join the group instead. I also want to learn how to make wheat bread and about loans to start a small business.

IMELDA: The manner in which this group is most helpful to me is that I get out of my house and forget about my problems and the problem I have with my nerves. That's because I suffer a lot from an illness of the nerves and sometimes I am really ill, but here I forget. What I would like is for the meetings to be more than once a week. For me that's not enough, because when I return home my nerves start acting up and I get sick.

The group's comments emphasized two very different needs. Some women needed the group for the convivencia and learning opportunities, while others—who were simply too busy to participate in any activities—chose to save. The focus here is on those who desired to learn and share their epistemological insight. These campesinas demonstrated similar women-centered epistemologies customary of many Latino and African American communities.*

The reason convivencia fosters survival (supervivencia) rests on the ontological significance and meaning of *vivencia* and the pedagogical practices of sharing. José Ortega y Gasset (2007a) theorizes the meaning of *vivir*—to live—that suggests an intimacy with oneself and with others. For Ortega y Gasset, "to be is to need one another" (2007a, 201). The self comingles with others and is nurtured by that presence and livelihood (vivencia) with others (con) (Antolínez 2008). "The Castilian term '*vivencia*' was coined by Ortega to translate the word Erlebnis, originated by Dilthey. The concept '*vivencia*' signifies to live something, that is, that the I is the life of things" (Osés Gorraiz 1989, 63). "It is necessary, therefore, to transcend from the interindividual life to a wider more whole being [*viviente*] that envelops the individual, the interindividual and the collective: the social life" (Ortega y Gasset 2007b, 94). Anzaldúa similarly acknowledges the significance of social relations when she states, "People bond because they want to work together. I'm hopeful because to be human is to be in relationship; to be human is to be related to other people, to be interdependent with other people" (Keating 2000, 26).

This conscious decision by members of the SSGs to convivir and be with other people is grounded on a cultural capital propio (of our own) of reflexive collective interaction (Arístegui et al. 2005). A conscious state of reflection on *lo vivido* (lived realities) is what makes convivencia an act of living in the company of others. A significant aspect of convivencia is the need to be consciously in the moment, living the moment with purpose among others. Said differently, the significance and notion of convivencia means or requires living and being in the moment with our experiences (vivencia) with others (con). Because we bring our entire being and experiences—always fused with others—our coming together creates a "social life" engagement with purpose.

The SSGs are the physical places of social relations and social life that enable the sharing of vivencias among women. As Julieta mentions,

---

* See Carrillo 2006; Collins 1991; Delgado Bernal 2001; Dyrness 2011; Gonzales 2001; González 2006; hooks 1993; Hurtado 1999; Pérez 1999; Villenas 2005, 2006.

*Estábamos aprendiendo nuevamente a convivir, compartir lo que tienes, lo que te ha dado Dios. Compartes tus alimentos, tus experiencias. Nosotros quisimos rescatar eso. Aprendemos a relacionarnos nuevamente . . . y aprender unida con las demás personas.*

We are learning again to convivir, to share what you have, what God has given you. Share your food, your experiences. We wanted to rescue that. To learn once again how to relate to others . . . and to learn united with others.

Women draw on lo propio to defy the negative effects of globalization. Women's mutual vivencias of economic hardship, family separation, and transmigration created the need to come together. On the day Carolina shared the news of her miscarriage, for example, the group was present in the moment in a different way than on other occasions. The group was attentive and existent, not in a hurry to save and leave. Women listened attentively and shared their experiences and knowledge openly. In my field notes for that day I pondered the following:

It was a great moment of sharing. I realized these moments have the potential of bringing women together through the memories and experiences they share with each other. The women today connected with Carolina in spoken and unspoken ways. I felt stillness in the room.

As evident in Carolina's miscarriage *testimonio*, community does not negate the individual (Cruz 2012; Delgado Bernal, Burciaga, and Flores Carmona 2012). During the gathering where Carolina shared her miscarriage, teaching and learning focused on Carolina's well-being and on the cultural epistemologies and traditions women needed in circumstances such as hers. What became evident from this and other gatherings was that in their meetings the sharing of cultural knowledge and vivencias turned into pedagogies of healing and survival (Trinidad Galván 2001). Indeed, they healed as they learned, questioned, and shared. These sites of dignity and resistance, as hooks (1990) asserts, surface as a result of a communal need and struggle to create spaces and places that sustain individuals and communities.

The need to create spaces and places that sustain was a crucial determinant for their supervivencia. This is precisely where convivencia ties to supervivencia. Our vivencia, according to Ortega y Gasset (2007a) is made of the mundane insignificant occurrences and every so often of great happenings, many times painful and others joyous, but always a relationship with a circumstance and others. While both words speak of living and being in the moment (vivencia), one emphasizes a sort of communion with others, a togetherness (convivencia), while the other word (supervivencia) claims a beyondness (*super/sobre*) to mere material survival. In the case of this group of campesinas, both convivencia and supervivencia were intimately related. To go beyond survival required the act of living with others. Anzaldúa reminds us that being in the presence of and with others provides opportunities of solidarity building and feminist alliances. Anzaldúa states in her interview with Keating (2000, 199), "You're trying to heal a community or a culture while healing yourself. That's all alliance work is: you're trying to heal the wounds. You're trying to bring in justice, human rights, to people who have been wounded and disadvantaged in their lives." Women, like Carolina, needed to heal and relied on the SSGs and other convivencias to do precisely that.

From this communion with others surfaces la supervivencia, a move beyond survival to creative, full lives. As Inez Talamantez states, "We are a god-damn walking miracle. . . . We do not simply survive, that would imply that we were no more than drones. We live lives full with meaning. Now that we know that we can endure any circumstances and that daily we prove that we must be reckoned with by dominant culture, we must have faith in our vision" (in Castillo 1994, 221). The impetus for this among the Black community, according to hooks, rested in the belief in "higher powers" and the secrets of healing. According to hooks (1993, 8–9), "They [Black folks] knew how to live well and long despite adversity (the evils caused by racism, sexism, and class exploitation), pain, hardship, unrelenting poverty, and the ongoing reality of loss. They knew joy, that feeling that comes from using one's powers to the fullest." The unrelenting adversities of many women belied the joyful possibilities of the SSGs. Carolina's stouthearted vivencias revealed a multifarious terrain of mere survival and beyond. This led me to explore the word and idea of supervivencia in two different ways here: supervivencia in the commonly understood idea of barely surviving or making do—as in "*Sobreviví el terremoto*" (I survived the earthquake) and supervivencia, where I employ it literally—beyond (super/sobre) livelihood (vivencia). This juxtaposition mirrors Ortega y Gasset's (2007a, 206) idea that to live, to be, is "to feel living, know oneself existing . . . to live is, for now, a revelation, not to be content with being, but rather understand or see that one is, a knowing."

These women were both in a state of barely surviving and going beyond survival. They accommodated, resisted, and transcended, for instance, their transborder state by relying on social networks, grassroots organizations, and cultural traditions. In Carolina's testimonial we witness women's conscious presence, attention, and support of her healing. As mentioned previously, in the weeks that followed the group took on a new sense of togetherness and creative drive. In a similar vein, bell hooks (1993) poignantly suggests that testimonies and strategies of sharing are the crucibles for individual *supervivencia* and the catalyst for political struggle. She states that "the power of the group to transform one another's lives seemed to be determined by the intensity of each individual's desire to recover, to find a space within and without, where she could sustain the will to be well and create affirm- ing habits of being [vivencia]" (hooks 1993, 13). If one is not actualized, one cannot be in the moment or present enough *to be* and work with others.

Upon further reflection on Carolina's experiences in the months that followed, this notion of merely surviving and going beyond survival is crys- tallized. Her eventual breakdown a few months after my departure clearly revealed the lasting effects of patriarchal oppression and persistent strug- gle—a reminder that at times we just manage. My visit in 2006 revealed that she no longer led the SSG, relations with her husband were faint, and she relied solely on her children and sisters for support. Indeed, Carolina's SSG, miscarriage, and the trials that followed highlight in empowering and heart-wrenching ways the everyday struggles of campesinas who stay be- hind and the reality that vivencias are constantly reconstituted and rene- gotiated. Her state of survival was keenly tied to the social relations she fos- tered or lacked. Hence, it was not surprising that during her last pregnancy, and the emotional turmoil an unplanned and unwanted pregnancy created, she isolated herself and terminated her SSG. Once again, patriarchal re- pression, this time in the form of obliged commitment to reproduction, won over. During that point in time (and space) she merely survived. Keenly aware that things were not right, her family came to the rescue and initi- ated new spaces and places of convivencia. Her gatherings then included only her sisters and immediate family. The essence of the convivencias, however, remained the same—a space and place of sharing and of living in the company of others.

Women who stay behind use an array of social and cultural resources to survive their transborder state. This chapter presented one cultural tradition— that of convivencia—to ensure their survival. Carolina's testimonial and SSG present an important dimension of teaching and learning, its space and place and potential to heal. Indeed, the many adversities and changing commu- nity dynamics required women to find spaces and places of support, teach- ing, and healing. As a result, the chapter discussed the importance of spaces and places and the social relations they create. The opportunity to convi- vir provides the chance for women and community members to share their knowledge and vivencias with each other. As was evident with Carolina, the sharing of knowledge also had the potential to heal, and her SSG provided curative knowledge after her miscarriage. Acknowledging ultimately that the opportunity to be present with others increases our possibility of not merely surviving but of joyfully and creatively remaining whole (sobrevivir), the chapter also demonstrated how our vivencias (lived experiences) rest at the center of both women's convivencia and supervivencia. While both words speak of living and being in the moment (vivencia), one emphasizes a sort of communion with others, a togetherness (convivencia), while the other word (supervivencia) claims a beyondness (super/sobre) to mere material survival. Carolina's life history makes clear that we move back and forth between survival and beyond survival. There are moments when we barely survive life's turmoil and others where we reach joy and wholeness. In the chapters to come, I discuss one last cultural resource women used to go beyond survival: their very personal yet culturally based spiritual expression.

# CHAPTER SEVEN

# *Jovita*

## Caring and Humble Woman

*On that day, I search for our essential dignity as a people, a people with a*
*sense of purpose—to belong and contribute to something greater than our*
*pueblo. On that day I seek to recover and reshape my spiritual identity.*
—ANZALDÚA 1990, 386

Jovita Gomez and I met for the first time during a workshop Guillermina
and Silvia conducted in La Vereda while I was still living in PLAMAC's
office. Guillermina, Silvia, and I entered La Vereda to find Jovita in her
yard attending to her garden. Through the first few months, she was in a
cast. She had fallen, and her wrist was slightly dislocated. During that visit
and others, she complained about her cast, stating, "With this cast I feel
really useless, because I can't accomplish my chores." A humble woman in
her early fifties standing relatively tall at about five feet, four inches, she had
bronze skin and was fairly thin. Her oldest daughter recently cut Jovita's
shoulder-length hair to about ear's length, since she found it too bother-
some to deal with long hair in a cast.

Jovita had nine children, five girls and four boys. The two oldest, a young
woman and young man, were out of the house and working. Her eldest
daughter worked in Sierra Linda after living with her godmother, Carolina,
and choosing to leave middle school to work. Jovita was not content with
her daughter's decision but felt consoled that she found employment. Her
second child left her home a few months earlier and moved to a larger city
in the state. She explained that her son was not educationally driven and
consequently opted not to finish middle school and to work instead. She
was especially disillusioned with him, because as the eldest son, she and
her husband worked hard to send him to school. Karina and Reina, who
followed, attended the local middle school. For the family, it was a great
blessing that soon they would have two middle-school graduates; however,

an education beyond middle school was not ensured. Although Jovita valued education tremendously, her economic situation hindered her ability to provide her children with all the schooling they needed. She often stated to me, "I am committed to giving my children up to a middle school education, but if they want to continue after that then they have to find the means to do it because I just simply can't." Her other three boys and two girls attended the local elementary.

Jovita's husband, Anselmo Acosta, was Carolina's father's younger brother. The families were close since they lived in proximity, interacted on a daily basis, and participated in each other's SSGs. Although Anselmo lived with Jovita all but one year during their twenty years of marriage, their grim economic situation forced Jovita to play a critical role in the economic survival of their family. Unless unexpected employment came their way, Anselmo and Jovita counted only on the income and personal use of their seasonal crop. Undoubtedly, for a family of nine, their crop was not sufficient, so Jovita took every opportunity PLAMAC offered to complement household needs. During the corn harvest, for instance, Jovita was at the forefront. She commented on one occasion, "I also go and harvest our crops, because my husband just can't go alone." Jovita prepared and sent her seven children off to school in the mornings, walked to the agricultural fields, worked under the hot sun for hours, came home to prepare dinner for her children, do the wash, attend to her chickens and garden, and lead her small savings group and other church-related activities. As her narrative throughout illustrates, she preferred the financial and work struggles she and her husband confronted together to being alone. Therefore Anselmo stayed, although other men encouraged him to migrate to the United States for work.

Jovita lived directly in front of Andrea's family store in the main courtyard. The property and three-room house actually belonged to Jovita's mother-in-law. The property was enclosed by a stone wall, and the house stood to the right of the entrance and the garden to the left. The first room was Jovita's mother-in-law's, Andrea, Carolina, and Julieta's paternal grandmother. The two adjacent rooms served as bedrooms by night and living spaces by day to two adults and seven children. Jovita's beautiful garden, which included most of the property, had an array of flowers, herbs, and medicinal plants. On this plot of land were also an outhouse, a chicken coop, and a harvest of prickly pear cactus.

At first glance I was surprised to hear Jovita was the animadora of a group in her community. She often excused herself for not knowing things and for her lack of formal schooling. However, it was she who initiated her small savings group. Unlike Andrea who was approached by Guillermina—as the daughter of the community's commissioner—Jovita was first a member of Andrea's SSG before embarking on her leadership role. As a member of Andrea's SSG, Jovita discussed the purpose and activities of the group to other women in the community and found they were interested but not invited to join Andrea's group. Jovita then took it upon herself, with the support of PLAMAC, to start her own group on a different night and at a different meeting place.

During that first encounter, we passed by her home on our way to a meeting in her community. She asked us to step onto her property and admire her chicken coop. She was not only one of the best savers in her small savings group, which PLAMAC rewarded with baby chicks or fruit trees, but also obtained baby chicks from a local government subsidy. These and other endeavors were part of her great effort to provide for her family's supervivencia. We went in and commented on how well her coop looked. Without knowing me, she immediately proceeded to explain how she dislocated her wrist and the quandary it caused. Her forthright and friendly personality eventually helped us build a close and strong relationship. Although she relied on her two older daughters for some of the chores, there was still a lot for her to do. She lamented that her broken wrist hindered her ability to participate actively in the small savings groups and PLAMAC's meetings. Accustomed to knitting, sewing, or helping with the preparation of the food dishes during the meetings, throughout those months she sat, observed, and talked.

Jovita and I connected immediately. My initial entrance into the community and relationship with Andrea and some of her family in La Vereda felt awkward and difficult. I often appreciated and longed for Jovita's cheery and talkative presence. On several occasions I stopped to see Jovita first and inquired if Guillermina, who was often late, had already arrived for the meeting. On other occasions it was even Andrea, who from her mother's property next door to Jovita's, yelled out to her to join us. We also connected because even though Jovita was very talkative, others sometimes ignored or dismissed her comments as too simplistic. I, on the other hand, was willing to listen, and she was always eager to share her life story and experiences. During my visits to La Vereda it was easy to inquire about her experiences, education, and interests. It was after her SSG meeting one evening that we sat on her patio and she shared her schooling experience and upbringing.

Jovita had little formal schooling. At times she attended school off and on but to no grade level she could remember and certainly with no consistency. She complained that she spent her upbringing looking after the family farm animals.

*Yo nomás sabia cuidar chivas, vacas, burros, caballos, borregos, de toda clase de animales del campo, pero nomás hasta ahí. Yo crecí muy sola. Entonces yo por eso a veces siento que pues hasta ni le caigo bien a la gente. Porque yo siento que me encierro nomás en mi soledad—que fue toda mi niñez hasta los veintiún años que hice ése quehacer. A los veintiún años yo me rebele contra mis papas—"No, no quiero cuidar mas animales." Pero mi papá regañaba mucho a mi mamá, nomás la maltrataba y yo pues me sentía mal y mejor prefería irme devuelta con los animales. Pero ya no andaba a gusto, ya andaba desesperada.*

I only knew how to take care of goats, cows, donkeys, horses, sheep, and all kinds of farm animals, but that was all. I grew up alone. And so sometimes I feel like people don't like me because of that. Because I feel like I shut myself in my loneliness, which was essentially my entire childhood until I was twenty-one that I did that chore. At the age of twenty-one I rebelled against my parents—"I don't want to take care of any more animals." Because my father scolded my mother a lot and mistreated her, that made me feel bad, and I preferred to go out and take care of the animals. But by then I was just not happy anymore. I was desperate for something else.

Because traditionally rural women married young, I was surprised to hear she was twenty-one, not married, and still caring for animals. Clearly, her opportunities, as a rural woman outside matrimony, were slim. However, her unhappiness changed when an important economic, social, and educational opportunity surfaced. She was offered child care work in the home of a wealthy engineer. She began by working weekly shifts and getting a day off. Then, because the couple lived in the state capital an hour away and had to either pick up or drop off Jovita, they decided to keep her for months at a time. Jovita explained that although her mother told her about the work opportunity, she also worried about her security and honor away from home.

*Por Alberto, que era muy querido por mi mamá, traían los ejidatarios un programa en el campo de plantar magueyes y hacer terrazas. Entonces el ingeniero quería una muchacha y [Alberto] le platico a mi mamá. Mi mamá fue la que me dijo que si quería irme a trabajar por allá, pero primero me tenía que meter susto diciéndome que, que iba hacer allá sola y quien sabe cuanto me iba pasar. Bueno ella me había dado esos consejos, verdad, pero como quiera para mi era meterme miedo. Le dije, "Yo, si me voy." Y fue*

*cuando vi crecer a una bebita de tres meses. Tenía tres meses la niña cu-
ando me fui a cuidarla, y para ser [también] la compañera de la señora.
Le caí muy bien a la señora porque según no estaba yo tan tirada a la
calle y le servía para compañía, en sus reuniones que tenía ella. Ya ve que
la gente de sociedad siempre tienen sus reuniones. Me visiteron al nivel
así más o menos, porque yo no me sentía que fuera sirvienta de ésa casa.
Sino yo me sentí de la familia. Porque me vistieron según ellos pa'que no
les diera, yo creo, pena conmigo. Hasta la señora también empezó a decirme
como hablar, como comportarme. Pero siempre yo era su compañera, como
quien dice su dama de compañía y también cuidando nomás a la niña.
Entre cuidando nomás a la niña y después ahí duré hasta que me enseñe
hacer el quehacer, hacer de comer.*

Because of Alberto, who was dear to my mother, a communal land program came to the community to plant maguey plants and make roof ter-
races. The engineer wanted a young lady and so [Alberto] informed my
mother. My mother asked me if I wanted to work over there, but first she
had to scare me by asking me what I was going to do over there all alone
and who knows what else was going to happen to me. So she gave me
that advice, which to me sounded like she wanted to scare me. I told her,
"Yes, I'll go." And so I got to see a three-month baby grow. The baby girl
was three months when I started to care for her and be the lady of the
house's companion. The lady liked me because apparently I wasn't so
shabby and I served as her companion during her meetings. You know
how high-society people always have their gatherings. They dressed me
at an appropriate level, because I did not feel like a maid in their home.
Rather I felt like part of the family. They dressed me in a manner that, I
think, didn't embarrass them. The lady of the house began to tell me
how to talk, how to behave. But always I was her companion, one would
say, her lady companion while also taking care of the baby. I started by
taking care of the little girl and was there until I learned how to do chores
and prepare meals.

During her description of this period in her life she made certain to emphasize her status as the companion of a wealthy woman. She was chosen
because both her appearance and the manner in which she carried herself were up to par with what a woman of position wanted. She also felt
that her new experience provided her new perspectives and an education
few in the community had. She was treated like part of the family, dressed
in the role of a lady's companion, educated on appropriate social etiquette,

taught how to cook and clean, and taken on family trips. No education in La Vereda or Sierra Linda gave her that. Jovita shared, "When I finally came back [at twenty-six years of age to marry] I felt I had learned from all those experiences to see people differently. So that stuck in my mind—I want to learn about everything I see, because I understood that when people attend meetings they learn. So now when I'm invited to something, I go."

By sharing her unique experience as the woman's companion, she expressed to me that even if she was presently poor her personal history was not always one of poverty. In an attempt not to dwell on her financial limitations, Jovita found it important to refer back to a time in her life when she lived comfortably and held a slightly higher social status. For instance, she often excused herself from certain projects or meetings because, as she stated, "I don't have the means." Yet she held her head high, because although she lacked wealth she had everything she needed. In discussing her marriage and husband, she described poverty as her only limitation. "Really I feel I am luckier than my sisters [finding a good husband]. The only obstacle has been poverty, because I am not lacking [emotionally]. I get my wishes granted, I'm pampered, listened to, given my place. Of all that, I am very proud."

## La Convivencia

Because both Jovita's and Carolina's groups met on Monday afternoons, I either left Carolina's group early or was late to Jovita's. On the days I stayed and talked at length with Carolina after her SSG I normally did not make it to Jovita's group. My lengthy everyday conversations occurred with Jovita either after her SSG or before PLAMAC's meetings. On those latter occasions I drove out to La Vereda and waited for Guillermina in Jovita's home. On one November day I approached Jovita's home at about noon and asked her youngest daughter if she was home. Jovita immediately yelled out from her kitchen to come in. We proceeded immediately to her chicken coop. Because many of her chickens were dying of some unknown disease, she was down to only a dozen from the two dozen she started with. We returned to the area near the kitchen where shade from nearby trees was plentiful to chat and wait for Guillermina. With her cast now off, Jovita kept busy with her needlework as we talked. Needlework was a task she took up with Guillermina, who also instructed the women on needlework and crochet. She wanted to finish the task Guillermina left her so that she could instruct Jovita as to what to do next. Under the shade she proceeded to explain her incorporation into the SSGs and the initial meeting where Andrea was selected as animadora of her group. She relayed,

No, I didn't even know about that meeting until later when Andrea told me about the groups. I joined her group, but later other women would see us leave and would say, "Where are you going that you don't invite us?" So I told them about the group. I thought they were going to join Andrea's group, but then Guillermina told me, "You invited them, start your own group." And that is how, without real intention, I started my group.

I listened to her attentively tell her story and made a mental note to continue to ask her questions about the other women in her group, when we started to hear noises next door. When we arrived at the workshop, Andrea, Andrea's sister Sara, Guillermina, and two other young women from nearby communities were already seated. Magdalena and Esperanza from La Mesa, another community in the area, drove with Guillermina. Their community was on the way to La Vereda from Irapuato where Guillermina lived. It was about an hour's walk, so Guillermina always picked them up and brought them to meetings.

Moments later Mariana walked in with a piece of fabric with which to make her daughter a pair of pants. Mariana was a member of Jovita's SSG and the wife of a migrant man. The first cooking and sewing class I attended in La Vereda was held in her home, because she had many of the modern kitchen appliances. On this day, all the women in the meeting worked on a new or existing sewing project. Guillermina always took advantage of individual projects to teach different tasks to the entire group. For instance, up to this point she had not taught the group how to make a pattern for a pair of pants. She explained that because pants were the most difficult to make she always taught that last, but since some of the women already had their fabric she would go ahead and teach them. Even though Guillermina's sewing lessons followed a particular order, she was always willing to adjust her teaching to meet the needs of the group and motivate them to continue attending the class.

All of the women arranged themselves around Sara's bedroom. Esperanza and Magdalena sat on a bench by the door and began to work diligently on their crochet. Although Guillermina provided these young ladies private lessons when she stayed overnight in their home for two-day workshops, she liked to bring them to other communities to serve as role models for other young women. On this occasion they worked on their own. Jovita sat directly to the right of the entrance and worked on her crochet, while the rest of us (Sara, Mariana, Andrea, and I) stood by Guillermina at the center table. Sara was also working on a pair of pants for herself; hence, Guillermina proceeded to measure her while she explained the instructions.

As Jovita continued her crochet she approached Guillermina for feedback. Guillermina ignored her and continued with the lesson. Once done, Guillermina turned to Jovita, took her cloth, and explained the next step. Guillermina helped Jovita while women moved around the room and talked about their projects. Except for Magdalena and Esperanza, all of the women had changed their positions around the room. Andrea found herself fastening her pants with a needle and thread, while Mariana cut her pair and Guillermina moved around the room helping and observing the women. At that moment, Jovita's comment about her daughter's grades initiated a discussion on the poor schooling system of the region.

JOVITA: *Mi niña vino contenta que no reprobó, dice, "Tengo 0's pero no reprobé." Pero ella se refiere a los 6's.*

ANDREA: *¿Con 6's y no la reprobaron?*

JOVITA: *Pues dice la maestra que hay otros peores.*

GUILLERMINA: *Entonces a la mejor la mala es la maestra y no los alumnos.*

RUTH: *Pues si, ¿cuántos alumnos tiene?*

JOVITA: *Como cuarenta.*

RUTH: *Pues con cuarenta y de primer año, no puede hacer milagros. Primero es un año crucial y difícil. Es cuando aprenden a leer.*

ANDREA: *También quizás no sea tan buena la maestra. Estaba otro maestro mejor.*

JOVITA: *Sí, pero se fue para tomar computación, porque dice que aquí nadie sabe. Dijo que le iban a mander ayuda a la maestra, pero no ha llegado.*

JOVITA: My daughter came home happy that she did not flunk first grade. She said, "I have 0's, but I didn't flunk." But she was referring to the 6's [a failing grade].

ANDREA: With 6's and they didn't retain her?

JOVITA: The teacher said there are others worse.

GUILLERMINA: Then the bad one could probably be the teacher and not the students.

RUTH: That's true. How many students does she have?

JOVITA: Like forty.

RUTH: Well, with forty and all first graders she can't perform miracles. First grade is a difficult and crucial year. That's when most learn to read.

ANDREA: Maybe the teacher is also not very good. There was another teacher that was better.

JOVITA: Yes, he left to take computer classes, because he said no one here knows about that. He said he was going to send the new teacher some help, but it hasn't arrived.

At first I found myself, like Guillermina, being judgmental of teachers in the community but then quickly recognized how extremely difficult their jobs were. They commute from long distances, must deal with ill-functioning roads that hinder their movement and accessibility to schools, face large class sizes, and have virtually no teaching materials. Many times new teachers with little experience are sent to rural areas to fulfill their practicum hours. Because of the conditions, teachers placed in rural communities rarely chose to stay. Jovita later voiced that her daughter had three different teachers that year. As the conversation wound down, the room filled with silence as the women went back to work. Most meetings were sporadic like that—with conversations surging in spurts. During the silence, the hustle and bustle of the food began. Like most hosts, Andrea's family was responsible for the food. I often felt for them, because since many of the meetings were held in her mother's home, they were responsible for feeding everyone. This was no small accomplishment not only in the preparation but also in providing for beans, nopales, and tortillas almost every week. I thought it was too much for one campesino family to undertake. Sara, Andrea, and their sister-in-law Elena were in charge of the cooking. The children swarmed in as we all sat around eating in silence. By now it was five in the afternoon and everyone began to finish up her respective tasks. At 5:30 the meeting ended, and each woman returned home with a particular task to undertake during the week to come. As was customary, Guillermina drove Esperanza and Magdalena home while stopping in other communities to inform other groups about the next meeting.

## The Small Savings Group

It was 6:15 in the evening in September when I drove out to La Vereda to try to make Jovita's group. It was the first time I would attend Jovita's SSG, since Carolina's group often went late. I went directly to the chapel given that they started promptly at six. The door to the chapel was locked and none of the women seemed to be nearby. My youngest daughter, Anayansi, often accompanied me to these meetings so we waited together. A few minutes later Mariana approached the church courtyard holding the savings box. She was the group's tesorera, a role she took very seriously. Upon her arrival we chatted briefly about the weekend festivities in La Laguna. My family and I attended the festivities after being invited by the small savings group in that community.

Two older women appeared with their literacy notebook in hand. This reminded Mariana that she did not have hers, and she became worried. Pilar and her twenty-year-old daughter Rebecca arrived next. Pilar was Jovita's sister-in-law and one of two sisters who participated in her SSG. Three young ladies from the church choir also entered the courtyard but sat on a bench to the far left while the rest of us sat on benches directly in front of the chapel doors. The courtyard had a concrete floor with an iron and brick hedge that circled the entire chapel area. These young ladies were far enough and detached from the group and conversation. They remained in that spot, giggling and whispering to each other throughout the duration of the meeting and in particular when Jovita attempted to lead the group reflection.

Two other women in their midthirties came in. They sat with the rest of the group but remained silent during most of the meeting. By this time Jovita showed up, and upon seeing me began to worry about attendance. She had seventeen members of whom twelve or thirteen attended at any one time. After the two last women arrived, Jovita proceeded to take roll and counted eleven members. After taking roll, Jovita read from a booklet Guillermina gave her that included moral stories or lessons. Neither Jovita nor the group could remember where they left off, so she chose one short story. This story in particular addressed the need to tap into our loved ones' history and stories while they are still alive. Even though it was apparent Jovita was nervous—after all, we hadn't known each other long—she read slowly and clearly.

After Jovita finished the story, she immediately turned to the group and asked, "What can we learn from this story?" I was impressed by her ability to come up with an activity under pressure but even more that she did not let the story go without analysis. I guess I too mistook the community's signals and underestimated Jovita's potential. I also misjudged her group's willingness to respond and participate. They quite willingly responded, and it was the older women in particular who engaged the discussion. They commented on the need to speak to community elders.

PILAR: *Creo que ya ni sabemos quien queda y a quien se le puede preguntar cosas de aquí.*

MUJER 1: *Sí, hasta en nuestra propia familia deberíamos de tratar de recuperar historias antiguas que se pueden perder, porque después no va haber ni a quien.*

MARIANA: *Podríamos ir de casa en casa preguntando como cuando anduvimos preguntando lo que paso durante la revolución y como comenzó el rancho. Yo por lo menos aprendí mucho.*
REBECCA: *Con sólo preguntarle a nuestra propia familia es algo.*

PILAR: I think we don't even know who's left and whom we can ask these questions.
WOMAN 1: We should begin to ask our own family and recover past stories that can be lost, because later there won't be anyone to ask.
MARIANA: We could go from house to house and ask like when we asked about the revolution and how the community got started. I learned a lot.
REBECCA: To just ask our own family is something.

During the entire discussion the choirgirls in the corner talked privately to each other but did not participate. Jovita did not seem concerned or surprised with their behavior. Instead she turned to me and asked if I had something to share with the group. I answered that I did but preferred they continue with their normal activities and if time permitted I could do another activity. Jovita agreed and took out the PLAMAC literacy booklet, which only one woman brought. Jovita started on the first page and with the first reflexive word—*familia* (family). Here Jovita grew more nervous. She sounded out the syllables of the word quickly while her voice seemed to break. She asked the women to repeat after her, just as Guillermina taught us, but much faster, and so the group repeated tediously and not out of any concern to learn. The choirgirls were snickering and turning away to laugh. I could not help but feel I put Jovita in that situation.

The atmosphere quickly changed as Jovita came to the first reflexive sentence: *La familia se separa por el trabajo* (The family is separated by work). At first I had a hard time deciding whether I should agree or disagree. The feminist movement in the United States came to mind immediately. The conservative right sometimes used concerns surrounding the family to convey sexist and heteronormative ideas about women's roles as mothers and caregivers. Women were blamed for contemporary ruptures in family structure, because women "chose" to work outside their homes. Unsure of what the sentence intended to bring out, I did not voice my ideas. The women, however, without any hesitation agreed. Lack of employment in the area forced men and women to leave their community for the United States, and dozens of families in the area were separated. The number of hours men and women worked in the agricultural fields also separated families. The women concluded that families were separated by need.

As they spoke, I realized I never thought of work in that way. Work seemed so cemented in our lives that I had not associated it with anything but family subsistence. Even though I certainly reflected on and felt guilty about leaving my daughters with a caregiver while I worked outside my home, I did not ponder how this affected the entire family. The discussion was still going well when Jovita jumped to the next question. Rebecca immediately stopped her and said, "Let's talk more about that. What do others think?" The women then continued to discuss the migration problem.

> MARIANA: *Yo digo que sí separa la familia porque mire cuantos hombres se van para los Estados Unidos, y aquí nos quedamos las esposas e hijos. Eso no está bien, pero que puede hacer uno, ni modo que nos muramos de hambre.*
>
> MUJER 1: *Es como decía no se quien—es por necesidad. No es que uno quiera sino que no tiene otra opción.*
>
> MUJER 2: *No hay trabajos. No hay suficientes tierras tampoco para que todos las trabajen, ni manera de darle de comer a todos.*
>
> JOVITA: *Por eso yo si le he dicho a mi viejo que mejor así pobres pero juntos. Porque yo si veo que las familias no están contentas aunque tengan de comer y todo lo demás.*

> MARIANA: I believe it does separate families, because think of all the men that leave for the United States and the women and children are left behind. That isn't right, but what can we do, starve to death?
>
> WOMAN 1: It's like someone else said—it's out of necessity. It is not what we want, but there is no other way.
>
> WOMAN 2: There aren't any jobs. There isn't enough land for everyone to work either or even means to feed everyone.
>
> JOVITA: That's why I tell my husband it's best to be poor but together. Because I see that families are not happy even though they have food to eat and everything else.

The conversation dwindled as Jovita turned to me. I prepared an ice-breaker activity for the group that required they answer ten questions about themselves and find ten other people from the group with the same answers. I proceeded to explain the activity and model an answer. The women seemed eager to participate, but I hesitated to include the choirgirls. I asked if they wanted to participate, to which they agreed. The meeting came to an end after they answered their questions and moved around to find similar answers. The group proceeded to save and end the meeting with a final prayer inside the chapel.

Jovita was by far the most economically disadvantaged of the women. Although it was an issue she brought up during many meetings, she was also outspoken about her priorities. She was not willing, for instance, to hinder her emotional state, marriage, and family union for some dollars. During her interview there was nothing she spoke of with more distress than her husband's absence. Anselmo had migrated once to the United States during their twenty-year marriage, and those were the worst nine months of her life.

*Yo me sentía como la peor pluma del aire que andaba volando. Yo me sentía feo. Pues mire yo ya no tenía mamá, mi papá pues no es igual. Mi suegra era la única que me entendía y me aguantaba. Y yo sentía que hasta me daba cariño. Yo sufrí mucho. Yo me acuerdo que era tiempo de lluvias cuando tenía que trabajar mucho. Y también a los niños les afecta, porque de todos mis hijos yo digo que mi Emilio no está normal. Cuando él se fue yo quede embarazada de mi muchachillo. Y como yo me sentía tan mal. Fíjese que él está dormido y se levanta hasta que mi señor le habla o la jala y lo acuesta. Yo pienso que es de eso.*

I felt like the worst feather that was flying in the air. I felt awful. I didn't have a mother anymore, and a father just isn't the same. My mother-in-law was the only one that understood and put up with me. I felt like she even gave me affection. I suffered a lot. I remember that it was during the rainy season that I had to work a lot. The children are also affected by it, because of all my children I believe my Emilio is not normal. When he left I was pregnant with my little one. And because I felt so bad, can you believe that asleep he gets up, and my husband has to talk to him or pull and lay him down. I believe it's because of that.

Jovita blamed her son's unusual sleeping habits on the fact that during her pregnancy she could not reconcile her husband's absence. Because his absence was so strenuous on her physically and emotionally, she could not help but believe these factors determined her son's state. Since she and her husband were ejidatarios (communal land owners), they paid for the use of the land whether or not they harvested. During Anselmo's absence, Jovita was also responsible for harvesting some of the land and making sure someone was paid to work the rest. The emotional stress she endured, however, was much more painful than the physical work. She felt alone, *desamparada* (unprotected), and unloved. On the contrary, with her husband at her side, she felt she could endure anything, even scarcity.

Like Andrea, Julieta, and Carolina, Jovita worked hard to find opportunities for herself and her family. This meant being involved and informed about various activities the Catholic Church, local or state government, or other nonprofit organizations offered. All four women wanted to create favorable conditions for their children in order to ensure a better life that did not include migration but instead an education and stable work at home. For Jovita, no less, it meant worrying extensively about the economic well-being and survival of her family. Indeed, schooling sometimes came second to feeding and clothing the seven children she was still raising. Jovita, like the other women, also relied considerably on her spiritual and cultural knowledge and beliefs to face her concerns. As her narrative demonstrates in the following chapter, since she was unable, financially, to provide her children with ample schooling and commodities, she felt it necessary to instill in them valuable spiritual and cultural knowledge she deemed necessary for their supervivencia.

# CHAPTER EIGHT

# Campesina Epistemologies and Pedagogies of the Spirit

*One needs to live everyday as if it were the last. The importance of these meetings is not just the saving, it's the sharing.*

—CAROLINA ACOSTA VALDÉZ

This chapter examines how campesina spiritual epistemologies—their way of knowing and being in the world and the source of their strength and supervivencia—shaped the pedagogies enacted in the small savings groups. In chapter 6, I presented how women appropriated the SSGs by using their own (lo propio) method of collective organizing and healing. In this chapter, I examine the more intimate, culturally based spiritual epistemologies as another means by which women self-define and remain whole, while operating within transborder and global spheres. While supervivencia may suggest barely surviving, it also entails going beyond survival (*super/sobre–vivencia*) as was the case with Carolina's life history. The very personal and intimate place of women's spirituality represented that source with which to ensure their survival and beyond.

In the educational and social space of the SSGs, campesina spiritual epistemologies inform their teaching and learning by providing them individual and collective purpose. Sierra Linda's women organically transformed the small savings group into spiritual and health-conscious spaces of teaching and learning. These cultural spiritual epistemologies include their indigenous roots, dreams, intuition, and use of alternative medicine.

A version of this chapter appeared in *Chicana/Latina Education in Everyday Life: Feminista Perspectives on Pedagogy and Epistemology,* edited by D. Delgado Bernal, A. Elenes, F. Gonzalez, and S. Villenas, pp. 161–79. Albany, NY: SUNY Press, 2006.

## Spiritual Epistemologies

*Spirituality is oppressed people's only weapon and means of protection.*
—ANZALDÚA IN KEATING 2000, 98

### The Significance of Faith

Even with the chore of caring and attending to the cooking and washing for her numerous family and their agricultural lot, Jovita still found time and strength to lead a small savings group, participate in devotional and prayer groups, and be involved in other equally important community projects (e.g., she was previously involved in the initiation and operation of a community mill and paving of the chapel courtyard). This humble woman led other women in group reflections, handwriting tasks, and prayer. She, of all the women I worked and interacted with, most vividly personified struggle, love, and joy. Because of her dire economic situation, conviction for community progress (evident in her SSG), and personal devotion to saints, she demonstrated a unique spiritual inclination that served as a catalyst for her community work and defiance of the transmigration plaguing her community. Part of this conviction came from her faith and participation in the Catholic Church.

Women in Sierra Linda have few opportunities outside the Catholic Church to participate in community public activities. Rather, the Church has been and continues to be a space and place for women's integration into the public and the discovery of a voice other than that of family member and mother (Naples 1998). Certainly the religious and cultural tradition Mexico holds to popular Catholicism—the meshing of indigenous ancestral beliefs and traditions with Catholic beliefs—keenly informs *campesina* religious and spiritual epistemologies. Jovita's devotion to El Sagrado Corazón de Jesus (Sacred Heart of Jesus) and involvement in the *honoraria* group are examples of community traditions passed down through mainly female figures. In her interview, Jovita described her religious and spiritual trajectory and epistemology from a line of spiritual women, the Catholic Church, and eventually her own spiritual inclination and devotion. In the following narrative, Jovita shares the source of familial and cultural spiritual epistemologies.

> *En la vida de mis papas nos bautizaban de recién nacidos. Si ahora nacíamos, iban horita en la tarde o en la noche. . . . Y luego ella [la partera] corría con el recién nacido a registrarlo y a bautizarlo, las dos cosas.*

*Cuando se levantaba mi mamá iba a Sierra Linda y compraba un escap-*
*ulario que era de la Virgen del Carmen. Y nos recibía. [Ruth: Qué es eso?]*
*Le reza como una bendición el sacerdote. Un recito y luego nos ponen el*
*escapulario, y ya éramos Carmelos. Y luego enseguida confirmaban y tam-*
*bién recibíamos el Sagrado Corazón. Por eso todos mis hermanos y mis*
*hermanas somos devotos del Sagrado Corazón, porque tenemos el distintivo*
*rojo y listón rojo con una medalla. Casi al año nos hacían todo eso. Su*
*creencia de ellos [sus papas] era si recibimos todo eso no nos chupaban las*
*brujas y no éramos de él, como dicen ellos del chamuco, que ya éramos de*
*Dios. Según así eran las creencias de nuestros papas, y yo creo que de sus*
*papas de ellos también. De mis abuelos míos.*

During my parents' lifetime we were baptized right away. If we were born
now, they'd go in the evening or at night. . . . Then she [the midwife]
would run with the infant to register and baptize it, both things. When
my mother got up [from the forty days of diet and rest] she went to Sierra
Linda to buy us a scapulary of Saint Carmen. And we were received [to
that faith]. [Ruth: What does it mean to be received?] The priest prays
like a blessing. A small prayer and then they placed the scapulary on us
and we were considered Saint Carmen devotees. Right after we were confirmed and then received the Sacred Heart of Jesus. That is why all of
my siblings are devotees of the Sacred Heart of Jesus, because we all have
the red emblem and the red ribbon with the medallion. All of this was
done during the first year. It was their [her parents] belief that having
received all of this then the witches wouldn't suck our blood, we weren't
his, like they say of the devil, and we became children of God. That was
the belief of our parents, and I believe of their parents as well. Of my
grandparents.

Jovita's spiritual epistemologies, like other Chicana epistemologies, have ancestral and indigenous roots dating back beyond her grandparents (Castillo
1994; Delgado Bernal 1998; Keating 2000). Her devotion to numerous saints,
like that of her mother before her, dates back hundreds of years to probably
Otomi and Chichimeca peoples. It is argued that Mexicans practice a form
of Nahuatized Christianity evident in the appropriation of particular rituals, myths, and beliefs by indigenous communities during the postcoloni-
zation era (Klor de Alva 1997; Marzal 1997). One such spiritual metamor-
phosis from ancestral beliefs to contemporary time is seen in Mexicans'
devotion to saints. Jovita continues her spiritual life history by emphasiz-
ing the importance of saints.

*Yo también agarre [las costumbres de mis padres y de los padres de ellos].*
*También mis hijas, ya todas están confirmadas. La único que no les hice*
*fue arrimarlas para ser socias del Sagrado Corazón [pero ahora lo está in-*
*tentando] y de la Virgen del Carmen, porque yo me incline mucho a lo*
*del Sagrado Corazón pero a lo de la Virgen del Carmen como que se me*
*hizo más trabajoso. Nos inculcaron que a la Virgen del Carmen, ya que*
*tuviéramos uso de razón, le debíamos rezar siete Padre Nuestros y Ave*
*Marías, diario. Y los sábados no debemos comer carne. A mi se me hizo*
*trabajoso. Dije, "Ayyy que tal si ése día tengo carne y nomás porque soy*
*de la Virgen del Carmen no como carne [risa]." Y no me gusto ésa idea.*
*Ser del Sagrado Corazón ésa si me gusta, y ser Honoraria. Eso yo lo es-*
*cogí con mi uso de razón. A ellas [las hijas más grandes] las hice que reci-*
*bieran [la Virgen del Carmen], pero a las demás las he dejado hasta el*
*día que ellas decidan. A Karina y a Reina las tengo en eso del Sagrado*
*Corazón. Es bonito, da mucho animo y los que son devotas del Sagrado*
*Corazón tiene el cielo seguro.*

I have also taken up [my parents' and grandparents' traditions]. My daughters have all been confirmed. The only thing I didn't do for them was make them devotees of the Sacred Heart of Jesus [although they are now working on being devotees] and Saint Carmen. Because I was kind of more inclined to the Sacred Heart of Jesus, but to be a devotee of Saint Carmen was harder for me. It was inculcated in us that to devote yourself to Saint Carmen, as soon as we came into reason, we should pray seven Our Fathers and Hail Marys every day. We also shouldn't eat meat on Saturdays. I found that to be difficult. I said to myself, "Boy, what if I have meat that day, and just because I am devoted to Saint Carmen I can't eat meat [laughs]." I didn't like that idea. I do enjoy being devoted to the Sacred Heart of Jesus and being an Honoraria. That I did choose myself with my use of reason and all. I did make them [older daughters] receive it [devotion to Saint Carmen], but I left the others to decide for themselves. I put Karina and Reina in the Sacred Heart of Jesus group. It's very nice, gives you lots of motivation, and if you are a devotee of the Sacred Heart of Jesus you have heaven secured.

Jovita's devotion, belief, and reliance on saints were part of that ancestral knowledge that ensures her *supervivencia*. Devotion to and worshipping of Christian saints by Nahuatl-speaking people, for example, came from the Christian appearance the Nahuatl gave their own gods so as to not suffer pagan persecution. One of the few images in Jovita's humble chapel,

besides Jesus Christ on the cross and Our Lady of Guadalupe, was El Señor San José (Saint Joseph), their community patron. Klor de Alva (1997)
argues Nahuatl-speaking people worshipped or placed themselves under
the protection of a god of the community. He notes, "These local deities,
small-scale avatars of the supernatural cosmic forces, could be counted on
to protect and advocate for parochial needs. They were the immediate, familiar gods with which the communities identified and around which they
articulated the rites and beliefs that guided their everyday spiritual and sec-
ular lives" (Klor de Alva 1997, 179). According to Klor de Alva (1997), part
of people's everyday being in the world was informed by the guidance and
protection of these deities. He goes on to argue that because a saint is said
to intervene on behalf of its devotee, the saint is much more real, human,
personal, and accessible.

Jovita's community, like many rural communities in Mexico, relied on
the protection and guidance of their patron. In turn, the community's largest yearly celebration does not surround the birth or resurrection of Christ
(even though those are certainly important events) but instead takes place
on the calendar day of their patron saint. The response of saints, their protection and advocacy during difficult times and on behalf of those most
requiring their protection, serves to uphold campesina supervivencia. Consequently, women's supervivencia is affirmed by spiritual epistemologies (belief in the healing power of saints) and inclinations (devotion to saints). For
instance, Jovita's devotion to Saint Carmen and other saints rests on the
saint's protective and cleansing powers.

In her interview, Jovita shared with me how she was handed down from
her mother the responsibility of caring for and securing the worshipping of
her mother's saint (image of the Sacred Heart of Jesus). From her death-
bed, Jovita's mother asked her to take her saint and make sure the community
continued to pay reverence to Him. Jovita consented and for a while actively
presented the saint to the community to worship and pray to. Numerous
children and her extensive work contributed to her carelessness with regard
to the saint, and months went by before she "showed" Him. Hence, the
saint came to her. He spoke to Jovita through dreams she had about her
mother. This is how she related her story:

*Cuando ya no podía caminar ni pararse, me pedía [su mamá], "Cámbi-
ame el santito [que lo moviera de casa y le rezaran]." Así estuvo todos los
días [recordándole]. Yo he tenido muy mala memoria desde que yo me acuerdo, entonces yo nomás le hacía la lucha. También me he valido de un li-
brito. En un papel de cuaderno había escrito lo que tenía que rezar y decir*

*para que respondiera la gente. Así fue como fui quitándome la vergüenza de hacerlo delante de las personas. Hasta que ya no tuvo remedio [la enfermedad de su mamá]. Como al año le seguí yo dando, pero empecé a sentir el cargo, y dejé de hacerlo un tiempo. Después como que ella se ha ido encargando de estarme acordando. Cada vez que tengo mucho de no cambiarlo la sueño. Pero cuando empiezo a cambiarlo ya no la sueño. Como que por medio de mis sueños ella quiere recordarme de seguir su tradición.*

When she [her mother] could not walk or stand, she would ask me, "Move my saint [move it from one house to another and pray]." For some time she went on every day [reminding me]. I have had a bad memory since I can remember, so I just tried my best. I also relied on a little book. In a sheet of notebook paper I wrote what I had to pray and to say for people to respond. That is how I started ridding myself of the embarrassment and started doing it in front of people. Until it was incurable [her mother's illness]. A year later I continued to do it, but I started to feel the weight [of the responsibility], and so I stopped doing it for a while. Later it is as if she [her mother] has taken it upon herself to continually remind me. Whenever time goes by since I've moved Him, I dream of her. But as soon as I start moving Him I stop dreaming her. Like if through my dreams she wants to remind me to continue her tradition.

The divine intervention Jovita experienced represents what naturalist Luisah Teish (1985, 82) suggests is the intervention of our ancestors and loved ones: our "ancestors function as guides, warriors, and healers." As healers, for example, they "help us maintain our physical, emotional, and mental health, in a number of ways. Sometimes they give us the impulse to try a particular diet; sometimes they introduce us to healers (doctors, midwives) who will help us care for ourselves. At other times they actually come and heal us in our sleep" (Teish 1985, 81). To my understanding, Jovita's dreams summoned her mother's guidance but also the saint's protection. In time of great frailty, when Jovita was overextended, her mother summoned the help of her adored saint.

As Jovita, Julieta, Carolina, and others spoke of their lives, they transmitted this spiritual knowledge. As mentioned by Espín (1996, 310), "The cultural 'idiom' of an individual or group will shape the language, symbols, and so on used by that individual or group in the process of interpreting religious experiences, thereby shaping the experience itself as 'religious' and the image(s) of the One encountered as 'divine.'" Here, I attempt to reveal those "cultural idioms" and the not so evident aspects of spirituality, as in

Jovita's saint's calling. Even though I identify these more obvious qualities (e.g., moving the saint around), it was after reading Teish (1985) and Anzaldúa (1987) that the not so obvious became clear and vital. That is, the significance of Jovita's dreams, her mother's calling, and the saint's protection contributed to her spiritual epistemologies and supervivencia. Her spiritual epistemologies were filled with familial and ancestral beliefs of the divine in time of need that ensured her wholeness. Anzaldúa's ideas of our connection with the divine and reclaiming our mind, body, and spirit union come to mind. To Anzaldúa, "being spiritual is awakening to the fact that you're a spirit, that you have this presence" (in Keating 2000, 98).

Espín (1996) also maintains that the cultural "idiom" of a people, the "place" of their religious experience and the oppressions they endure in society contextualize groups of people's religious experience. How people experience that higher source "is necessarily culturally and socially contextualized in ways possible only to them and expressive of the language, symbols, understandings, and image(s) of the divine shaped by their culture, by their social place, and by the conflict" (Espín 1996, 311). Likewise, being conscious of women's material conditions helps us understand their spiritual epistemologies, what makes and helps them remain whole and eventually how it shapes the manner in which they learn and teach. Similarly, Anzaldúa suggests, "I didn't have the money, privilege, body, or knowledge to fight oppression, but I had this presence, this spirit, this soul. And that was the only way for me to fight—through ritual, meditation, affirmation, and strengthening myself. Spirituality is oppressed people's only weapon and means of protection. Changes in society only come after that" (in Keating 2000, 98).

Although Chicana feminisms acknowledge and embrace many Catholic beliefs as important rituals and ontological insight, Hurtado (2003, 104) posits that they also "provided a powerful critique of the role of institutionalized religion in women's oppression." Hence, some of these female figures, such as Saint Carmen or Our Lady of Guadalupe, historically served as oppressive images and cultural frames as well as liberating figures. Chicana feminisms reimagined religious female figures by appropriating historically repressive interpretations of these figures and transforming them into positive female images (Anzaldúa 1987; Elenes 2011; Hurtado 2003; Moraga 2000).

Campesinas' implication in transborder relations and the conditions in which they find themselves regarding the transmigration of family members influence women's identities, the spiritual female images, and the funds of knowledge they draw from (González, Moll, and Amanti 2005). That is, they turn to different sources—regional NGOs and their spiritual episte-mologies—to respond to their oppressive conditions.

## The Significance of Dreams and Intuition

Julieta's life and narrative provide an equally important dimension to campe-sina spiritual epistemologies through women's cultural intuition, dreams, and healing. Even though Julieta's friendly nature surrounded her with ac-quaintances, the responsibilities and workload created by her husband's absence and life in the United States intensified her physical and emotional ailments. Julieta discussed relying on her spiritual epistemologies to com-bat her physical and emotional afflictions when she nonchalantly described her use of dreams and intuition to determine the source of an illness or problem. After months of interaction and a well-developed friendship, we had become for each other a source of *desahogo* (relief), especially with re-gard to ailments of the body and spirit. As evident in her personal narra-tive, it was with Julieta that I often visited curanderas (traditional healers) and *sobadoras* (traditional chiropractors) for a spiritual cleanse or curative massage. She and her sister Carolina had great insight as to whom did what and where in Sierra Linda, and they often recommended different sources of energy. After not interacting with Julieta for a number of days and won-dering how she was doing, I dropped in unexpectedly and found her clean-ing nopales to sell in town. As I sat next to her to talk, she remained quiet and uninterested in the conversation. Apparently weekend troubles with her daughter affected her health and she opted to stay home all weekend. She proceeded to reveal the problem and source of her ailments by using her intuition.

> Yo tampoco me he aliviado del estomago, todavía no me siento bien, y de todo me achicopalo. Dejó que cualquier cosa me tumbe. Hoy me la pasé todo el día acostada, también porque me está queriendo dar gripa. Hasta el apetito he perdido por ese problema que te platiqué. Yo sí siento que me afectó mucho y a la mejor hasta asustada quedé. Por eso te digo que a la mejor estoy haciendo algo grande de algo pequeño. No sé, pero sí siento que me afectó.

> I have not recovered from my stomach ailments, I still don't feel well, and I let everything get me down. I allow any little thing to affect me. Today I spent the whole day bedridden but also because I am getting a cold. I even lost my appetite, because of the problem I told you about.

I do feel it affected me greatly, and I am probably suffering from fright. That's why I say maybe I'm making something big out of something small. I don't know, but I do feel it affected me.

Julieta relied on her intuition to read her body's response to this emotionally driven situation. Like Delgado Bernal's (1998, 563) discussion of "cultural intuition"—which she defines as the "unique viewpoints" that come with personal experience—campesina intuition is informed by both personal experiences and ancestral community beliefs, traditions, and sources (e.g., dreams; signs from nature, such as moon stages; visual power of some individuals). Julieta's intuition signaled the source of her problem as *susto* (fright) so she did not waste time using mainstream medicine or consulting conventional doctors that she believed would misdiagnose her condition. Instead she relied on her intuition and other sources like traditional healers and spiritual guides to heal her emotions. In the following testimony, she further describes how her dreams revealed a solution days later.

*Ya me siento mejor. Fui con una señora que me sobara. Fíjate que soñé que iba con ella y que me aliviaba. Así que nomás me levanté y me fui. Y creo que hoy me he sentido mejor. Ya tuve hasta ánimo de cocinar, porque ni de eso tenía ganas y hasta la comida me salía mala. Me alivió de espanto. Le conté todo y le dije que sentía que estaba espantada. Y sí, no me encontró el pulso hasta por acá [pone su mano cercas del dobles del brazo]. Y dicen que uno está espantado cuando no tiene el pulso acá abajo [en la muñeca]. Yo le dije que era espanto porque yo recuerdo cuando estaba chica, antes de casarme, a mí me curaron de espanto. Me sentía como me he sentido estos días, como decaída, que el cuerpo no te responde, desganada, sin ganas de comer. Y ahora también así me pasaba. Mi mamá conocía una señora que le iba hacer no se que trabajo, y ella era curandera. Mi mamá le dijo, "Oiga no me ve esta niña que sabe que tiene." Y ya le dijo la señora, "No pues es que su hija está espantada." "No me la puede curar?" "Sí." Así que la señora vino al día siguiente y me agarraba y sobaba y sabe cuanto. Me hacía cosquillas y yo ni decía nada, así estaba mi cuerpo que ni respondía. Y me curó otra vez, pero tenía que ser tres. Como ya tenía que ir a la escuela, porque estaba queriendo terminar la primaria, no me hizo la última. Por eso yo digo que como que me faltó otra. Quizás tengo rezagado el espanto de hace mucho. No sé, eso creo yo. Si creo que lo que te dije me espanto.*

I feel better now. I went to a woman to get a chiropractic massage. I even dreamt that I went to her and got better. So as soon as I got up I went to

her. And I believe I feel better today. I even felt like cooking, because I
didn't even want to do that, and the food I made tasted bad. She cured
me of fright. I told her everything that happened and that I felt I was
frightened. And yes, she found my heart pulse way up here [points to
her inner elbow]. And they say that one is frightened when one doesn't
have a heart pulse down here [on the wrist]. I told her it was fright because I remember that when I was young, before I got married, I was
cured of fright. I felt then like I did these last few days, weak, like your
body doesn't respond to you, apathetic, without an appetite. My mother
knew of a woman who did I-don't-know-what work for her and she was a
folk healer. My mom asked her, "Won't you check this girl, because I
don't know what is wrong with her." And so the woman told my mother,
"Your daughter has fright." "Can you cure her?" "Yes." So the woman
came the next day and moved me and massaged me, and I don't know
what else she did. She would tickle me, and I wouldn't say anything, that
is how my body was that it didn't respond. And she cured me another
time, but it had to be three times. Since I had to go back to school, because I was trying to finish grade school, she didn't finish the last one.
That is why I say I needed another and that I might have fright from a
long time ago. I don't know, that is what I think. And I do believe that
what I told you did frighten me.

If, as Teish (1985) highlights, dreams are means by which ancestors trans-
port their knowledge to people, then Julieta's ancestors helped heal her in
her sleep by referring her to a curandera. In these traditions, dreams are
respected as sources of the material or real world. As Laguna scholar Paula
Gunn Allen (1998, 44) argues, unlike Western "divisions between mind
and material reality," for indigenous peoples dreams represent reality. She
claims that in indigenous traditions "such divisions [between dreams and
waking experience] do not exist." For Julieta, the visit to the curandera in
her dream was not only a calling or sign but also a real occurrence that
needed to be carried out to rid herself fully of the fright.

Campesinas overlooked on the basis of their gender, class, and racial or
ethnic status are left with little choice but to rely on their own sources and
entrust themselves to their spirituality and bodies' signals, dreams, and
intuition for survival. The spirit world is a place where we "derive strength
and perseverance" (Moraga 2000, 122). Ana Castillo (1994, 146) further
argues that

this apparent synthesis of belief systems for mestiza consciousness is her
way of coping in a society that does not give her humanity substantial

value. It is not a contradiction of irreconcilable ideologies. At this junc-
ture in her history, by recalling her blood-tie memories to the Americas
and relying upon the guidance of her dreams and intuitions, she gradu-
ally reawakens her female indigenous energies.

These spiritual epistemologies of ancestral knowledge, dreams, and intuition are the crucibles for transborder feminist pedagogies. As I will explain,
it is this epistemological foundation that shaped and informed another form
of pedagogy surging in the SSGs. While the SSGs brought women together
to convivir and collectively heal, women's personal spiritual expressions
shaped the SSGs and their teaching and learning approach.

## Pedagogies of the Spirit

*Third World feminism is about feeding people in all their hungers.*
—MORAGA 2000, 123

Throughout this chapter I argue that spirituality represents women's intimate ways of knowing and defiance of their transborder state. Just like the
cultural tradition of convivencia in and outside their SSGs has healing po-
tentials, spirituality represents women's strength and catalyst from which
to struggle against and combat the daily turmoil of home, work, and transborderism. Their spiritual epistemologies serve as one more medium and
motivation for personal and collective action. For Carolina, it was the impulse to start her own savings group; for Jovita, the drive to provide for her
family; for Andrea, the motivation to rally around community projects; and
for Julieta, the vigor to educate her children alone and for them to thrive in
their rural and urban communities.

Of keen importance is the understanding that campesinas' supervivencia and happiness is intimately tied to their sense of spirit, which organically surfaced in the SSGs to shape their teaching and learning. Even when
the SSGs intended to bring people together to save and organize for common causes, the women renewed the SSGs into spaces of convivencia as
well as moments of teaching and learning that revitalized and affirmed their
spiritual ways of knowing (epistemologies). For instance, Carolina's SSG's
association to the local church structured the discussion and activities, such
that they often talked about their various roles and responsibilities in the
church. Carolina's narrative also describes the spiritual connections women
in her group made when she shared her miscarriage. At that moment a
sense of spirit organically surfaced in her SSG that molded their teaching

modalities. Dillard notes, "Many writers, particularly people of color, have called for attention to spirituality and other ways of knowing in research, theory, and practice. Spirituality is seen to help people claim their internal sense of power, leading to and grounding social action, while fostering a sense of hope" (in Tisdell, Brown-Haywood, Charaniya, and Walsh 2012, 230). Moreover, Anzaldúa reminds us "spirituality and being spiritual means to be aware of the interconnections between things" (in Keating 2000, 9).

Campesina pedagogies are thus imbued with spiritual epistemologies of ancestral knowledge and intuition that give meaning and purpose. Indeed, spirituality, as women's conviction and supervivencia, broadens traditional notions of pedagogy enacted in classrooms (Delgado Bernal 2001; Dillard, Abdur-Rashid, and Tyson 2000; Gonzales 2001). For example, Freirian notions of pedagogy are clearly tied to the everyday material and social conditions of people. From Freire (1998) I came to understand that people's worldviews and how they respond to their overall situation are informed by their everyday living and being in the world. Spirituality constitutes a powerful source of wholeness and sustenance that is seldom associated with people's teachings and learning. While people's social and material conditions are usually considered, their emotional state and how their supervivencia may also inform their teachings and learning remain ignored.

It is imperative to portray the women of Sierra Linda in their complexities and contradictions (Anzaldúa 1987; Gargallo 2006; Mohanty 2008). The fact that they find solace in the patriarchal structures of the Catholic Church, for instance, suggests a contradiction from the differential consciousness that guides their activist work. However, as Chicana feminists argue, women also redefine traditionally oppressive figures like Malintzin and the Virgin of Guadalupe in order to recenter female knowledge (Anzaldúa 1987; Behar 1993; Castillo 1996; Elenes 2011). Highlighting women's differences and contradictions sheds light on multiple ways of being and knowing. Indeed, recognizing and uncovering multiple ways of knowing reveals alternative realities that may build inroads for transborder coalitions and supervivencia (Gargallo 2006; Mohanty 2008; Suárez Navaz and Hernández 2008). For instance, uncovering campesina spiritual epistemologies reveals other sources of knowledge many times unexplored and invalidated (Dillard et al. 2000). By presenting spiritual knowledge as valid and crucial, we reimagine the potential of culturally based epistemologies to counter hegemonic patriarchal and imperialist knowledge that separates oppressed communities around the globe.

A transborder conceptualization also requires what Moraga (1981, 23) suggests is a "theory of the flesh . . . where the physical realities of our lives—our skin color, the land or concrete we grew up on, our sexual longings—all fuse to create a politic born out of necessity." This "theory of the flesh" recenters women's holistic and transborder existence. That is, a theory—founded on our knowledge, history, and struggles; a holistic approach to self; and the wholeness of our people—does not deny women's intersectionality, personal struggle, and commitment to community. In previous work I used a womanist lens precisely because of its intersectionality, everyday situatedness (*en lo común*), social vision of change, and focus on wholeness so integral to the lives of these women (Trinidad Galván 2001). Phillips (2006, xx), for instance, describes womanist sensibilities as "a social change perspective rooted in Black women's and other women of color's everyday experiences and everyday methods of problem solving in everyday spaces, extended to the problem of ending all forms of oppression for all people, restoring the balance between people and the environment/nature, and reconciling human life with the spiritual dimension."

The women of Sierra Linda also demonstrate womanist sensibilities, as they forge forward but not alone. They walk in the company of their families and community. Their pedagogies and visions are about all of us "committed to the survival and wholeness of entire people" (Walker 1983, xi). Spirituality is unique to this holistic tradition precisely because it has ties to theology and indigenous/traditional spiritualities of communities of color in the United States and abroad.* Most important is la supervivencia, the ability to name ourselves, record our history, and choose our own destiny. We want to move beyond the daily bread, as argued by Isasi-Díaz (1993, 16): "Today we need a roof over our heads, but we also need to have possibilities for a better future for ourselves and our children—a future with some cultural continuity to our past and our present." Just like ancestral knowledge informs campesinas' spiritual epistemologies, it also shapes their pedagogies and gives them purpose.

## Pedagogies with a Purpose

In their attempt to explore and explain the meaning spirituality has for women professors and students of color in education, Dillard et al. (2000, 447) conclude the intersection of spirituality and education is "education with purpose." By focusing on teacher and student spirituality, what it means, how it is embodied and then enacted in the learning process, and finally

---

* See Collins 1991; Dillard et al. 2000; Grant 1989; Hudson-Weems 2006; Isasi-Díaz 1993, 1994; Kinser 2004; Ogunyemi 2006; Phillips 2006; Trinidad Galván 2001; Walker 1983.

how it might impact praxis, they attempt to unearth the success of "African-American female teachers, and, as such . . . reveal otherwise obscured clues about culturally relevant teaching and liberatory pedagogy" (Dillard et al. 2000, 449). Like other women of color, their assertions are based on the belief that spirituality pervades our entire being and hence is present in our meetings, teaching, and social relations (convivencia) (Anzaldúa 1987; Castillo 1994; Moraga 2000).

Gudorf (1992, 75) acknowledges individuals as "whole persons" who, unlike objects, cannot and should not be compartmentalized. To understand and know individuals as spiritual beings who rely on particular sources—knowledge, dreams, and intuition—to struggle with life's lesions and live happy and creative lives is to understand people holistically in all of their conditions. Furthermore, to understand pedagogy as encompassing the whole person contextualizes and humanizes the entire process. If we truly come to understand spirituality as that essence that moves us, makes us whole, and gives us the strength to go beyond survival, then essentially spirituality gives us a purpose. As with convivencia, where we bring our entire being to create communal engagements with purpose, so does spirituality give purpose to teaching and learning endeavors.

Moraga (2000, 123) posits "it is about feeding people in all their hungers." As people who long to quench that centuries-long hunger, women appeal to the source of that strength in order to battle the oppression, anger, and emptiness. That which strengthened for centuries can continue to be the source of struggle, teaching, and learning. Moraga (2000, 120–21) too argues that spirituality drives and inspires politics and activism.

> History has taught us that the effectiveness of a movement often depends on its ability to provide what, at least, feels at the time like a spiritual imperative. Spirituality that inspires activism and, similarly, politics that move the spirit—drawn from the deep-seated place of our greatest longings for freedom—give meaning to our lives. Such a vision can hold and heal us in the worst of times, and is in direct opposition to an apolitical spiritualist view of the world or a totally materialistic perspective.

Because spirituality has a purpose, it can also be a source of unification that brings meaning to teaching and learning. Pizarro (1998), for instance, critiques the education Chicano/a students receive as filled with consumerism and lacking any spiritual connection to the community. In turn, Pizarro uses Anzaldúa's (1987) and Castillo's (1994) idea of the need to turn to ancestral spiritual beliefs to find meaning in education. Through spiritual connection, Pizarro (1998, 61) argues a "creation of strong bonds within communities based on shared notions of the sanctity of life (and the greater forces behind this life)" can be a source of empowerment. This is precisely what is organically surfacing among these women. Carolina engages the idea of mutual responsibility when in her interview she makes reference to Jesus Christ's vision and work on earth.

> *Nuestro Señor cuando vino a la tierra hizo la última cena y ahí ofreció su cuerpo y su sangre y Él los consagro. . . . Pero al momento de leer el ritual, el libro o la biblia o textos bíblicos vez que no es la oración solamente, tienes que trabajar afuera también. Al momento de leer el párrafo, ahí te dice que no basta solamente con orar, sino que afuera también tienes que trabajar con tus hermanos.*

> When our Lord came to earth He made the last supper and there He offered His body and blood and consecrated them. . . . But at the time of reading the ritual, the book, or the Bible or biblical texts, you understand that it is not enough to pray, you have to work outside as well. The moment you read the paragraph, it tells you it is not enough to pray, rather you must also work outside with your brothers and sisters.

Here Carolina describes campesina spirituality with a purpose. That purpose is the survival and wholeness of her community. Women's pedagogies emanate from their personal and communal experience and inseparable ties to their community's socioeconomic and transborder conditions. These pedagogies of the spirit are intimately tied to women's beliefs, epistemologies, community, and supervivencia and consequently have a purpose.

As women who rely on their spirituality as a source of strength to combat life's struggles, they also rely on this source to create bonds and unity among community members. This is quite apparent in the women's involvement with each other through their participation in church-related groups and convivencias. For example, I participated in a forum put on by the archdiocese of the state titled Jubileo de la Mujer (Women's Jubilee) whose intention was to celebrate women and focus on their needs and aspirations. The forum brought together two other neighboring cities, while farther south in the state the same summit took place in other cities. Because more women than I could fit in my minivan wanted to attend, Julieta, her family, Carolina, and her daughter took the bus while Andrea, her sisters Sara and Sandra, and two other women rode with me. We arrived to find a long line of other women waiting to register. Apparently this jubilee had taken place every year now for several years, and Carolina and Julieta had attended for the last three years.

Through various skits and sociodramas—Woman Fight for Your Right to Be, Defining Our Qualities, and Maria Walks with Us—the forum attempted to answer one central question: What does it mean to be a woman? For instance, one of the sociodramas highlighted female oppression at the hands of males in the family, while contrasting that with biblical and spiritual claims that we are all made equally in God's image. Another sociodrama touched on the migration phenomenon and the strong role women play in the absence of men. Yet another critiqued some women's sole devotion to prayer and church attendance while they allow society to remain unchanged. One truly powerful speaker and representative of the archdiocese touched on numerous critical points in order to make clear to all of us our multifarious positions and duty to society. She stated:

> Por ser mujer, por ser pobre y por estar enferma, estamos marginadas tres veces. Dios viene a darle a la mujer un lugar muy especial, pero entonces un sistema patriarcal no se lo valora. Pocas veces se escucha de mujeres que luchan por la palabra. ¡Mujer adquiere una dimensión! Las mujeres somos muy importantes, somos el amor de Dios hecho mujer. Dios se vale de ti para dar un beso de amor, curar al enfermo, cargar al recién nacido. Nosotros somos la ternura de nuestros esposos, hijos, y papás. Ahora más que nada es importante ver como le damos a la sociedad, como criamos a nuestros hijos. Es importante reflexionar sobre lo que debemos hacer para cambiar está sociedad. Ya no somos la mujer que sólo barre y trapea. Somos mujeres que conocemos nuestro ser y eso nos empuja a reaccionar.

Because we are women, poor, and ill, we are marginalized threefold. God came to give women their special place, but then a patriarchal system doesn't validate her place. Few times you hear women fight for their right to speak. Women, gain a new dimension! As women we are very important; we are God's love made into woman. God gives a kiss of love, cures the ill, and carries the infant through you. We are the loving care of our husbands, sons, and fathers. Now more than ever it is important to see how we give back to society, how we raise our children. It is important to reflect on what we should do to change this society. We are no longer women who simply sweep and mop. We are women that know our being [in this world], and that propels us to react.

Indeed, campesinas embody their spirituality and in turn carry with them a sense of purpose. Because poor racialized women must always contend with oppressive structures and exploitation, even spiritual and teachable moments like this one are saturated with a plea for change. This forum encouraged women to also feel compelled to create those changes and envision that place in and for themselves and their families. They were urged to envision a place where women are valued for who and what they are and, as this woman so eloquently put it, "define our being as a woman, as a person, that we are no one's floor mat."

These pedagogical spaces were also self-defining moments. I was astonished at first to hear throughout the conference the Virgin Mary's name in the same breath with that of campesinas. I later understood that like Chicanas in the United States, campesinas in Mexico also want to appropriate and self-identify with those familiar religious female icons traditionally considered oppressive (Behar 1993; Rodriguez 1994) and refashion the Catholic Church's patriarchal structure. Mary is no longer placed on an unreachable pedestal. According to one sociodrama, "she walks with us, she is us." That same powerful woman continued her discourse and stated:

> *Tenemos que tener un objetivo, no sólo vivir por vivir. Es mejor luchar por el pueblo. Vemos como la mujer a ido evolucionando. Ya vemos que María no sólo está en la iglesia. Hoy encontramos a muchas Marías que están escuchando, que están en casa, que están en el campo tratando de salvar la cosecha. No se quedan en casa, como quisiéramos a cuidar a nuestros hijos. Eso ya es un lujo. Las Marías prostitutas que las dejó el esposo para ir al norte y no tienen alternativa para criar a sus hijos. Las Marías de Acteal [Chiapas] que salieron a enfrentar a los soldados y fueron asesinadas y les sacaron a sus hijos del vientre. Las Marías de Argentina que protestaron contra sus hijos desaparecidos. Quisiera que este júbilo fuera una toma de conciencia para ir descubriendo nuestro lugar como mujer y como debemos luchar para nuestra sociedad.*

We need to have an objective, not just to live life to live. It is better to fight for our people. We see how women have evolved. We now see that Mary is not just in church. Today we have many Marys listening, at home, in the agricultural fields trying to save their crops. They don't stay at home like we would like to take care of our children. That is now a luxury. The prostitute Marys whose husbands left to go North and don't have any other alternative to raise and support their children. The Marys of Acteal [Chiapas] who confronted the army, were assassinated and their children taken from their womb. The Marys of Argentina that protested against the disappearance of their children. I hope this jubilee would be a consciousness-raising to continue discovering our place as women and how we can fight for our society.

These pedagogies of the spirit are a cry for campesina self-determination and action. That day was truly a jubilee and celebration of women and an invigoration of the spirit. I also left spiritually rejuvenated and even more convinced that spirituality forms pedagogies with a purpose for individual and collective change.

This chapter explored one remaining resource women used to defy the transmigrant and transborder condition of their communities and households. Women's spiritual inclination underscored how faith, dreams, and intuition ensured their survival and also shaped their teaching and learning. Women's spirituality and its connection to pedagogy demonstrate a holistic understanding of what people bring to teaching and learning relationships. Because spirituality is intimately connected to campesina supervivencia, it also propels women to struggle and enjoy relationships across spatial boundaries. Locally their personal and collective wholeness is attached to their traditions, to what they know and feel and makes them whole. Consequently, we see how their spiritual epistemologies shaped the pedagogies enacted in the small savings groups and other meetings. As in the Women's Jubilee, it was clear that to be spiritual and able to transmit it, epistemologically, pedagogically, or otherwise, requires a level of consciousness, of self-definition and passion. Pedagogically, spirituality has what it takes to move us beyond the personal to a unifying source reminiscent of a particular struggle. As Allen (1998) argues of tribal peoples, I also argue of detribalized peoples—our spiritual purpose is communal. Allen (1998, 47) states, "For tribal peoples, spirituality and mysticism are communitarian realities. The community and every individual within it must ever be mindful of the human obligations to spirit, balance, and the relationship (or kinship) that exists among all beings, so that all might prosper." I see clearly now campesinas' spirituality and supervivencia as threefold: as a catalyst for change, their vision for that change, and their strength to carry it out.

# Conclusion

*Desde otros lugares de enunciación y desde unas voces que nos hablan a partir de lo cotidiano, las mujeres con las que trabajamos han venido construyendo también sus propias teorizaciones y conceptualizaciones sobre las desigualdades de género.*

—HERNÁNDEZ CASTILLO AND SUÁREZ NAVAZ 2008, 12

As Hernández Castillo and Suárez Navaz (2008) indicate, women speaking from "the everyday," like Sierra Linda's women, are inadvertently constructing their own theories and conceptualizations. From the everyday and attempts at collective activism they taught me about supervivencia and convivencia. These conceptualizations about survival and living in the company of others are complex and theoretically sophisticated constructs of what it means to be women who stay behind to lead, care, and change family and community dynamics. Their theories of the everyday are about attending to their transborder conditions and purposeful efforts at creating change and confronting the inequities that lead community members to migrate. It is their conceptualizations that I tried to convey.

I detail how women's spirituality, convivencia, and social relations with family, a grassroots organization, and transmigrant loved ones sustained them. I pointed to the fact that their pedagogies of survival at times meant barely surviving and at others going beyond survival. At an innermost level, their personal and collective wholeness was attributed to cultural traditions, to what they know and feel and makes them whole. Their spiritual tradition was one source from which to ensure a "beyond survival" (supervivencia) precisely because it came from an intimate place that could always be accessed. Women's narratives and work revealed how their spiritual

"From other places of enunciation and from voices that speak to us from the everyday, the women we work with have also been building their own theories and conceptualizations about gender inequities" (Hernández Castillo and Suárez Navaz 2008, 12; translated by the author).

epistemologies shaped the pedagogies enacted in the small savings group and how a transborder decolonial feminist framework—couched in their material, social, ideological, and spiritual complexities—captures that essence. I also elucidated that while their spiritual epistemologies resulted in pedagogies with purpose, the convivencia they fostered in their meetings also had the potential to heal when engaged with purpose. That is, the spaces, places, and social relations of members also determined the focus, dialogue, and praxis of their meetings.

Regionally, their wholeness was connected to social movements, to the creation of a community "we" and collective action. While they drew from familial and traditional beliefs, they also faced new and changing transborder communities. The migration of the men forced women to be leaders in their homes and communities. These new leadership tasks were new and uncomfortable, personally and collectively. Traditionally campesinas are not bestowed the tools to assume public-oriented responsibilities, and their community was also not socially and culturally prepared to accept their leadership. Through the SSGs and other workshops, PLAMAC created spaces and experiences that prepared women and communities to confront and change their transborder community. Essentially, PLAMAC helped communities counter the negative effects of global restructuring and inadvertently "globalize from below."

Since my relationship with the women of Sierra Linda spans many years, I also witnessed and understood women's and communities' supervivencia across time. My periodic visits uncovered the notion that our supervivencia does not always consist of *sobre-viviendo*, going beyond survival, but that indeed it many times consists of just surviving. I questioned my understanding of "beyond survival" when in my trips back I witnessed women's trials and tribulations. It's not that I did not see them during my initial eighteen-month study but rather that my immersion into the community and the immense strength, accomplishments, and learning I witnessed shaded the hardships and long-term struggles. Indeed, Carolina's miscarriage, Andrea's community marginalization, and Jovita's financial hardship were present during our initial encounters and analyzed from the onset. Nonetheless, it was later Carolina's emotional breakdown in 2001, Andrea's further marginalization after the return of her husband in 2005, Julieta's husband's death in 2006, and many other situations that brought forth a reexamination of supervivencia as discussed in chapter 6 and the epilogue. Hence, the book concludes by revisiting the women's lives after fourteen years and revealing how their supervivencia continues.

## Transmigration, Children, and Education

Jovita, Carolina, Andrea, Julieta, and other women frequently said migration was both a blessing and a curse. Migration provided economic well-being but in the process added emotional distress and loneliness (Parreñas 2005; Pribilsky 2004; Salazar Parreñas 2001, 2008; Zentgraf and Stoltz Chinchilla 2012). With time, women's activism and community involvement provided their children educational opportunities and the possibility of dissuading migration. In essence, given opportunities at home, families can deter the migration of their children and create opportunities in their native communities.

Sierra Linda's women's narratives demonstrate with complexity the impact transmigration has on families and communities that stay behind. Their narratives leave behind migration push and pull claims that do not address the urgency of understanding not only the migrant but also those the migrant leaves behind, and in so doing, potential ways of deterring further migration are not addressed. In that respect, it's essential to underscore the crucial role NGOs and feminist grassroots organizations play in preparing citizens of sending nation-states to question, problem-solve, and act on their conditions. PLAMAC's role is a critical piece to the overall story of women's transformation and missing in many other studies of women and families left behind (Salazar Parreñas 2005; Stephen 2007). In other words, transnational communities require support to confront the changes, challenges, and transformative possibilities of their transborder state. Although cultural knowledge and traditions are catalysts for change, it is only possible to access that knowledge if women and families engage in critical thought and consciousness-raising dialogue. PLAMAC's role in providing those spaces and ideological insight cannot be emphasized enough. Communities need the tools and opportunity to engage in dialogue and praxis if indeed change is the ultimate goal.

The work of campesinas also signals the type of accommodation immigrant families—once in a new country—can make and offer schools and communities in host societies. While it is crucial to learn the many ways immigrant families accommodate to their host community, there is also plenty to learn from established and successful programs families back home build and rely on for their survival. The types of community organizing that women of rural communities in Mexico create are important examples for immigrant communities in receiving countries. Learning of the ample experience of native communities can generate similar community groups in and around schools and communities in receiving countries

(Dyrness 2011). This is important for both host countries, like the United States, as they explore ways to support and integrate immigrant communities, and sending countries, like Mexico, who need to make greater efforts to provide social programs and deter emigration.

While children were not a focus of the study, with time it was apparent that women's long journey and community work resulted in the educational advancement of mostly daughters. While in some cases sons' migration was prevented, the result was not educational and professional advancement. This was the case for all four women's sons. In cases when sons did not migrate, such as Carolina's and Jovita's cases, they did not resort to schooling for their professional preparation. Several of Sierra Linda's daughters (see epilogue), on the other hand, did demonstrate unprecedented success by extending their schooling beyond middle school. Gender-focused migration studies are further needed to address these inequities and expose the underlying effects of migration on children overall but gender differences in particular (Salazar Parreñas 2001, 2005). The few studies that do exist suggest school performance results are mixed, with children leaving school due to depression, misbehavior, school peer pressure, or lack of academic support (Dreby 2006), while in other cases the economic resources of remittances actually enable young people to stay in school (Battistella and Conaco 1998). Children's academic performance is further negatively affected when the mother migrates even if they are left with female extended family (Battistella and Conaco 1998). Yet again, of the few studies on children left behind, emotional strain and loss of intimacy are significant outcomes that cannot be replenished with commodities, material security, or educational opportunities (Battistella and Conaco 1998; Salazar Parreñas 2001, 2003).

# *Epilogue*

Through the years and in every visit since the time that I lived among these women (1999–2000), my understanding and analysis of supervivencia became ever more profound. I returned to Sierra Linda on four occasions, most recently in 2012. As I revisited our lives, I could see more clearly their survival beyond mere subsistence but also the complexity the concept entails. With each visit, I understood that at specific moments in our lives we merely survive, but in others we might actually satisfy our hopes and dreams beyond barely making do. I witnessed from these repeated visits the highs and lows of their lives.

## Julieta

Since 2000, Julieta had become the primary breadwinner and head of household of her family. One day in 2003 she decided she could not be away from her husband Manuel any longer. She made the difficult decision to leave her four children in the care of her sisters and without proper documentation crossed the border with the help of her younger brother. Julieta spent months alongside her husband for the first time in her marriage and learned about Manuel and her brothers' lives in the United States. While those months rekindled their relationship, the time also exposed the realities of her husband's existence in the United States. Although she was aware of her husband's cocaine addiction, something she never mentioned to me until later visits, the toll that it took on his body led to a fatal cerebral hemorrhage during her stay in Houston. Her happy reunion was short-lived, and after only a few months together, she returned home to bury him just weeks before my visit. I arrived in Sierra Linda that summer of 2003 without knowing anything about her tragedy.

The crux of our conversations and convivencia during the 2003 visit focused on the family's financial survival. Julieta's precarious situation following her husband's death forced her to cross the border on two more occasions before my next visit in 2006. She intended on those two occasions to gain employment and the social security benefits due to her as a result of Manuel's twenty years of employment and contribution into the system. However, her unauthorized entrance into the United States consistently impeded her from receiving those funds. She then tried from Mexico to apply for a visa to enter the country legally and reapply for Manuel's retirement benefits. Suffice it to say, the U.S. consulate's clear reading of her rural demarcation denied her legal entrance on the grounds that she might decide to stay. Her assurance that her only intention was the opportunity to arrange all the necessary documentation to receive what was rightfully hers fell on deaf ears.

During one of her entries into the United States, she traveled with her sixteen-year-old son. He initially attended high school in Houston but found himself unable to accommodate to a new language and education system. Instead he joined the workforce and successfully worked for several months in a factory. The factory, however, required that this young man use heavy and dangerous machinery without adequate training and bodily protection, and as a result he lost a finger on his right hand. Julieta felt like dying. She never thought her attempt at a new life in the United States would harm her son. After several months of working as a babysitter, earning little income, and unable to resolve anything with the government's social security authorities, she returned home. During my visit in 2006 she shared all of this and lamented the fact that Manuel never legalized his family's residency or visas in the United States. She felt that his lack of foresight left her and her children unprotected and financially unstable. At that moment, I could not help but recollect my conversation with Manuel back in December 2000 when I asked him if he considered providing his family with the proper documentation to travel back and forth to the United States. His response at the time reflected the patriarchal notion that the imminent freedom awaiting women in the United States would only challenge his authority and result in permanent separation.

Opportunely in 2006, I also participated with Julieta, Andrea, and Carolina's daughters' high school graduations. Miztli graduated and planned to attend a community college in Sierra Linda. To provide for her family, Julieta worked at a local restaurant making tortillas but also relied on the remittances her eldest son sent from the United States. Although she was not able to convince her son to return to Mexico, she was proud that her only daughter continued with her schooling. Indeed, that was the case with all three sisters: it was the daughters who continued their education and, possibly, impeded further migration.

During my visit in 2012, Julieta was in Houston visiting her two sons and new partner. Before my visit and on numerous occasions since 2006, we spoke on the phone about her new life. She finally secured a visa and her deceased husband's retirement funds but also endured the migration of her second son and started a new romantic relationship. Although her new partner was also a migrant man, she joyfully shared that he lived with and took care of her two oldest sons in Texas. Although Miztli did not continue in higher education, she and Julieta were professionally trained in the lucrative sale of alternative medicine. When I visited in 2012, it was Miztli and Jovita who welcomed my students and me to the community.

As of 2014, Julieta's eldest son returned to the community after, as she stated, "misbehaving" in the United States. He works in Sierra Linda and does not have plans to return to the United States. Unfortunately, upon gaining one son, Julieta lost another. Her youngest son, now eighteen years old, migrated to the United States a year ago and just recently left Texas to work in Oklahoma. Her middle son has continued to work in Texas since 2011. Miztli, now in her late twenties, continues, with Julieta, to participate as an entrepreneur. They receive training from a nutritional supplement company and sell their products. Julieta feels she gained knowledge and a healthier lifestyle with the product. Her sales success won her and Miztli several trips in the last two years to tourist destinations in Mexico.

## Andrea

When I returned in 2003, Andrea's group had organized and led their community's September 15 celebration. Although she still found it difficult to lead her SSG, her participation in PLAMAC afforded her lots of satisfaction and motivation. *La convivencia* with other women distracted her from the mundane chores of the home, the absence of her husband, and her solitude. She also mastered her sewing and tailored several new outfits. Although many of our conversations during that visit surrounded her brother-in-law

Manuel's death and increased anxiety as a woman who stays behind, she found herself in a good place. All three of her children were in school, and although money was tight she had the support of extended family.

In 2006 I encountered a different story. Just months before my arrival her husband's yearlong stay provoked such unease and problems that she left her SSG altogether. Instead a different woman from the community led her small savings group. At the time she shared with me how demoralized she felt at giving up her group.

> The year that he was here, he made it very difficult to continue with the savings group. And no, I couldn't stand it. I was sick and tired of it. And so I left the group [SSG]. Although he isn't here, he's still reproaching me. He says, "and don't go back again." That's something that frustrates your dreams, because you can't do what you want. Because although I know I'm not very capable, I know if I set my mind to it, I can. All of these meetings are like therapy, because they help you forget what you have inside. Because it isn't good to always be thinking.

Her husband's stay in La Vereda was difficult and life changing. It was the first time she opened up about her marriage and the way her husband consistently repressed her throughout their entire marriage. Her experience reconfirmed the power patriarchal control has on women even in men's absence and her efforts to disregard him in order to accomplish what she wanted.

Although none of the sisters led or participated in a small savings group, they formed convivencias. For example, the day I arrived in 2006 they organized a get-together in Imelda's home. With the exception of Carolina, all of the sisters and their families celebrated Imelda's eldest daughter's birthday. After a good discussion on the results of the previous elections, all the women commented that the convivencias took the place of the SSGs. Before returning home, I participated in yet another conviviality in Carolina's home where we celebrated her birthday.

In 2012, Andrea was also away visiting her husband in the United States. Since securing a visa in the last few years, she traveled occasionally to Texas to visit him. As she stated once to me, she was not content with the idea of living her marriage in complete separation. Like Julieta, she made the effort to rekindle her relationship. I was able during this trip to visit with her middle daughter Mayela who, like Miztli, did not finish her college education but worked in Sierra Linda. Andrea's eldest daughter Lorena was the pride of the family as she lived and studied in a neighboring city. As of 2014,

Andrea's daughters were all married or in committed relationships, and it was not clear if Lorena finished her degree.

## Carolina

During my visits, I had few opportunities to interact with Carolina. She seemed so busy with household chores and childrearing that we participated in few convivencias. Her two older children took over the family business, and her husband sold alternative medicines from another part of town. Because her oldest daughter Lupe remained close to her aunts and always participated in their get-togethers, I saw her during each of my visits except my most recent in 2012.

As I did with Julieta's daughter, during my visit in 2006, I participated in Carolina's fifth child's high school graduation ceremony. To Carolina's great fortune, all of her children were in Sierra Linda either attending school or working in town. Even her eldest son who spent time in the United States during my residency in Sierra Linda managed to make a career of managing the family mill. Although the situation with her husband was unstable and he now lived in a different home on the other side of town, she managed to expand her home and comfortably accommodate all of her children. Carolina's daily mission was the nutrition of her children, and she remained attentive to the preparation of every family meal. Since my most recent visit in 2012 focused on La Vereda, I was unable to see Carolina or any of her children in their Sierra Linda neighborhood.

In 2014, Julieta shared that several of Carolina's children married and lived independently. Her eldest son was married and had two children, while Lupe was engaged, and one of her younger daughters was also married with children. While also attending to grandchildren, Carolina continued her involvement in church-related activities.

## Jovita

Jovita was the only one who still led her small savings group during my last visit in 2012. It seems ironic that, of all four women, Jovita, who received the least formal schooling, raised the most children, and counted on the least financial means, maintained her SSG. She was not only responsible for leading her SSG but also managed her community's National System for the Integral Development of the Family (Sistema Nacional para el

Desarrollo Integral de la Familia—DIF). The DIF is a federally funded program that boosted her SSG membership and also expanded its objectives. She shared in 2006:

> I have not left my group. Before there were just eight, but this year and last it occurred to me to reach out to the DIF. I heard on the radio that they were encouraging groups for the elderly. One day a month I go to their training session. So now I have a group of twenty people. Not all of them are saving, because there is still not enough trust. The ones that are saving money are fourteen. Others are there because DIF gives food. The requirement is that we meet once a month and the organization comes to visit us when they can.

Jovita's husband remained in the community, but several of her children had married and migrated. In 2006 she shared that her eldest daughter was married and lived in the United States together with a younger son. At the time, three of her unmarried children worked in Sierra Linda, while her eldest son was married and living in a neighboring city. With so many children already out of the house, she only had three unmarried daughters living at home. At the time she lamented that although her husband built new rooms in her home they were unoccupied. Nevertheless, she spoke proudly of her husband's efforts to build the two rooms that her grandchildren might inhabit when they visit. She was also pleased to be the grandmother of three children, despite not knowing any of them.

With grown and employed children, Jovita's economic conditions also improved. At no point during that visit did she mention suffering such severe financial straits as to drive her husband to leave La Vereda for the United States. She actually kept her promise to provide all her children up to a middle-school education if they applied themselves. Some finished— mostly women—but none made an effort to continue high school in Sierra Linda.

In 2012, Jovita was the only woman I saw as she welcomed my students and me to her home and SSG. With the help of Miztli and Mayela, her SSG met and spoke with us about their work and continued community activism. For our students, the group's testimonio was by far the most enlightening aspect of the course that summer. Jovita generously accommodated and fed the entire group of thirteen students and three instructors during our visit. It was truly wonderful to see her so happy and successful in her community. Things changed in 2014 when her husband suffered a major heart attack. I was not surprised to hear that she was deeply affected by the severity of his medical condition. Julieta and I reminisced over the phone about Jovita's unwavering love and commitment to her husband even after thirty years of marriage.

## Ruth

My supervivencia has also included blissful and challenging realities. When I returned from Sierra Linda in 2000 to finish graduate school, my husband and I welcomed our third daughter, Nemiliztli. Along with her two older sisters Xiomara and Anayansi, her father and I could not have been more ecstatic and proud. Since I was still in graduate school and writing at the time, I stayed home with her during her first year. I was fortunate to secure a tenure-track position in New Mexico, and so my family and I gladly moved in 2002 to the place I now call home.

In the process, however, I suffered a miscarriage, and by the time I visited Sierra Linda in 2003, my marriage was in shambles and divorce was inevitable. During that visit I only shared with the women the glories of motherhood and photographs of my new baby and two older daughters. Thereafter I raised my three daughters alone and with the support of friends and collegues in New Mexico also battled breast cancer in 2004. The trauma and shock of confronting my own mortality at thirty-seven years old further epitomized the notion of "barely making do." Survival was about making it through the next chemotherapy and ensuring my daughters were taken care of during the entire ordeal.

In 2006 I shared the entire traumatic journey of the divorce and illness as well as the great news that I was cancer-free, in a relationship with a wonderful man, and happy with my life. I felt I had moved beyond being a survivor of cancer to actually having a fulfilling life as a woman, partner, mother, friend, and professional. My only regret during my most recent visit in 2012 when I cotaught a course in Guanajuato was the missed opportunity of seeing Guillermina, who had been battling breast cancer herself. My regret was exacerbated when I found out months later that she had lost her battle with cancer and passed away on December 16, 2012. I was beside myself. I wrote these words to her sister Silvia and family.

Muy querida Silvia y familia,

No sabes cuanto me entristece saber del fallecimiento de Guille. Con todo mi corazón te mando a ti y a toda tu familia mi mas sincero pésame, pues se que fue tan querida por todos los que la conocimos. Me duele mas saber que estando en Guanajuato durante el verano no se me haya hecho verla.

Te confieso que cuando Melissa me dijo que estaba enferma batalle mucho con la noticia y sinceramente se me hacia tan difícil hablarle para darle animo y simplemente escucharla. Como te puedes imaginar, por mis antecedentes con cáncer del seno, pase varias semanas reflexionado con mi propia enfermedad y volvieron a surgir muchos sentimientos y miedos. Su fallecimiento me recuerda lo frágil que es la vida y tengo simplemente que recordar que Guille vivió una vida plena y—por su sonrisa y risa—también llena de alegría. La recordare siempre por su gran dedicación a las comunidades y por sus esfuerzos a la justicia social. Nos toco a todos de manera profunda y única . . . la extrañare.

Con mucho afecto,

Ruth

Dearest Silvia and family,

You do not know how saddened I am to learn of Guille's death. With all my heart I send you and your family my sincere condolences, as she was beloved by all who knew her. It hurts more to know that being in Guanajuato during the summer I was unable to see her.

I confess that when Melissa told me she was sick I struggled with the news and honestly could not get the courage to call to encourage her or simply listen to her voice. As you can imagine, as a result of my own history with breast cancer, I spent several weeks reflecting on my own illness and struggled with resurging feelings and fears. Her death reminds me how fragile life is, and I can only reconcile with the idea knowing Guille lived a full life and—from her smile and laugh—also a joyful one. I will remember her always for her dedication to marginalized communities and her social justice efforts. She touched all of us in deep and profound ways . . . I will miss her.

With great affection,

Ruth

Indeed, Guillermina's life, work, and dedication to rural and marginalized communities across the country are an inspiration. Her legacy sobrevive.

# *Appendix*

## Genealogy

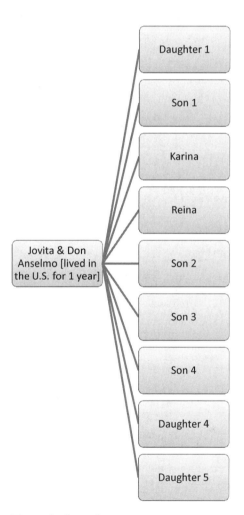

*Figure 4.* Genealogy.

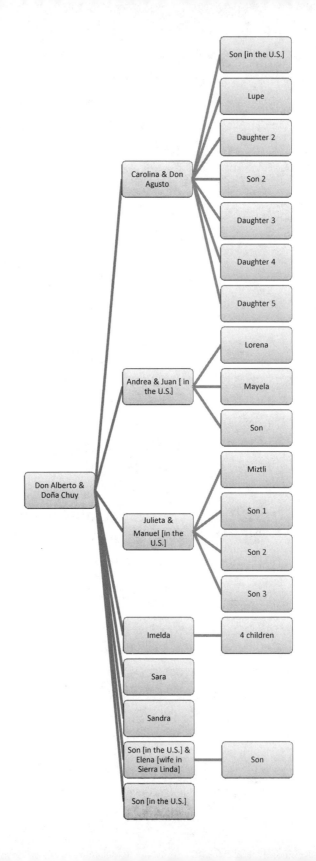

# References

Abu El-Haj, T. 2007. "I was born here, but my home, it's not here": Educating for democratic citizenship in an era of transnational migration and global conflict. *Harvard Educational Review* 77(3): 285–316.

Acosta-Belén, E., and C. E. Bose. 1995. Colonialism, structural subordination, and empowerment: Women in the development process in Latin America and the Caribbean. In C. E. Bose and E. Acosta-Belén (eds.), *Women in the Latin American development process*, pp. 15–36. Philadelphia: Temple University Press.

Alexander, M. J., and C. T. Mohanty. 1997. Introduction: Genealogies, legacies, movements. In M. J. Alexander and C. T. Mohanty (eds.), *Feminist genealogies, colonial legacies, and democratic futures*, pp. xiii–xliii. New York: Routledge.

Alfabetización Laubach Mexicana, A. C. 1976. *Documento de educación de adultos: Post-alfabetización guía para instructores*. Mexico City.

Allen, P. G. 1998. *Off the reservation: Reflections on boundary-busting, border-crossing, loose canons*. Boston: Beacon Press.

Angrosino, M. 2005. Recontextualizing observation: Ethnography, pedagogy, and the prospects for a progressive political agenda. In Denzin and Lincoln (eds.), *The Sage handbook of qualitative research*, 3rd ed., pp. 729–45. Thousand Oaks, CA: Sage.

Antolínez, R. C. 2008. Derechos humanos y pedagogía de la convivencia: Fundamentos antropológicos de la convivencia. *Cuadernos de Filosofía latinoamericana* 29(99): 125–39.

Anzaldúa, G. 1987. *Borderlands/la frontera: The new mestiza*. San Francisco: Aunt Lute Books.

Anzaldúa, G. 1990. La conciencia de la mestiza: Towards a new consciousness. In G. Anzaldúa (ed.), *Making face, making soul, haciendo caras: Creative and critical perspectives by feminists of color*, pp. 377–89. San Francisco: Aunt Lute Books.

Anzaldúa, G. 2009. From now let us shift . . . the path of conocimiento . . . inner work, public acts. In F. Adler, D. Busman, and D. Garcia (eds.), *Fire and ink: An anthology of social action writing*, pp. 198–208. Tucson: University of Arizona Press.

163

Appadurai, A. 1996. *Modernity at large: Cultural dimensions of globalization*. Minneapolis: University of Minnesota Press.

Appadurai, A. 2000. Grassroots globalization and the research imagination. *Public Culture* 12(1): 1–19.

Arias, P. 2004. Old paradigms and new scenarios in a migratory tradition: U.S. migration from Guanajuato. In J. Durand and D. Massey (eds.), *Crossing the border: Research from the Mexican migration project*, pp. 171–83. New York: Russell Sage Foundation.

Arístegui, R., D. Bazán, J. Lieva, R. López, B. Muñoz, and J. Ruz. 2005. Hacia una pedagogía de la convivencia/Towards a pedagogy of coexistence. *Psykhe* 14(1): 137–50.

Batalla, G. B. 2009. *Mexico profundo: Reclaiming a civilization*. Austin: University of Texas Press.

Battistella, G., and M. C. G. Conaco. 1998. The impact of labour migration on the children left behind: A study of elementary school children in the Phillippines. *Sojourn* 13(2): 220–41.

Behar, R. 1993. *Translated women: Crossing the border with Esperanza's story*. Boston: Beacon Press.

Borland, K. 2007. Decolonizing approach to feminist research: The case of feminist ethnography. In S. Hesse-Biber (ed.), *Handbook of feminist research: Theory and praxis*, pp. 621–28. London: Sage.

Brah, A., M. Hickman, and M. Mac an Ghaill. 1999. Introduction: Whither "the global"? In A. Brah, M. Hickman, and M. Mac an Ghaill (eds.), *Global futures: Migration, environment and globalization*, pp. 3–26. New York: St. Martin's Press.

Buch, E. D., and K. M. Staller. 2011. The feminist practice of ethnography. In S. J. Hesse-Biber and P. L. Leavy (eds.), *Feminist research practice: A primer*, pp. 223–48. Thousand Oaks, CA: Sage.

Burdick, J. 1992. Rethinking the study of social movements: The case of Christian base communities in urban Brazil. In A. Escobar and S. Alvarez (eds.), *The making of social movements in Latin America: Identity, strategy and democracy*. San Francisco: Westview Press.

Callejo Pérez, D., S. Fain, and J. Slater. 2004. Introduction: Understanding place as a social aspect of education. In D. Callejo Perez, S. Fain, and J. Slater (eds.), *Pedagogy of place: Seeing space as cultural education*, pp. 1–5. New York: Peter Lang.

Carrillo, R. 2006. Humor casero mujerista—womanist humor of the home: Laughing all the way to greater cultural understandings. In D. Delgado Bernal, A. Elenes, F. Godinez, and S. Villenas (eds.), *Chicana/Latina education in everyday life: Feminista perspectives on pedagogy and epistemology*, pp. 186–96. Albany: State University of New York Press.

Casey, E. 1997. *The fate of place: A philosophical history*. Los Angeles: University of Calfornia Press.

Castellanos Llanos, G. 2006. *Sexo, género y feminismo: Tres catgorías en pugna*. Colombia: Universidad del Valle.

Castillo, A. 1994. *Massacre of the dreamers: Essays on Xicanisma*. New York: Plume Books.

Castillo A. (ed.) 1996. *Goddess of the Americas: Writing on the Virgin of Guadalupe*. New York: Riverhead Books.

Castillo, D., and M. S. Tabuenca Córdoba. 2002. Reading the border, north and south. In D. Castillo and M. S. Tabuenca Córdoba (eds.), *Border women: Writing from la frontera*, pp. 1–32. Minneapolis: University of Minnesota Press.

Cervone, E. 2002. Engendering leadership: Indigenous women leaders in the Ecuadorian Andes. In R. Montoya, L. J. Frazier, and J. Hurtig. (eds.), *Gender's place: Feminist anthropologies of Latin America*, pp. 179–96. New York: Palgrave Macmillan.

Chase, S. 2005. Narrative inquiry: Multiple lenses, approaches, voices. In N. Denzin and Y. Lincoln (eds.), *The Sage handbook of qualitative research*, pp. 651–79. Thousand Oaks, CA: Sage.

Clover, D. 2012. Feminist artists and popular education: The creative turn. In L. Manicom and S. Walters (eds.), *Feminist popular education in transnational debates*, pp. 193–208. New York: Palgrave Macmillan.

Collins, P. H. 1991. *Black feminist thought: Knowledge, consciousness, and the politics of empowerment.* New York: Routledge.

Consejo Nacional de Población (CONAPO), Secretaria de Gobernación (SEGOB). n.d. *Migración a Estados Unidos durante el quinquenio, 1997–2002*. México City. http://www.conapo.gob.mx/mig_int/series/0704.htm. Accessed September 29, 2007.

Cruz, C. 2012. Making curriculum from scratch: *Testimonio* in an urban classroom. *Equity and Excellence in Education* 45(3): 460–71.

Dandavati, A. G. 1996. *The women's movement and the transition to democracy in Chile.* New York: Peter Lang.

Delgado Bernal, D. 1998. Using a Chicana feminist epistemology in educational research. *Harvard Educational Review* 68(4): 555–82.

Delgado Bernal, D. 2001. Learning and living pedagogies of the home: The mestiza consciousness of Chicana students. *International Journal of Qualitative Studies in Education* 14(5): 623–39.

Delgado Bernal, D., R. Burciaga, and J. Flores Carmona. 2012. Chicana/Latina *testimonios*: Mapping the methodological, pedagogical, and political. *Equity and Excellence in Education* 45(3): 363–72.

Dillard, C., D. Abdur-Rashid, and C. Tyson. 2000. My soul is a witness: Affirming pedagogies of the spirit. *International Journal of Qualitative Studies in Education* 13(5): 447–62.

Dreby, J. 2006. Honor and virtue: Mexican parenting in the transnational context. *Gender and Society* 20(1): 32–59.

Durand, J., and D. Massey. 2006. *Crossing the border: Research from the Mexican migration project.* New York: Russell Sage Foundation.

Dyrness, A. 2011. *Mothers united: An immigrant struggle for socially just education.* Minneapolis: University of Minnesota Press.

Elenes, A. 2011. *Transforming borders: Chicana/o popular culture and pedagogy.* Lanham, MD: Lexington Books.

Elenes, A., and D. Delgado Bernal. 2010. Latina/o education and the reciprocal relationship between theory and practice: Four theories informed by the experiential knowledge of marginalized communities. In E. Murillo Jr., S. Villenas, R. Trinidad Galván, J. Muñoz, C. Martinez, and M. Macado-Casas (eds.), *The handbook of Latinos and education: Research, theory and practice*, pp. 63–89. New York: Routledge.

Ellsworth, E. 1992. Why doesn't this feel empowering? Work through the repressive myth of critical pedagogy. In C. Luke and J. Gore (eds.), *Feminism and critical pedagogy*, pp. 90–119. New York: Routledge.

Espín, O. 1996. Popular Catholicism: Alienation or hope? In A. M. Isasi-Díaz and F. Segovia (eds.), *Hispanic/Latino theology: Challenge and promise*, pp. 307–24. Minneapolis, MN: Fortress Press.

Espiritu, Y. L. 2003. Gender and labor in Asian immigrant families. In P. Hondagneu-Sotelo (ed.), *Gender and U.S. immigration: Contemporary trends*, pp. 81–100. Los Angeles: University of California Press.

Fanon, F. [1963] 2005. *The wretched of the earth.* New York: Grove Press.

Finkler, K. 1994. *Women in pain: Gender and morbidity in Mexico.* Philadelphia: University of Pennsylvia Press.

Fontana, A., and J. Frey. 2005. The interview: From neutral stance to political involvement. In Denzin and Lincoln (eds.), *The Sage handbook of qualitative research*, 3rd ed., pp. 695–728. Thousand Oaks, CA: Sage.

Freire, P. 1998. *Pedagogy of the oppressed.* New York: Continuum.

Gargallo, F. 2006. *Ideas feministas latinoamericanas.* México City: Universidad Autónoma de la Cuidad de México.

Glesne, C. 2006. *Becoming qualitative researchers: An introduction.* Boston: Pearson.

Glick Schiller, N., L. Bash, and C. Blanc-Szanton. 1992. Transnationalism: A new analytic framework for understanding migration. In N. Glick Schiller, L. Bash, and C. Blanc-Szanton (eds.), *Towards a transnational perspective on migration: Race, class, ethnicity, and nationalism reconsidered*, pp. 1–24. New York: New York Academy of Sciences.

Gonzales, F. 2001. Haciendo que hacer—cultivating a mestiza worldview and academic achievement: Braiding cultural knowledge into educational research, policy, practice. *International Journal of Qualitative Studies in Education* 14(5): 641–56.

González, N. 2005. *I am my language: Discourses of women and children in the borderlands.* Tucson: University of Arizona Press.

González, N. 2006. *Testimonios* of border identities: "*Una mujer acomedida donde quiera cabe.*" In D. Delgado Bernal, A. Elenes, F. Godinez, and S. Villenas (eds.), *Chicana/Latina education in everyday life: Feminista perspectives on pedagogy and epistemology*, pp. 197–213. Albany: State University of New York Press.

González, N., L. C. Moll, and C. Amanti. 2005. *Funds of knowledge: Theorizing practices in households, communities, and classrooms.* New York: Routledge.

González Pérez, C. 2011. *Se voltearon los papeles: La migración de mujeres a Estados Unidos.* Jalisco: Universidad de Guadalajara.

Grant, J. 1989. *White women's Christ and black women's Jesus: Feminist Christology and womanist response.* Atlanta, GA: Scholars Press.

Gruenewald, D. 2003. Foundations of place: A multidisciplinary framework for place-conscious education. *American Educational Research Journal* 40(3): 619–54.

Gudorf, C. 1992. Renewal or repatriarchalization? Responses of the Roman Catholic Church to the feminization of religion. In J. Conn and W. Conn (eds.), *Horizons on Catholic feminist theology*, pp. 61–84. Washington, D.C.: Georgetown University Press.

Gutiérrez, G. 1991. *A theology of liberation.* New York: Orbis Books.

Hernández Castillo, R., and L. Suárez Navaz. 2008. Introducción. In L. Suárez Navaz and R. A. Hernández (eds.), *Descolonizando el feminismo: Teorías y practices desde los márgenes*, pp. 11–28. Madrid: Ediciones Cátedra—Grupo Anaya, S.A.

Hesse-Biber, S. J. 2011. The practice of feminist in-depth interviewing. In S. J. Hesse-Biber and P. L. Leavy (eds.), *Feminist research practice: A primer*, pp. 111–48. Thousand Oaks, CA: Sage.

Hirsch, J. 2007. "En el norte la mujer manda": Gender, generation, and geogrpahy in a Mexican transnational community. In D. Segura and P. Zavella (eds.), *Women and migration in the U.S.-Mexico borderlands: A reader*, pp. 438–55. London: Duke University Press.

Hondagneu-Sotelo, P. 1992. Overcoming patriarchal constraints: The reconstruction of gender relations among Mexican immigrant women and men. *Gender and Society* 6(3): 393–415.

Hondagneu-Sotelo, P. 1994. *Gendered transitions: Mexican experiences of immigrations.* Los Angeles: University of California Press.

Hondagneu-Sotelo, P. 2000. Feminism and migration. *The ANNALS of the American Academy of Political and Social Science* 571: 107–20.

hooks, b. 1990. *Yearning: Race, gender and cultural politics.* Boston: South End Press.

hooks, b. 1993. *Sisters of the yam: Black women and self-recovery.* Boston: South End Press.

hooks, b. 1999. *Yearning: Race, gender and cultural politics.* Boston: South End Press.

hooks, b. 2013. *Writing beyond race: Living theory and practice.* New York: Routledge.

Hudson-Weems. 2006. Cultural and agenda conflicts in academia: Critical issues for Africana women's studies. In L. Phillips (ed.), *The womanist reader*, pp. 37–54. New York: Routledge.

Hurtado, A. 1999. *The color of privilege: Three blasphemies on race and feminism.* Ann Arbor: University of Michigan Press.

Hurtado, A. 2003. *Voicing Chicana feminisms: Young women speak out on sexuality and identity.* New York: New York University Press.

Hurtig, J., R. Montoya, and J. Frazier. 2002. Introduction: A *desalabrar*: Unfencing gender's place in research on Latin America. In R. Montoya, J. Frazier, and J. Hurtig (eds.), *Gender's place: Feminist anthropologies of Latin America*, pp. 1–18. New York: Palgrave Macmillan.

Instituto Nacional de Estadística y Geografía. 2011. *Principales resultados del censo de población y vivienda.* Mexico City.

Isasi-Díaz, A. M. 1993. *En la lucha/In the struggle: A Hispanic women's liberation theology.* Minneapolis, MN: Fortress Press.

Isasi-Díaz, A. M. 1994. The task of Hispanic women's liberation theology—Mujeristas: Who we are and what we are about. In U. King (ed.), *Feminist theology from the third world: A reader*, pp. 88–102. New York: Orbis Press.

Jacobi, T. 2012. Twenty-year sentences: Women's writing workshops in US prison and jails. In L. Manicom and S. Walters (eds.), *Feminist popular education in transnational debates*, pp. 111–28. New York: Palgrave Macmillan.

Karpinski, E. 1999. Choosing feminism, choosing exile: Towards the development of a transnational feminist consciousness. In A. Heitlinger (ed.), *Émigré feminism: Transnational perspectives*, pp. 17–29. Toronto: University of Toronto Press.

Kearney, M. 1996. *Reconceptualizing the peasantry: Anthropology in global perspective*. Boulder, CO: Westview Press.

Kearney, M. 2000. Transnational Oaxacan indigenous identity: The case of Mixtecs and Zapotecs. *Identities* 7(2): 173–95.

Keating, A. L. (ed.) 2000. *Gloria E. Anzaldúa: Interviews/Entrevistas*. New York: Routledge.

Kim, H. S. 2007. The politics of border crossing: Black, postcolonial, and transnational feminist perspectives. In S. Hesse-Biber (ed.), *Handbook of feminist research: Theory and praxis*, pp. 107–21. London: Sage.

Kinser, A. 2004. Negotiating spaces for/through third-wave feminism. *National Women's Studies Association Journal* 16(3): 124–53.

Klor de Alva, J. 1997. Aztec spirituality and Nahuatized Christianity. In G. Gossen (ed.), *South and Meso-American native spirituality: From the cult of the feathered serpent to the theology of liberation*, pp. 173–97. New York: Crossword.

Laubach, F. 1999. La campaña de alfabetización comienza en Lanao. *Revista Debate en Educación de Adultos* 10: 25–29.

Leavy, P. L. 2011. The practice of feminist oral history and focus group interviews. In S. J. Hesse-Biber and P. L. Leavy (eds.), *Feminist research practice: A primer*, pp. 149–88. Thousand Oaks, CA: Sage.

Lefebvre, H. 1991. *The production of place*. Boston: Blackwell.

López, N. 2002. *Hopeful girls, troubled boys: Race and gender disparity in urban education*. New York: Routledge.

Low, S. M., and D. Lawrence-Zúñiga. 2003. *The anthropology of space and place: Locating culture*. Boston: Blackwell.

Manicom, L., and S. Walters (eds.) 2012a. *Feminist popular education in transnational debates*. New York: Palgrave Macmillan.

Manicom, L., and S. Walters. 2012b. Feminist popular education: Pedagogies, politics, and possibilities. In L. Manicom and S. Walters (eds.), *Feminist popular education in transnational debates*, pp. 1–23. New York: Palgrave Macmillan.

Marchand, M. H., and A. S. Runyan. 2000. Introduction. In M. H. Marchand and A. S. Runyan (eds.), *Gender and global restructuring: Sightings, sites and resistances*, pp. 1–22. New York: Routledge.

Marzal, M. 1997. Transplated Spanish Catholicism. In G. Gossen (ed.), *South and Meso-American native spirituality: From the cult of the feathered serpent to the theology of liberation*, pp. 140–69. New York: Crossword.

Massey, D. 1994. *Space, place and gender*. Minneapolis: University of Minnesota Press.

Mendez, J. B., and D. Wolf. 2007. Feminizing global research/globallizing feminist research: Methods and practice under globalization. In S. Hesse-Biber (ed.), *Handbook of feminist research: Theory and praxis*, pp. 651–62. London: Sage.

Mies, M. 2007. A global feminist perspective on research. In S. Hesse-Biber (ed.), *Handbook of feminist research: Theory and praxis*, pp. 663–68. London: Sage.

Mignolo, W. (2005). *The idea of Latin America*. Malden, MA: Blackwell.

Mohanty, C. T. 2003. Introduction. In C. Mohanty (ed.), *Feminisms without borders: Decolonizing theory, practicing solidarity*, pp. 1–13. London: Duke University Press.

Mohanty, C. T. 2008. De vuelta a "Bajo los ojos de occidente": La solidaridad feminist a través de las luchas anticapitalistas. In L. Suárez Navaz and R. A. Hernández (eds.),

*Descolonizando el feminismo: Teorías y práctices desde los márgenes*, pp. 407–64. Madrid: Ediciones Cátedra—Grupo Anaya, S.A.

Moraga, C. 1981. Theory in the flesh. In C. Moraga and G. Anzaldúa (eds.), *This bridge called my back: Writings by radical women of color*, p. 23. New York: Kitchen Table, Women of Color Press.

Moraga, C. 2000. *Loving in the war years: Lo que nunca paso por sus labios.* Boston: South End Press.

Moraga, C., and G. Anzaldúa (eds.) 1981. *This bridge called my back: Writings by radical women of color.* New York: Kitchen Table, Women of Color Press.

Municipio de Dolores Hidalgo Cuna de la Independencia Nacional. 2012. *Plan municipal de desarrollo.* Dolores Hidalgo, Mexico.

Naples, N. 1998. *Grassroots warriors: Activist mothering, community work, and the war on poverty.* New York: Routledge.

Ogunyemi, C. O. 2006. Womanism: The dynamics of the contemporary black female novel in English. In L. Phillips (ed.), *The womanist reader*, pp. 21–36. New York: Routledge.

Ojeda de la Peña, N. 2007. Transborder families and gendered trajectories of migration and work. In D. Segura and P. Zavella (eds.), *Women and migration in the U.S.-Mexico borderlands: A reader*, pp. 327–40. London: Duke University Press.

Olesen, V. 2003. Feminisms and qualitative research at and into the millenium. In N. Denzin and Y. Lincoln (eds.), *The landscape of qualitative research: Theories and issues*, pp. 332–97. Thousand Oaks, CA: Sage.

Ortega y Gasset, José. [1957] 2007a. *Qué es filosofía?* Madrid, Spain: Editorial Espasa Calpe, S.A.

Ortega y Gasset, José. 2007b. *Hegel: Notas de trabajo.* Madrid: Abada Editores, S.L.

Osés Gorraiz, J. M. 1989. *La sociología en Ortega y Gasset.* Barcelona, Spain: Editorial Anthropos.

Parreñas, R. 2005. Long distance intimacy: Class, gender and intergenerational relations between mothers and children in Filipino transnational families. *Global Networks* 5(4): 317–36.

Pascale, C. M. 2011. *Cartographies of knowledge: Exploring qualitative epistemologies.* London: Sage.

Pérez, E. 1999. *Decolonial imaginary: Writing Chicanas into history.* Indianapolis: Indiana University Press.

Pessar, P. R. 2003. Engendering migration studies: The case of new immigrants in the United States. In P. Hondagneu-Sotelo (ed.), *Gender and U.S. immigration: Contemporary trends*, pp. 20–42. Los Angeles: University of California Press.

Pessar, P. R., and S. J. Mahler. 2003. Transnational migration: Bringing gender in. *International Migration Review* 37(3): 812–46.

Phillips, L. 2006. *The womanist reader.* New York: Routledge.

Pillow, W. 2003. Confessions, catharsis, or cure? Rethinking the uses of reflexivity as methodological power in qualitative research. *Journal of Qualitative Studies in Education* 16(2): 175–96.

Pillow, W., and C. Mayo. 2007. Toward understandings of feminist ethnography. In S. Hesse-Biber (ed.), *Handbook of feminist research: Theory and praxis*, pp. 155–72. London: Sage.

Pizarro, M. 1998. Contesting dehumanization: Chicano/a spiritualization, revolutionary possibility, and the curriculum. *Aztlán: A Journal of Chicano Studies* 23(1): 55–76.

Plantenga, D. 2012. Shaping the magic: Reflections on some core principals of feminist popular education. In L. Manicom and S. Walters (eds.) *Feminist popular education in transnational debates*, pp. 25–40. New York: Palgrave Macmillan.

Pribilsky, J. 2004. "Aprendemos a convivir": Conjugal relations, co-parenting, and family life among Ecuadorian transnational migrants in New York City and the Ecuadorian Andes. *Global Networks* 4(3): 313–34.

Rionda, L. M. 2000. Guanajuato: Pobreza, desarrollo desigual y comportamiento politico. Paper presented at the Latin American Studies Association (LASA), Miami, FL.

Rodman, M. 2004. Empowering place: Multilocality and multivocality. In S. Low and D. Lawrence-Zúñiga (eds.), *The anthropology of space and place: Locating culture*, pp. 204–23. Boston: Blackwell.

Rodriguez, J. 1994. *Our Lady of Guadalupe: Faith and empowerment among Mexican-American women*. Austin: University of Texas Press.

Rojas, M. 2009. *Women of color and feminism*. Berkeley, CA: Seal Studies.

Runyan, A. S., and M. Marchand. 2000. Conclusion: Feminist approaches to global restructuring. In M. H. Marchand and A. S. Runyan (eds.), *Gender and global restructuring: Sightings, sites and resistances*, pp. 225–30. New York: Routledge.

Saavedra, C. M., and E. D. Nymark. 2008. Borderland-Mestizaje feminism: The new tribalism. In N. Denzin, Y. Lincoln, and T. Smith (eds.), *Handbook of critical and indigenous methodologies*, pp. 255–76. Thousand Oaks, CA: Sage.

Salazar Parreñas, R. 2001. Mothering from a distance: Emotions, gender, and intergenerational relations in Filipino transnational families. *Feminist Studies* 27(2): 361–90.

Salazar Parreñas, R. 2003. The care crisis in the Phillipines: Children and transnational families in the new global economy. In B. Ehrenreich and A. R. Hochschild (eds.), *Global woman: Nannies, maids, and sex workers in the new economy*, pp. 39–54. New York: Metropolitan Books.

Salazar Parreñas, R. 2005. *Children of global migration: Transnational families and gendered woes*. Stanford, CA: Stanford University Press.

Salazar Parreñas, R. 2008. Transnational fathering: Gendered conflicts, distance disciplining and emotional gaps. *Journal of Ethnic and Migration Studies* 34(7): 1057–72.

Salazar Parreñas, R. 2009. Inserting feminism in transnational migration studies. MigrationOnline.cz: 1–13.

Saldívar-Hull, S. 2000. *Feminism on the border: Chicana gender politics and literature*. Berkeley: University of California Press.

Sampaio, A. 2004. Transnational feminisms in a new global matrix: *Hermanas en la lucha*. *International Feminist Journal of Politics* 6(2): 181–206.

Sánchez, P. 2001. Adopting a transnational theory and discourse: Making space for transnational Chicana. *Discourse: Studies in the Cultural Politics of Education* 22(3): 375–81.

Sandoval, C. 1991. U.S. third world feminism: The theory and method of oppositional consciousness in the postmodern world. *Genders* 10: 1–24.

Sandoval, C. 2000. *Methodology of the oppressed.* Minneapolis: University of Minnesota Press.

Silvey, R. 2004. Power, difference and mobility: Feminist advances in migration studies. *Progress in Human Geography* 28(4): 490–506.

Soja, E. 1989. *Postmodern geographies: The reassertion of space in critical social theory.* New York: Verso.

Stephen, L. 1997. *Women and social movements in Latin America: Power from below.* Austin: University of Texas Press.

Stephen, L. 2007. *Transborder lives: Indigenous Oaxacans in Mexico, California, and Oregon.* London: Duke University Press.

Suárez Navaz, L. 2008. Colonialismo, governabilidad y feminismos poscoloniales. In L. Suárez Navaz and R. A. Hernández (eds.), *Descolonizando el feminismo: Teorías y prácticas desde los márgenes,* pp. 31–73. Madrid: Ediciones Cátedra—Grupo Anaya, S.A.

Suárez Navaz, L., and R. A. Hernández (eds.) 2008. *Descolonizando el feminismo: Teorías y prácticas desde los márgenes.* Madrid: Ediciones Cátedra—Grupo Anaya, S.A.

Teish, L. 1985. *Jambalaya: The natural woman's book of personal charms and practical rituals.* San Francisco: Harper.

Tisdell, E., F. Brown-Haywood, N. Charaniya, and J. W. Walsh. 2012. The intersecting roles of religion, culture, and spirituality in feminist popular education in a post-9/11 US context. In L. Manicom and S. Walters (eds.), *Feminist popular education in transnational debates,* pp. 227–46. New York: Palgrave Macmillan.

Trinidad Galván, R. 2001. Portraits of mujeres desjuiciadas: Womanist pedagogies of the everyday, the mundane and the ordinary. *International Journal of Qualitative Studies in Education* 14(5): 603–21.

Trinidad Galván, R. 2005. Transnational communities *en la lucha*: Campesinas and grassroots organizations "globalizing from below." *Journal of Latinos and Education* 4(1): 3–20.

Trinidad Galván, R. 2006. *Campesina* pedagogies of the spirit: Examining women's *sobrevivencia.* In D. Delgado Bernal, A. Elenes, F. Gonzalez, and S. Villenas (eds.), *Chicana/Latina education in everyday life: Feminista perspectives on pedagogy and epistemology,* pp. 161–79. Albany: State University of New York Press.

Trinidad Galván, R. 2008. Global restructuring, transmigration and Mexican rural women who stay behind: Accommodating, contesting and transcending ideologies. *Globalizations* 5(4): 523–40.

Trinidad Galván, R. 2010. Calming the spirit and ensuring super-vivencia: Rural Mexican women-centered teaching and learning spaces. *Ethnography and Education* 5(3): 309–23.

Trinidad Galván, R. 2011. Chicana transborder vivencias and autoherteorías: Reflections from the field. *Qualitative Inquiry* 16(6): 552–57.

Tuan, Y. 1977. *Space and place: The perspective of experience.* Minneapolis: University of Minnesota Press.

Vila, P. 2000. *Crossing borders, reinforcing borders: Social categories, metaphors, and narrative identities on the U.S.-Mexico frontier.* Austin: University of Texas Press.

Villenas, S. 1996. The colonizer/colonized Chicana ethnographer: Identity, marginalization, and co-optation in the field. *Harvard Educational Review* 66(4): 711–31.

Villenas, S. 2000. This ethnography called my back: Writing of the exotic gaze, "othering" Latina, and recuperating Xicanisma. In E. St. Pierre and W. Pillow (eds.), *Working the ruins: Feminist poststructural theory and methods in education*, pp. 74–95. New York: Routledge.

Villenas, S. 2005. Latina literacies in convivencia: Communal spaces of teaching and learning. *Anthropology and Education Quarterly* 36(1): 273–77.

Villenas, S. 2006. Pedagogical moments in the borderlands: Latina mothers teaching and learning. In D. Delgado Bernal, A. Elenes, F. Gonzalez, and S. Villenas (eds.), *Chicana/Latina education in everyday life: Feminista perspectives on pedagogy and epistemology*, pp. 147–59. Albany: State University of New York Press.

Villenas, S. A. 2010. Thinking Latina/s education with and from Chicana/Latina feminist cultural studies: Emerging pathways—decolonial possibilities. In Zeus Leonardo (ed.), *Handbook of cultural politics and education*, pp. 451–76. Rotterdam, Netherlands: Sense.

Villenas, S. 2012. Ethnographies *de lucha* (or struggle) in Latino education: Toward social movement. *Anthropology and Education Quarterly* 43(1): 13–19.

Villenas, S., and M. Moreno. 2001. To valerse por si misma between race, capitalism and patriarchy: Latina mother-daughter pedagogies in North Carolina. *International Journal of Qualitative Studies in Education* 14(5): 671–87.

Visweswaran, K. 1994. *Fictions of feminist ethnography*. Minneapolis: University of Minnesota Press.

Vizenor, G. 1999. *Manifest manners: Narratives on postindian survivance*. Lincoln: University of Nebraska Press.

Walker, A. 1983. *In search of our mothers' gardens: Womanist prose*. San Diego, CA: Harcourt Brace.

Wilkerson, J., N. Yamawaki, and S. Downs. 2009. Effects of husbands' migration on mental health and gender role ideology of rural Mexican women. *Health Care for Women International* 30: 614–28.

Wilson, S. 2008. *Research is ceremony: Indigenous research methods*. Winnipeg, Canada: Fernwood.

Zentgraf, K., and N. Stoltz Chinchilla. 2012. Transnational family separation: A framework for analysis. *Journal of Ethnic and Migration Studies* 38(2): 345–66.

# Index

Page numbers in *italics* represent illustrations.

rural communities, xi, 25, 33, 34; and
association with PLAMAC, 95, 151;
and community competition, 35–36;
and community organizing, 151–52;
and cultural beliefs on women's place
and education, 37–38, 76; globalizing
from below in, of Sierra Linda, 92; and
history recovery project, 89–91; and
lack of jobs in, 8–9, 76, 77; and
married women living with in-laws,
32–33; and migration, 3–4, 56–57, 76;
and negative effects of migration on,
80, 84; and patriarchal roles assumed
by women, 46–47; and protection of
patron saint, 135; schools of, 27; of
Sierra Linda, 11–12, 40–42; and SSGs,
6, 105; stagnation of, 84; and
subsistence from agricultural economy
in, of Sierra Linda, 41; and teachers,
124–25; and transmigrant and
transborder state of, 107, 148, 150; and
transmigration, 15. *See also* La Vereda,
Mexico; migration

Salazar Parreñas, Rhacel, 43, 44, 51, 55
Saldívar-Hull, Sonia, 17
Sandoval, Chela, 18, 80, 82, 84, 88
Sierra Linda, Mexico, xiv, 4, 7, 14, 25, 59,
122; and Carolina Acosta Valdéz,
67–68, 101, 108, 138; and composer
José Alfredo Jimenez, 70; and
dispensary of Catholic Church, 30, 31;
and Imelda Acosta Valdéz, 30; and
international migration, 9; and jobs in
rural communities of, 8; and literacy
manual of, 83, 84; and political
connections of Andrea Acosta Valdéz's
father, 60; and pottery production, 8;
and poverty, 9; and property of Julieta
Acosta Valdéz, 26; and return visit of
Ruth Trinidad Galván, 153–59; rural
communities of, 11–12, 40–42, 92;
and SSGs, 5, 11; and tourism, 8. *See
also* women, of Sierra Linda
small savings groups (SSGs), 4–7, 6, 89,
118; and Andrea Acosta Valdéz, 10, 25,
31, 62–64, 69–73; and *animadoras*, xii,

xiii, 5, 6–7, 101, 108; and birthday
celebrations, 70–71; and Carolina
Acosta Valdéz, 25, 93–94, 95, 96–97,
101–4, 105, 106, 115, 141–42; and
collective groups, 19, 131; and
education, 106–7; and the everyday
(*lo cotidiano*), 99–100; and healing,
18, 92, 106, 108, 111, 114, 115, 131,
150; and histories of living relatives,
126–27; and Jovita Gomez, 66, 69,
125–30, 157; knowledge transfer and
social mobilization in, 78, 85–88, 92,
108; and literacy activities, 5, 19,
64, 76, 105; number of members of,
6–7, 102, 126; and participation in
organizing process, 81, 106; and
pedagogies of survival, 110; purposes
of, 5, 76, 93–94, 102, 106–7; and
saving money, 5, 6, 70, 96, 102,
105, 111, 112; and sharing of lived
experiences, 107, 111, 112–13; as
spaces of *convivencia* and healing, 106,
107, 110–13, 141; as spaces of praxis,
18, 92; and *supervivencia*, 18, 106;
and teaching and learning in, 19–20;
and *tesoreras*, 5, 70, 101, 125; and
*vigilantas*, 5, 70, 93. See also
*animadoras* (educators/motivators)
spaces of teaching and learning, 3, 11,
23, 77; led by PLAMAC, 12, 78–79,
92, 107; and sense of place, 107–8; and
use of indigenous roots, dreams, and
intuition, 131. *See also* women-
centered spaces
spirituality, 4, 19, 106; and connection to
pedagogy, 143–50; and *convivencia*,
144; and cultural idioms, 136–37; and
intuition, 139; and Jovita's story, 22;
and *Jubileo de la Mujer* (Women's
Jubilee), 146–48; and local deities,
135; and pedagogy in classrooms, 142;
as resource for fighting oppression,
137–38, 142, 144; and self-
determination, 148; and significance
of dreams and intuition, 138–41, 148;
and significance of faith, 132–38, 148;
and significance of faith in Catholic

# About the Author

Ruth Trinidad Galván is associate professor in the Language, Literacy, and Sociocultural Studies Department at the University of New Mexico and adjunct faculty in Women's Studies and Chicana and Chicano Studies Program. She was awarded the prestigious Fulbright Scholar's Grant in 2008 for research and teaching in Ecuador; the AERA/Spencer Fellowship for her research in rural Mexico; and the University Libraries Faculty Acknowledgment Award and Faculty of Color Research Award at the University of New Mexico.

Dr. Trinidad Galván is the coeditor of the *Handbook of Latinos and Education,* which received the Critics Choice Award in 2010 from the American Educational Studies Association (AESA). She has published over twenty-five peer-reviewed articles in journals such as *International Journal of Qualitative Studies in Education; Qualitative Inquiry; Globalizations; Encyclopedia of Race and Racism; Sage Handbook of Curriculum and Instruction;* and *National Women's Studies Association Journal,* among others. She has served as associate editor of the *Journal of Latinos and Education* since 2005.

Dr. Trinidad Galván earned her PhD in education, culture, and society from the University of Utah on her research with rural Mexican women, her MA in educational foundations and Bilingual/Bicultural Teaching Certification from California State University, Los Angeles, and her BA in economics and international relations with an emphasis on Latin America from the University of California, Los Angeles (UCLA). She grew up in the East Los Angeles area the daughter of Mexican immigrant parents and was an adult English as a Second Language (ESL) instructor and bilingual educator in inner-city schools in Los Angeles for seven years before entering academia. Her research foci include gendered analyses of global, transnational, and migration issues; popular education; transborder feminist epistemologies and pedagogies; and qualitative research in education.